CW01426238

Why Baby Boomers Turned from Religion

Why Baby Boomers Turned from Religion

Shaping Belief and Belonging, 1945–2021

ABBY DAY

OXFORD
UNIVERSITY PRESS

OXFORD
UNIVERSITY PRESS

Great Clarendon Street, Oxford, OX2 6DP,
United Kingdom

Oxford University Press is a department of the University of Oxford.
It furthers the University's objective of excellence in research, scholarship,
and education by publishing worldwide. Oxford is a registered trade mark of
Oxford University Press in the UK and in certain other countries

First Edition published in 2022

Impression: 1

Published in the United States of America by Oxford University Press
198 Madison Avenue, New York, NY 10016, United States of America

British Library Cataloguing in Publication Data
Data available

Library of Congress Control Number: 2022937070

ISBN 978-0-19-286668-4

DOI: 10.1093/oso/9780192866684.001.0001

Printed and bound in the UK by
Clays Ltd, Elcograf S.p.A.

For Alex and Jake, and their futures.

Contents

Acknowledgements

This book was created from a project that, due to the massive impact of a global pandemic, took a slightly different course than originally intended. Fortunately, due to the solid support of academic and personal networks, it continued more or less on track. I am very grateful for those networks and the wonderful, generous people who inhabit and sustain them.

Thanks to the support of the Sociology Department at Goldsmiths, University of London, I had been granted a six-month research leave period from April to September 2020 to conduct the majority of the interviews and secondary research for the project. I was due to spend three months of that time as a Visiting Research Fellow at my institutional home-away-from home, the Centre for Studies in Religion & Society at the University of Victoria, Canada. But, as readers will be aware, that did not, and could not have, happened. Instead, in March 2020, still planning to go to Victoria in May, I faced, as did the whole world, the shock of the Covid-19 pandemic. Rather than brave it out alone, I 'bubbled' with my extended family, Liz and Terry Hooper. I am so grateful to them for their hospitality, the near-exclusive use of their office room, their kindness, wonderful food, and our many conversations about my research.

I was sad that my 2020 University of Victoria trip had to be cancelled and therefore was thrilled a year later when travel restrictions were lifted and I was able to re-book it for December 2021. Unfortunately, 'Omicron' wreaked havoc on travel logistics, supply chains, and the university's ability to open normally. The trip was therefore postponed yet again. I am so grateful to everyone at the Centre for their support and continued enthusiasm, particularly its director Paul Bramadat. This enabled me, in January 2022, to present my research findings in a Public Lecture hosted by the Centre to a large, international audience over Zoom. I am grateful to attendees at the lecture, and those Fellows who participated in a smaller discussion group the following day, for supporting my conclusions and offering further important suggestions and insights. I look forward to seeing them again, in person, in safer, less chaotic times.

Throughout all the turbulence and uncertainty was the certain prospect that working yet again with Tom Perridge at Oxford University Press would mean that a book from the project could take shape under his keen and professional eye. Through his feedback, and the detailed, supportive comments from anonymous reviewers, I was able to write a book confident that it would be focused, interesting, and suitable for its academic audience. Readers will judge if I have met those objectives, and any failure to do so is mine alone. I am grateful, as always, to Tom and his team and to my academic peers who give so freely of their precious time.

Were it not for the individuals who agreed to be interviewed, this book would never have been written. They have been kind, open, fascinating, and flexible with their time and resources. Interviewing people exclusively online was a new experience for me, and for them, and I am grateful to them for cheerfully going along with the experiment. I reflect for the benefit of students, on the experience of online interviewing in Chapter 1.

It was to my original church networks I first turned in my search for the people who had left, and, from there, tapped into other academic networks, ranging from the British Sociological Association's Sociology of Religion Study Group, and the Centre for Studies in Religion & Society at the University of Victoria, Canada, to networks of people who identified as non-religious, such as UK Humanists and the BC Humanist Association. Many of the individuals I talked with recommended other people I should interview and so, using the highly technical academic term, it 'snowballed'.

There have been several individuals who have been particularly helpful in talking through with me my initial ideas, and offering useful comments and encouragement, especially: Alp Arat, Eileen Barker, Lori Beaman, Callum Brown, Grace Davie, Michele Dillon, Conrad Hackett, Allyson Jule, Lois Lee, Pete Ward, and Paul Wink. I am also grateful for the generous help of the polling company *YouGov,* particularly Tanya Abraham, Associate Director.

Finally, no one gets through an intense work period, and in this Covid-19 case, one tinged with background anxiety, occasional isolation, and uncertainty, without emotional support. I am grateful to my friends, my colleagues at Goldsmiths, and my Goldsmiths students for their support, interest, and often simply good humour. Mostly, I thank my immediate family for aways being willing to listen and for keeping me company during challenging times for us all. I dedicate this book to all of them, but mostly to my children Alex and Jake, and to their futures.

1
Who Are the Baby Boomers?

Introduction: 'Maybe You Should Ask Them'

In 2020, half the UK population was aged over 50. The UK population became rapidly less Christian during the last 50 years, and many scholars argue that the catalyst was the Baby Boomer generation, the post-World War II babies who were born, roughly, between 1944 and 1960, raised in the 1950s' consumerist boom and were the chief architects and agitators of the 1960s' cultural revolution. Similar patterns exist in North America, principally Canada, whose national census and other data mirror closely the UK's religious demography and connection to the Anglican church. The Boomers were less religious than their parents, 'Generation A',[1] and they then raised a generation of even less religious children, born in the 1970s, the 1980s, and early 1990s. These generations, now known as Generation X, Millennials, and older members of Generation Z, are dominating the category of the non-religious 'Nones'. The effect of these generations on the current 'Generation Z' is one of continued irreligiosity combined with ethics formed partly through family transmission and through new, digitally mediated, connectivity.

At the time of writing, the most recent British Social Attitudes (BSA) survey (BSA 2019) showed that the number of people with no religion and who were raised without religion increased from 11 per cent in 1998 to 23 per cent in 2018. In these ways, I suggest, Boomers have been the catalyst of this century's intense religious change. Yet why so many gave up religion and transmitted non-religious values and practices to the next generation remains something of a mystery. A review of Gallup surveys covering religion from 1939 to 1999 (Field 2015) reveals that most respondents affirm that their religious values were set as children. And yet, I puzzled, despite their upbringing, many Boomer Anglicans left the church, never to return apart from participation in occasional cultural and lifecycle events. Although scores of academic scholars have advanced substantial theories about why that might be so, most lack in-depth empirical work. As a result, the ensuing arguments about secularisation and religious change rely either

Why Baby Boomers Turned from Religion: Shaping Belief and Belonging, 1945–2021. Abby Day, Oxford University Press. © Abby Day 2022. DOI: 10.1093/oso/9780192866684.003.0001

on opinion and speculation or in some cases on quantitative datasets that lack any in-depth information gathered from the perspectives of Boomers themselves. There was also an added mystery: what was it about Anglicanism in particular that may have provoked such a response? Significantly, as Linda Woodhead discussed (2016, 248), Anglicanism, the national religion of the UK, that particularly implicated in a narrative of Christian decline:

> This shows that it is decline in the number of Anglicans that is the most important cause of overall Christian decline. Anglican numbers have halved since the 1980s, as has attendance in the Church of England, and the decline continues. BSA data reveal that for every one convert, the C of E currently loses 12 people, mainly through death.

That is why the research upon which this book is based focused on the non-religious lives of ex-religious Boomers, baptised and confirmed as Anglicans before rejecting religion, and on their influence on subsequent generations of Generation X, Millennials, and Generation Z. The Anglican Boomer withdrawal seemed a puzzle not only to me but to many of their mothers I interviewed. As one observant Anglican laywoman, born in the 1920s, told me during my Generation A research (Day 2017), she could not explain why her Boomer children had rejected her religious example: 'Maybe you should ask them,' she suggested. Now, before that Boomer generation, in their late 60s and 70s, disappears, it seemed important to do just that, building on my earlier work by collecting new data and producing analyses about that century of religious change from the 1920s to the 2020s.

This study is therefore important because theories maintain that the key to religious sustainability is inter-generational transmission and yet most of those Boomers rejected the religiosity of their parents in their teens or early adulthood and have never reclaimed it, and nor have they raised religiously observant children, contributing to generational decline in Euro-American Christianity (and see Barker 2012 for non-Christian and also new religions).

Also, beyond that initial question of why they left religion another question arose: what, if anything, replaced it? While scholars have suggested numerous, usually large-scale societal, explanations for the Boomer mass retreat from religion, one aspect has been insufficiently explored: If religion is often seen as a reliable source of morality, meaning-making, spirituality, and community, what different and perhaps new values or practices have been transmitted over these three generations, from the religious oldest generation, through to the less religious Boomers, and then to the generations following? These may include, for example, progressive ideals of equality, diversity, autonomy over their bodies, and respect for diverse sexual identities. And yet, where do these values come from? Are they inventions, or reassertions of earlier, non-religious values?

I found, and argue further in this book, that inter-generational transmission is familial (and see also Bengston et al. 2018; Bengtson et al. 2019; Bengston and Silverstein 2019) and that the Generation A, church-attending parents successfully transmitted important values to their Boomer children. They were just not religious values. Further, I suggest the values that parents transmitted enabled their Baby Boomer children to leave religion. Those Boomers then successfully transmitted their non-religious values to subsequent generations.

When I studied the generation of elderly Anglican laywomen (Day 2017), my fieldwork ended with a prediction that, when that generation died out, their non-attending Boomer children would not return to churches to replace them. I did not understand why, but it seemed to me that decades of non-religious belief and behaviour would not be reversed. This change would, I concluded, have important consequences as the women of Generation A contributed significantly to church and related charities' incomes through fund-raising and legacies and often acted as informal social workers (see also Middlemiss Lé Mon 2009 for her study of an Anglican church in northern England).

A report in 2015 from the think-tank *Respublica* cited fund-raising, legacies, and congregations' donations as the most significant form of church income (http://www.respublica.org.uk/our-work/publications/holistic-mission-socialaction-church-england); in the same year, the Mothers' Union's (an international charity) annual report cited the problem of losing income due to that ageing and dying demographic. Similarly, structural changes that distinguish the social realities of Boomers vis à vis Millennials are well-documented. The latter now find themselves in an era of relatively slow economic growth; a shrinking labour market; rising living costs; the coming of age of the digital era; and the growing pressures of the climate crisis (Roberts 2012). This raises important questions as to whether Millennials' religious and non-religious subjectivities and practices are influenced by traditional agents of socialisation (denominations, parents, and schools); life-course factors (marriage, divorce, and childrearing); or, indeed, participation in contemporaneous mass-scale political protests akin to the countercultural movements of the 1960s and early 1970s. I discuss in this book why the answer is 'all of the above', in varying degrees, but with family remaining as the most important.

This new research is the first to focus exclusively on the Boomers as the pivotal, formerly religious generation in the history of religious change over the last century asking: Why did the Boomer generation *not* follow their parents' church-based practices or transmit religious beliefs and practices to their own children? What kind of beliefs and practices were transmitted instead from Generation A to B and beyond? It does so by focusing first on the people from the churches and the families of the Generation A women I studied in the UK and Canada, between 2012 and 2014, and then extends to other people through purposive sampling matching four combined criteria: Boomers who 1) were born roughly between 1945 and 1960 to church-attending Anglican parents; 2) were baptised and attended church regularly as children; 3) ceased to engage with the church in teenage or early adulthood; 4) have not socialised their own children into religiosity. Substantial research exists on Millennial beliefs and practices and a systematic review of that literature showed how Millennials make sense of their relationships with their Boomer parents, shaping the formation of their non-religious and existential beliefs and cultures. And yet, while studies of young people abound, few studies focus exclusively on the older generations.

Research questions explored in this book include:

1) How and why did ex-religious Boomer's religious beliefs and practices change over time?
2) What, if any, alternative forms of moral, meaning-making, spiritual, and community values are believed in and practised by the non-religious Boomers?
3) How and why did ex-religious Boomers decide to raise their own children in non-religious ways and what beliefs and practices were transmitted instead to the next generations?
4) What academic theories need to be generated, amended, or challenged?

The research questions were answered here by producing oral history evidence of how and why ex-religious Boomers' beliefs and practices changed over time and influenced the next generations, providing a detailed and nuanced account of the ex-religious Boomer generation's current moral, meaning-making, spiritual, and community beliefs and practices. I have also explored secondary and survey data and analyses to widen the findings beyond the UK to other regions experiencing the same phenomena, principally North America, Europe, and Australia and, finally, I have tried to enrich knowledge about the specific mechanisms contributing to inter-generational religious decline.

Research Context and Theoretical Debates

There is broad scholarly agreement that Euro-American Christian decline quickly gathered pace from the 1960s onwards. The evidence, drawn from a variety of sources, appears to be robust, with the most common pattern for religious decline being generational: as elderly churchgoers die, they are not being replaced by the next generation, and nor are the churches attracting or retaining children or teenagers (Woodhead 2016; Ashworth and Farthing 2007; Brierley 2006, 2000; Voas and Crockett 2005).

In November 2015, the Church of England director of finance, John Spence, said that the evidence for decline was 'indisputable' (http://www.theguardian.com/world/2015/nov/21/justin- welby- church- englandnew-synod). While there is some evidence that an Anglican turn towards evan-gelicalism and more spiritual practices may, in some regions, slow that decline (Goodhew 2012) it does not reverse the general trend. Many scholars cite the 1960s' cultural revolution as the critical period when Boomers apparently rejected church, religion, respect for institutions, care for com-munity, and obedience to a higher moral authority. Scholars tend to agree amongst themselves that the causal influences are likely to include feminism, consumerism, pluralism, the power of choice, and a preference for an individualised, non-institutional authenticity (Brown 2001, 2015, 2017; Brown and Lynch 2012; Snape and Brown 2016; McLeod 2007; Roof 1993, 1999; Wuthnow 1998; Bellah et al. 1985; Wilson 1966). Brown's claim for the death of Christian Britain: 'the demise of the nation's core religious and moral identity' (Brown 2001, 1) rests on what he perceives as a sudden shift in 1963 amongst the two generations who matured in the last 30 years of the twentieth century. These would be the Boomers and their progeny. The shift in the following decade was, he argued (Brown 2001,176), sudden and violent with a quick series of major changes as the 'institutional structures of cultural traditionalism started to crumble in Britain'. Some scholars (Brown and Lynch 2012, 2015, 2017; Cook 2004; McLeod 2007) suggest the 1960s' cultural milieu, particularly the feminist turn, may have had a longer tail. Brown (2017); Snape and Brown (2016); and Brown and Lynch (2012) refer to the 'long sixties' of 1957–1975, in which there arose a new moral cosmos as people began to increasingly doubt the supposed truths and authority of religion and turned to broader ideas of human and natural rights. It has also been observed that the porous boundaries between religion and spirituality may shift over time (Wink and Dillon 2003). While Boomers have been studied in historical reviews of inter-generational change following World War II, the stock analytical variables continually relate to uncontested notions of religious beliefs and practices and institutional accounts of religious identity, practice, and expression (Sherkat 1998; Sherkat and Ellison 1999).

Framework for Analysis: 'A Shared Zeitgeist'

First, central to my recent and current study is the concept of 'generation'. While not a homogenous group, the majority of the elderly women I previously studied (Day 2017) had always attended church with their families since they were children, and usually stressed the importance of their mother's influence on their religiosity. Further, I argued that evidence about the particularities of wartime, nation re-building, post-war austerity, domestication, and the consumerist boom helped draw the broad strokes that characterised this Generation A. I operationalised then, and again here, the concept of 'generation' as suggested by Mannheim (1952)—that a generation is not simply a cohort of people sharing similar birth years, but a collection of people born at a time of historical note and even trauma that, in their own view, has shaped their identity. Belonging to a generation, he argued, requires a self-awareness of that cohort's location in a certain time and place. Generation, I argue, is therefore performative and imagined, but no less 'real' for that (Day 2013, 2017). (See, for example, Beaudoin 1998; Pardun and McKee 1995; Nelson and Cowan 1994; Rushkoff 1994; Roof 1993, 1999; Coupland 1991; Lipsky and Abrahams 1994.)

I discuss in more detail in later chapters how the Baby Boomers I interviewed saw themselves as a generation, but here I would like to note that whether they thought their influence was good, bad, or indifferent, it is indisputable that their effect is felt significantly. The Boomers were, as the name suggested, a large cohort. They are sometimes referred to as 'the pig in the python', a metaphor to show that their size continues to be visible over time. Writing in a business magazine, Cam Marston (https://www.generationalinsights.com/wp-content/uploads/BA_April_2011.pdf) drew attention to the sheer size and weight of the Boomer effect:

The pig in the python—that's the metaphor for Baby Boomers that resonates with most people. It refers to their population bulge as it moves through life's stages. From the beginning of the Baby Boom in 1946 right through the beginning of Boomers' retirement this year, they have changed every phase of life that they have passed through. They were a huge population explosion to a nation unprepared and soon gave birth to the 'youth market.' Ever since, media, manufacturers and marketers have vied to supply Boomers' new demands as this momentous generation reaches each new milestone.

There has, in the last few years, been more discussion of inter-generational conflict as Baby Boomers are seen as being much more advantaged compared to younger generations. Sometimes referred to as part of 'culture wars', there does seem to be a clear trend of conflict. Announcing the result of their study into generational culture wars, Bobby Duffy and Kirstie Hewlett of King's College London point out that there has been a 'huge surge in media coverage of culture wars, and how public understanding of the key concepts in the debate has evolved ... [In] 2015, there were only 21 articles in mainstream UK newspapers that discussed a "culture war" in the UK—in 2020, there were 534' (https://www.kcl.ac.uk/news/how-culture-wars-start).

Examining those attitudes in Australia for example, researchers identified an emerging and dominant public discourse where younger people's poorer life prospects are juxtaposed with the wealth of older Australians. Similar discourses exist, I would argue, in countries such as the UK and Canada, with many of my interviewees saying that their generation has had unique advantages of, for example, inexpensive higher education and decades of prosperity.

As Yvonne, a Canadian teacher born in 1952, said, while she identified with the term 'Baby Boomers' such a term has its 'issues, its own baggage now. I don't like being hated, being told we ruined the earth'. Viv, a retired British scientist born in 1948, said she felt a 'shared zeitgeist' amongst Boomers, but also pointed to generational divides. Her generation was, she said, 'lucky'. They had nearly free university education, 'the pill', and unlike current young people, they could buy their own houses. I will revisit those insights in future chapters, particularly Chapter 11.

Such comments resonate with an Australian study (O'Loughlin et al. 2020, 2), showing how Baby Boomers are 'often viewed as significant beneficiaries of social change, and economic circumstances affording them lifelong opportunities' as well as being the architects of neoliberal, late capitalism polices and ideologies. They suggest that 'The generations following the baby boomers, usually referred to as Generations X and Y or "Millennials" (born before 1980 and after 1980, respectively), are faced with changing social and economic circumstances' and, because those challenges are often not as acutely felt by the Boomers, this disparity puts the generations at odds, particularly because 'there is increasing recognition that more recent birth cohorts are subjected to downturns in employment markets, expensive entry into the housing market in major urban areas, and the prospects of decreasing public benefits and services together with likely increases in taxation' (O'Loughlin et al. 2020, 4). They also noticed gendered, as well as generational, differences particularly in regard to whether the age of eligibility for pension benefits should be increased; more women than men opposed such a move.

While secularisation was the principal paradigm in the study of religion in the last century, the gendered aspect needed, I argued (and see also Woodhead 2001), more analysis. As my ongoing research in this field continues to highlight in greater detail, gender-blind understandings of secularisation overlook the pivotal role that women have and continue to play in trajectories of religious change over the long term.

There is, accordingly, a slightly higher proportion of women interviewed for this study. The 1960s period was, as Brown (2001) says, the time when the British population stopped going to church or marrying, getting confirmed, or being baptised. Consequently, the majority of churchgoers are older women. Penny Marler (2008) advised scholars in her eponymously titled chapter to 'Watch the Women' as she and others pointed out that during the post-industrial era the family moved from a site of production to a site of consumption and, as fertility declines, women engage in more external work. Indeed, women did not sink quietly into enforced domesticity in spite of (or perhaps in response to) societal pressure that in the 1950s promoted a vision of women as happy homemakers. In the 1950s, roughly 40 per cent of women with young children, and at least half of women with older children, chose to remain in the workforce (https://www. khanacademy.org/humanities/us-history/postwarera/1950s-america/a/women-in-the-1950s).

While the numbers in my study are too small to make any generalisations, it was striking that both men and women talked about the damaging effects of the church's patriarchy. The main gendered effect I could discern was the women's propensity to share more personal insights into the emotional, visceral effects of being discriminated against, overtly or covertly, because of their gender.

Moving away from exploring how Boomers became ex-religious, a question remains as to what, if anything, replaced religion in their lives. The field is rich with a variety of, often competing, theses and studies. For example, have they participated in a 'quest' (Roof 1999, 2003); become involved in alternative religions through a spiritual revolution and contributed to the 'spiritual turn' (Arat 2016, 2017; Heelas, Woodhead et al. 2005); found something in between the binary categories of religion and secular (Day et al. 2013); made discoveries of goddess or pagan movements or new forms of spiritual relationality (Utriainen and Salmesvuori 2014); or developed and elaborated new and complex forms of atheist worldviews (Lee 2015)? Are they part of a religious transformation, rather than decline (Woodhead and Catto 2012), continuing to believe if not belong, either directly or vicariously (Davie 1994, 2007), or become, if somewhat passively 'secular' (Bruce 2011), or 'non-religious' but with other, significant, beliefs and values (Lee 2015; Baker 2013; Day 2013; Baker and Miles-Watson 2008)? Perhaps they find comfort in small groups (Wuthnow 1994) or happiness and purpose through humanism (Copson 2017; Copson and Grayling 2015; Engelke 2015; Lee 2015; Zuckerman 2010)? Or have they, and their children, lost a sense of purpose and become instead individualistic and consumerist (Mason et al. 2007; Taylor 2007; Smith and Denton 2005; Savage et al. 2006)?

Method

The multi-method research involved three components with the sample being the formerly religious Anglican Boomer generation:

1) Oral histories obtained through interviews;
2) Archival and textual research;
3) Secondary-data comparative analyses.

The approach is sociological in method, meaning that its goal is to reveal micro-level beliefs, values, and practices that are set within larger social structures. It is primarily qualitative and inductive and therefore did not begin with a hypothesis to prove but rather sought to identify themes that emerged which were then analysed and related to existing, and amended, sociological theory.

This multi-mode approach reflects current academic practice as scholars have moved away from analysing religious change through the grand, top-down, and all-encompassing narratives of modernisation and secularisation. Focusing instead on the lived reality of people on the ground, the qualitative nuances and contradictions found there have provided a greater understanding. It is within this wider context that oral history interviews have emerged as a valuable method in increasingly interdisciplinary research designs (Thompson 2017), due in large part to their unique capacity for offering systematic insights into the full complexity of social, cultural, and historic areas of concern, by way of highly rich and nuanced lived accounts (Portelli 2017). As a method, oral history thus allows for the construction of a detailed picture of societal change based on the systematic gathering of targeted personal accounts unavailable in written sources.

The next methodological question was the extent to which I could create a sample of ex-Anglican Boomers based on my criteria. I was looking for those who had 'turned from religion': ex-Anglican Baby Boomers who had been raised in church-attending families and who had stopped attending as they grew older. I was not sure if I was asking too much—was there an identifiable, accessible category of people born roughly between 1945 and 1960 out there who had been baptised in the Anglican church, attended church when young, been confirmed, left, and now assumed a non-religious identity?

To verify the robustness of my sample, I consulted several sources, including Conrad Hackett, Senior Researcher in the US-based research organisation PEW, and other academic colleagues. My hunch that there were Boomers who conformed to my sample criteria was confirmed through working with Tanya Abraham, Associate Director of the polling company, *YouGov*. We were able to test assumptions about the sample through their standard Daily Polling survey wave of the UK population (weighted, 1675 respondents). We constructed questions to find if people who were baptised and attended church as Anglicans subsequently left the church and religion more generally.

Significantly, we found that 38 per cent of them (644) self-identified as former practising Anglicans who had attended church as children, were baptised, but gave up church attendance in their teens. The largest such group was over the age of 55 (the top age band included in the survey). I therefore became convinced that constructing research using a Boomer sample based on that criteria would be achievable. It may also shed more light on reasons for Christian decline more broadly.

I then needed to find them, and so reached out to a number of sources and from there found others through direct referrals—the academic 'snowballing' technique. My existing church networks were helpful, following on from my former study about the oldest, active, Anglican generation (Day 2017). Those were the mothers of the Baby Boomers who raised them to attend church and who then, for the most part, witnessed their permanent withdrawal from church activities and religion more generally. I then advertised my request for Boomers fitting my criteria in a number of areas, ranging from the British Sociologist Association's Sociology of Religion Study Group, and the Centre for Studies in Religion & Society at the University of Victoria, Canada, to networks of people who identified as non-religious, such as UK Humanists and the BC Humanist Association. On the Humanists, I was slightly concerned that I might recruit too many people who were strongly atheistic and committed to campaigning against religion. In practice I found, unsurprisingly, that 'Humanist' is not a homogenous category. Many had joined years earlier and their only contact was receiving the newsletter; some occasionally signed petitions the group created, for example, to pressure government into allowing assisted dying; a handful were active organising members. Most significantly, I did not find that their attitudes, beliefs, and practices differed from the non-Humanist-group Boomers I interviewed. Indeed, I was surprised by the consistency of people's answers. Whether in Canada or the UK, the recollections of early church experience were mostly similar, reflecting a common approach to worship and other church practices as part of a worldwide Anglican communion (see Day 2015). In practice, the Boomers I interviewed seemed genuinely enthusiastic about sharing their experiences and their often quite lengthy stories about themselves and, usually, their families. While some struggled to remember an exact date or two, they seemed remarkably close to the emotional impact of church and family on their religious and non-religious lives. This is consistent with identity theories of relational behaviour, and memory as a social product (see, for example, Carsten 2007; Fortier 2000; Hervieu-Léger 2000; Halbwachs 1992). As Michael Lambek (1996, 237) put it, memory expresses and validates individual experiences and seems to exist as a 'function of social relationships'.

I interviewed 55 people between April 2020 and August 2021, by which the time I had reached 'saturation', where I was not finding contrasts or substantially new information. To follow previous research carried out mostly in England with a small Canadian sample (Day 2017), most (38) of the 55 interviewees are British; 17 are Canadian; and 34 are women.

Following socio-economic classification systems, all but four are situated within middle class strata.

Social class is a complicated and contested issue, not least because there has been no definite, wide-scale study of social class, however defined, amongst Anglicans in the UK and Canada (Stringer 2015) and yet the impression is that the congregations are overwhelmingly middle class. I discuss this in more depth in Chapter 6. In assigning a social class category to my research participants, I followed the classification system I adopted in my earlier study of Anglican women (Day 2017) created by researchers (Savage et al. 2013) who analysed the largest survey of social class ever conducted in the UK, the BBC's 2011 Great British Class Survey. They identified seven new categories: elite; established middle class; technical middle class; new affluent workers; traditional working class; emergent service workers; precariat. On that basis, I assigned the values of middle class to most of my research participants, and traditional working class to four.

Names have been changed, and some details altered to protect confidentiality. As most appear in more than one chapter, I do not always repeat the key characteristics of exact age, occupation, and other qualities. The most important characteristics were that they all shared the four criteria mentioned earlier, being born in the 1940s and 1950s, being baptised and confirmed in the Anglican church, and eventually leaving church and religion permanently. As discussed above and in Chapter 6, the sample matched the general demographic composition of Anglicans in the UK and Canada: largely white and middle class.

The interview questions employed here were designed to focus on Boomers' memories of direct experiences and events related to their early religious lives. I always began by asking them to tell me about their earliest memories of church, or religion, including the types of cultural products, such as books or films, that influenced them, how they recall leaving church-related religion, what kinds of other, perhaps spiritual activities, they might engage in, how they decided to raise their children in non-religious ways, and what kinds of activities they engaged in to give them, and perhaps their children, a sense of morality, community, and purpose. Interview questions for the Boomers were drawn from the already-tested question schedule I have used before (Day 2013, 2017 and see also Lee 2015) that are designed to probe beliefs and values, asking about morality, social and cultural influences, relationality, and ontology (beginning, end, and purpose of life).These were enriched through more specific generational questions such as what role religion played in their parents' lives, what religious practices they engaged in at home, what conversations they had with their parents about religion, what provoked their move away from the church and religion more widely, and how, if at all, they engaged with matters of religion/spirituality with their own child/ren. Although the term 'religion' could be interpreted in a variety of ways, no one paused to discuss it. They seemed relaxed about describing themselves as 'non-religious' by which they meant as having no beliefs in deities, no practices such as prayer, or loyalties to religious institutions. Most also distanced themselves from concepts such as 'spirituality'.

Themes and findings from the primary material are compared with other relevant national and international studies and sources. Through secondary analysis of relevant data from large quantitative datasets used by a wide variety of scholars, the work provides indications of how findings may be generalised, for example (and see individual chapters for details): Gallup Poll overviews of religious attitudes, international surveys on non-believers from the Kent/Templeton Understanding Unbelief programme; PEW; the British Social Attitudes Survey, Tearfund, *Christian Research*, the UK census, the USA's General Social Survey, European Social Survey, European Values Survey, American Religious Identification Survey, National Congregational Life surveys (the USA, the UK, Australia), World Values Survey, International Social Survey Programme, and Eurobarometer.

Findings

This research was necessary to shed light on those questions described above, finding a more complicated story of Boomers who for the most part drifted, rather than fled, from institutionalised religion and found instead meaning, morality, belonging, and contentment in their affective, relational lives. Chapters are written along chronological lines, reflecting the Boomers' own journeys to becoming non-religious. Further, the book is structured into three parts to represent a trinity of separate but interconnected phases in their lives.

Part I, 'And in the Beginning Was the End', looks at the Boomers' early lives when they were still living at home. In Chapter 2 I discuss how in their childhoods the church was a social community to which their families belonged, both for social contact and to meet society's wider expectations about an important mode of 'respectability'. I expose here the negative impact of Sunday school on sustained church attendance. The Boomers were the generation who, for the first time in most church's practices, did not go to church as children, other than for a brief moment before or after Sunday school. In many ways, as I discuss in Chapter 3, the Boomers' parents, particularly their mothers, projected a sense of ambivalence that enabled their children to withdraw from the church. For many Boomers their withdrawal occurred, as I discuss in Chapter 4, around the time of their confirmation, and it was striking how many Boomers articulated why this was the case.

Part II, 'Believing in Leaving', covering Chapters 5–8, discusses what happened as the Boomers left their family homes and created their own adult lives. As they moved away from home, for university or for jobs, most Boomers gently 'drifted', as I discuss in Chapter 5, while some, as I explore in Chapter 6, had a more sudden, 'blinding' light. Boomers shared key events that helped shape their generational identity and in Chapters 6 and 7 I summarise those and what they mean to Boomers.

The argument here operationalises the concept of 'generation' as suggested by Mannheim (1952) and shows how particular events and their interpretations shaped a shared non-religious generational identity.

There were, and often remained, some lingering trails of what appeared to be religiosity but, on closer examination as I show in Chapter 8, there were more often examples of more secular ways of experiencing transcendence. Attending Christmas carol services, for example, was a non-religious, nostalgic event for many. Boomers' affection for 'church music' was not, it transpired, related to the hymns they recalled from their childhood but to the largely Baroque period of High-Church choral music. That is perhaps one reason why cathedrals, specialising in such music, have become increasingly popular.

Part III, 'Shaping Belief and Belonging', explores the Boomers' later lives to date and the effect they had on later generations' religiosity. Belief in spirits, I argue in Chapter 9, is not only a common definition of religion but also a way to describe many Boomers' experiences of non-religious other worlds populated by deceased loved ones.

Reflecting on the way Boomers have shaped beliefs of later generations, I suggest that how Baby Boomers report and understand 'supernatural', non-religious experiences is significant and may help explain why the generations that followed are more likely than previous generations to be both non-religious *and* open to such other-worldly, numinous experiences.

Chapter 10 discusses how Boomers find significant, meaningful, and morally grounded ways of believing and belonging. Baby Boomers are the parents of younger, less religious generations, and grandparents of the generation most likely to be non-religious. They are, therefore, at least partly responsible for those cohorts' upbringings and turn away from religion. I examine that process in Chapter 11, exploring the kinds of values the Boomers say they transmitted to their children. The chapter turns from the 'subtraction story' of secularisation theses which discuss what is *not* in less religious worlds to one of an 'addition narrative', exploring how Baby Boomers transformed belief and belonging for, arguably, generations to come. I conclude that different modes and styles of practice, belief, habit, and the turn to legitimate authority all suggest less religious, but profoundly connected and ethical futures.

In conclusion, this nuanced story of ex-religious Baby Boomers demands a revision of several theories prominent in the sociology of religion, particularly concerning causes of secularisation. Apparent turns to modernity, individualism, and consumerism are popular themes within the discipline, yet are found wanting in this current analysis. Far more robust are theories provided here relating to relationality, belonging, cultural change, ethics of care, significance of 'elsewhere', and less obvious forms of 'transmission'. Indeed, as I argued in my research about the older, active Anglican generation of women, the values held sacred by that generation—male leadership, God, Queen, and country—were precisely those rejected by the Boomers.

Interviewing Online: Reflections for Fellow and Future Researchers

Covid-19 restrictions meant that most of my research participants (48) were interviewed over a digital platform: Zoom, Skype, or Face Time. All interviewees appeared willing and relaxed with such technology, and all permitted the interview to occur with video and audio, and to be recorded. Several people followed up the interview with emails, sometimes with photographs, to expand on points discussed in the interviews.

I reflected on the experience of online interviewing and compared this to my previous research (Day 2011, 2017) where I used face-to-face, in-person interviews and ethnographic methods. My conclusion is that although we may not be physically co-present in the same place, we can be 'face-to-face' in a social, digitalised space. Recall human geographer Doreen Massey's (2005) brilliant formulation of the reality beyond physical 'place' to 'space' created by and performed through social relationships. Others have also problematised and worked towards the notion of de-territorialising 'place' or 'field', reminding us that the 'field' is ultimately our creation and, if we are to focus on themes, people, and global connections, is multi-sited and mobile (see, for example, Lövheim and Lundmark 2019; Caliandro 2018; Caliandro and Gandini 2017; Hjorth et al. 2017; James and Busher 2009; Coleman and Collins 2006; Amit 2000; Hine 2000; Marcus 1995).

The notes following are from a Postdoctoral Seminar I conducted at Goldsmiths, University of London. I include them here for researchers who may find them useful when planning and conducting online interviews. It is also the kind of reflection and discussion I encourage amongst colleagues and students, mindful of Ann Oakley's observation that 'Very few sociologists who employ interview data actually bother to describe in detail the process of interviewing itself' (Oakley 1981, 31).

I am also aware of the limitations of interviews, which is why I had originally designed, pre-pandemic, periods for participant and non-participant observation.

Most of us choose interviews because we want to:

a) get 'below the surface';
b) find new vocabulary;
c) elicit stories; and
d) sometimes engage emotion.

There is often an assumption that such objectives require a close, friendly, trusting relationship between researcher and research participant, and a worry that such conditions cannot be met during an online interview. But, just as in a physically co-present interview, the researcher will use specific strategies to try to address those.

Setting up the online interview

Let them choose the platform. People may have different preferences about the technologies available, so ask them what they prefer: Zoom, Skype, Teams, Face Time, WhatsApp. Giving them a choice of interview venue is what I would do anyway with physically co-present interviews: your place or mine? (subject to safety and security considerations). During my online research experience, I used them all. The only common factor that seemed to make the difference was the extent to which we could see each other. Being able to look at someone, smile, shrug, laugh, raise our eyebrows, frown in thought, sigh, shake, or nod our heads—these are all the visual cues we depend on face to face, and which are vital for the rich online experience. That is why I prefer the term 'physically co-present' for offline interviews. Online, especially on a screen close to our bodies, I felt definitely 'face to face'. There were times when the technology failed through freezing or connections dropping, and we had to switch to audio only. That really did seem to matter. Speaking without facial communication, in my experience, reduced the sense of being human.

Obtaining consent. Just as with any research, the Ethics Form, Consent Form, and Information Sheet all set out the purpose of the research and the method. Participants should be sent digitally the Information Sheet and Consent Form. In practice, many will not be able to sign the Consent Sheet digitally, so ask them to send an email saying they have read everything and agree.

Agree expectations. Time: Let them know how long the interview will last. Realistically, given how tiring online work is, 30–45 minutes is adequate. If you feel you need longer, schedule a new interview. Recording: Let them know that the interview will be recorded. In practice, you may wish to record both in Zoom or equivalent, and also on your phone or another hand-held, for backup.

Conducting the online interview

Because the process can be quite tiring through multi-tasking (conducting the interview, keeping an eye on the related technologies, perhaps having to reconnect a few times, note-taking) I recommend having no more than two interviews per day.

Control your environment. Think through the space available to you and any distracting elements. Try to eliminate these, and external noise, as they will interfere with both your ability to concentrate and your research participant's sense of trust in you. Particularly if the interview will contain confidential or sensitive information, I find it's helpful sometimes to rotate the screen so that the participant can see the room is empty.

Build rapport. While we are often told we should 'build rapport' with research participants, we should also be careful not to abuse or fetishise this—online or off. We are not their best friends: this is a professional, instrumental relationship. We are interviewing them because we assume they have something we need—mostly, their experiences, insights, and opinions. A professional researcher is not trying to trick research partici-pants into letting their guard down and telling us something they, on reflection, may wish they hadn't. The online experience can be one way to recalibrate the research relationship because at least in one sense we are all sharing something: the experience of living through a global pandemic. I started my interviews with just that fact, asking people how they were coping and keeping healthy, and sharing my feelings as well.

Keep focused. Try to limit questions to six or seven. Yin (2003) described qualitative interviews as 'structured conversations'. Fewer questions will allow you to keep focused and for the experience not to seem like a rapid-fire interrogation.

Conclude the interview. It's a good idea to let people know when you are nearing the end of your interview so that they might be able to draw together any thoughts. An online interview can feel like it has ended abruptly with you, literally, shutting it down. Once you do finish your questions and feel you are at the end of the interview, let that last question be shaped by them, asking something like: 'Before we stop, is there anything we haven't talked about that you would like to add, or perhaps there's a question I should have asked that I haven't?'

After the interview

With so much going on in an online interview, your memory may not be at its best. I found writing up notes immediately after the interview helped me capture, and seemed to embed, key phrases, themes, and other main points. Much later, I returned to each recording for a transcription. After every interview I wrote to each person to thank them for their time; each person responded by saying how much they enjoyed it and several wrote again to offer a new thought or a link to a book or event they thought might help. I also wrote a few notes reflecting on how I thought the interview went and what I might choose to do differently next time.

Note

1. Generation A is the moniker I gave to the current oldest, living generation of Anglicans I studied (Day 2017), signalling that they are the lead generation in the subsequent alphabet style used in common parlance: Generations X, Y, and Z. I also use Generation B to signify Baby Boomers.

PART I

AND IN THE BEGINNING
WAS THE END

2

Church

A Social Thing

Introduction: 'It Was a Social Thing'

Church was what you did because church was what you did. Although this sentiment was widely expressed by the Boomers I interviewed, it would be more accurate to say, 'Sunday school was what you did'. The Boomers were the generation who, for the first time in most churches' practices, did not go to church as children, other than for a brief moment before or after Sunday school. For the purpose of this study, the Boomers' first and early 'religious' activities have special significance because those first regular religious activities were largely their last. Most Baby Boomers studied here, and in related wider studies, ceased regular church attendance in their early their teens and never returned.

Large-scale social surveys corroborate a trend of declining church attendance from the late 1950s onwards. In the USA, Gallup's longest-running question about religious attendance asks, 'Did you, yourself, happen to attend church, synagogue or mosque in the last seven days, or not?' In 1939, when Gallup first asked this question, 41 per cent said 'yes'. That percentage dropped to 37 in 1940 and rose to 39 in 1950. It continued to climb, reaching as high as 49 at multiple points in the 1950s before declining again.[1]

Commentators usually put that North American (and a comparable UK) spike down to a brief surge created by evangelist Billy Graham's popular rallies (see, for example, Ellwood 1997). Callum Brown suggested (2001) that another explanation for a religious revival between 1945 and 1958 may be a need for post-war domestication, justifying women's removal from the workplace in favour of returning soldiers. Whatever the reason, the wave of evangelicalism spurred by Graham's missions was not sustained, Brown notes. Of the millions who attended the rallies in the mid-1950s only a tiny percentage converted to that form of Christianity. Attendance in the UK and USA, as with other countries, then settled down to lower figures

Why Baby Boomers Turned from Religion: Shaping Belief and Belonging, 1945–2021. Abby Day. Oxford University Press. © Abby Day 2022. DOI: 10.1093/oso/9780192866684.003.0002

(https://www.news.gallup.com/poll/200186/five-key-findings-religion.aspx last accessed 17.08.21).

When the Baby Boomers discussed with me their childhood memories, the phrase that often cropped up in my study, and comparable work to be explored further, was 'it was a social thing'. Their earliest memories were mainly about practice, rather than belief, and it is important to see how that may have affected their trajectory. The impact of values and beliefs is investigated in more detail in later chapters, notably Chapter 6.

In this chapter, I will explore the varieties of 'practice' and 'social' and the way those shaped the Baby Boomers' approach to religion then and now. I will conclude with some reflections on other studies and prominent theories to help explain what I observed.

The 'Thing' of the Social

Childhood religious practices did not, for the Baby Boomer children here, signify anything spiritual, moral, or existential. Significantly, they did not appear to signify anything particularly religious or spiritual for their parents either, an important feature I analyse more deeply in the following chapter.

Practice, in this context, will focus on what the Boomers did and, to some extent, on how it made them feel and may have influenced their future withdrawal from church specifically and religion more generally. Robert Wuthnow (2020, 1) suggests that the study of practice has been neglected in scholarship, defining it as 'the interconnected strings of activity that constitute our personal lives and the social relationships that shape the contours of our collective experience'. Such a definition is particularly relevant for this book as it stresses both the individual and collective experience. Wuthnow found that the difficulties in analysing religious practice were compounded by the variety of ways in which religion has been defined by different disciplines, such as sociology, anthropology, psychology, and history, and the way practice may change amongst different religions in different parts of the world. He offers three main frameworks that span disciplinary approaches. The first he suggests is the increasingly applied concept of 'lived religion' to enable a focus on lay rather than formal hierarchies and, he says, to allow scholars to examine 'ordinary' activities such as street festivals, prayer groups, holidays, and home altars. While a useful observation, I am not convinced that Wuthnow conflating and insufficiently engaging with the concepts, and the origins, of 'lived' and 'everyday' religion helps scholars understand their importance. Further, in the spirit of current moves to prevent the erasure of female scholars, I will add here comment on the two women behind those revolutionary concepts: Nancy Ammerman (2007) and Meredith McGuire (2008). Ammerman (2007, 5) developed the idea of the 'everyday' as a way of privileging the experience of laypeople. These are, she argued, the non-professionals, the 'nonexperts, the people who do not make a living being religious or thinking and writing about religious ideas'. McGuire (2008, 5) described the importance of 'lived religion' as a necessary corrective to studies of 'dubious value' because they solely focus on quantitative data. I agree that both approaches considerably enrich the study of religion and, increasingly, non-religion (Day 2020, 46):

> Just as Ammerman suggests that people do not often experience everyday religion in ways that match existing theological standards or categories, Meredith McGuire (2008) argued that how people 'live' religion often differs from how scholars suppose they do. Researching religion as it is lived requires more diverse research methods than a survey or question-naire. She explored how researchers should consider more fine- grained methods to understand lived diverse experiences of religion and spirituality as everyday, embodied, material and often gendered.

Wuthnow points to a second 'turn' in scholarship that affects practice: a contemporary emphasis on materiality influencing the way scholars analyse, for example, architecture, icons, and photographs. His third observation was to highlight the attention scholars now pay to the discursive structures of sermons, stories, and conversations. He argues that those three foci helped scholars shift from Protestant-centric research to investigating other religions and spiritualities. They also prompted a wider range of epistemological analyses to emerge around such areas as structure, agency, gender, power, and mind-body distinctions.[2]

Wuthnow's review and analysis of practice[3] has been relevant to my work here, as it demonstrated the importance, to Baby Boomers I interviewed, of what actually happened at church, Sunday school, and at home. One of the most significant related findings was, as I discuss in this chapter and in more depth in the next, that religion was not practised within the Baby Boomers' homes. Its practice outside the home seemed mainly related to 'the social'. The Baby Boomer choice of the word 'social' brought with it, I suggest, at least three different meanings, namely:

1) social contact;
2) social place; and
3) social respectability/expectations.

In this chapter, I will explore Boomers' experience and creation of social contact and place; in the next chapter the topic of social respectability and expectations will be explored.

Social Contact: 'More Social than Actually Believing'

When Philip, a retired British researcher born in 1939,[4] went to church as a child, he did not give it much thought; everyone seemed to be doing the same thing. He described himself and his family as 'fairly conventional'. Like a lot of people he knew, he met his friends through the church: 'going to church was a social thing,' he said, 'it was more social than actually believing'.[5] An added bonus for Philip was that, as teenagers, they went on a church-organised holiday to Spain. Two vicars went with the group. 'There were no religious things,' he said, 'but we didn't misbehave'.

Church also provided, for some, a social function beyond the formal services and activities. Eleanor, a retired British teacher born in 1949, said that as a child and a teenager church helped her to cope with her mother's depressions. The people and her engagement with them provided emotional and psychological support, she said, during the 'terrible times' with her mother's depression: 'If I hadn't fallen in with church and guides, I don't know. I would have become depressed,' she said.

Jennifer, a Canadian college lecturer born in 1952, said her father was alcoholic and violent. She suggests that a main reason her mother insisted they attended church every Sunday (in the 1950s and 1960s) was to get away from her father:

> I'm not 100 per cent sure my mother even believed in God, even though she'd probably tell you that she did, but a lot of going to church for us was the social part because my father was an alcoholic who beat the shit out of his wife and kids and so for us the church was a place of quiet and of safety.

Were it not for people at the church, she says, 'we would have all been dead'. Her elder siblings were nearly killed by their father, and left home as a result. 'For the rest of us,' she continued, 'the Church was a kind of social refuge, a place to go and hang out with nice people without father around'. For a child living in fear of her father's next drunken rage, this was one part of the week she treasured. Sunday school, church picnics, the choir where she sang every Sunday, the food parcels left on the doorstep ('we were very poor'), and, she added emphatically, the fellowship with other members of the congregation who 'were just really *nice*'. It is a word she used frequently in our interview when talking about a Mrs Smith, a Mrs Jones, a Mrs James, and other women from the church who supported the family with kindness and sustenance.

I asked if the church did anything to help her mother or siblings with abuse. She said that 'I can't recall, but I suspect the answer to that is yes, they would have offered it to mother'. She said she remembered that they brought food when they family did not have any food:

> There was one woman, Mrs James. And some of the others were pretty nice as we were very poor. They didn't give us money, but I remember some hampers coming from the Salvation Army, and also from the church, giving us food. But they were just also really nice, the church, the Sunday school events. People were really nice, and it was a network for mom.

That Jennifer stresses the laywomen and their practical help fits a larger pattern of how churches respond to domestic abuse. Following 20 years of fieldwork, Nancy Nason-Clark and Catherine Holtmann (2015, 75) conclude that:

> Religious women often look to their pastors, priests or 'sisters in the faith' when violence strikes in the family. What happens next gives pause for thought: few religious leaders know what to do, some are dismissive of the severity or the longer-term consequences of the acts of violence or suggest that the victim needs to change her ways. Others are overly optimistic that a violent man can and will alter his abusive thoughts and actions.

The authors found that priests or pastors are generally unwilling to refer abused women to non-church agencies, although those are the experts in domestic violence and best-suited to helping the women. Help comes, they found, from other women in the church's congregation who offer practical assistance and continue to support the abused woman and her children. Jennifer had strong words to say about the lack of support from the church's priest and the way in which his actions drove her further away from religion. I explore that in later chapters.

The main form of social contact Boomer children experienced at church did not come from the attending the actual church service as they usually went to a separate room or annex for the Sunday School. I did not find any Boomers who described that as a moving religious or spiritual event. Michele, a Canadian scientist born in 1956, described her experience as 'colouring pictures' and remarked that it felt like a 'baby-sitting service'. There did seem to be a lot of 'colouring in' according to my interviewees, usually involving crayons or colouring pencils and large black and white books with pictures of Mary and Joseph, Jesus, loaves and fishes, stars, camels, and churches.

In some cases, the children were adept at playing the system. When Robin, a retired British tech administrator born in 1950, was seven, she became jealous that all her friends were joining the Brownies. It meant that they could go out in the evening, and come home alone in the dark, sometimes stopping at the chip shop. Eager to become one of that daring crowd, she tried to join the Brownies, but couldn't because she wasn't a member of the local church. Brownies were required to attend Sunday school and the church once a month for parade. It didn't take long for Robin to claim a new allegiance to the local church, agreeing that she would regularly go to Sunday school. She didn't like the school, although she was quite impressed by the massive church organ she saw at the back of the church one Sunday morning when they were in the main service.

'I was told off by Brown Owl for not facing front,' she recalled, oblivious to one of the finer points of Anglican etiquette. Nor did she know the words of the Lord's Prayer. When they were given an exercise to write out neatly, she rendered the opening words 'Old Father wishard how be thy name'. She also did not agree with the words of the Brownie promise to do her best to God, the Queen, and her country.

Her parents, she explained, were left-wing political activists who would not approve of such things. On balance, she said, she didn't mind reciting the promise because 'I knew I didn't believe in it, so what did it matter?'[6] She recalled that Sunday school involved reading the Bible and singing hymns. For her, it only meant that she earned a stamp in a book for attending. 'It didn't impress me at all,' she said, 'God or Jesus went over my head. I just ignored it, didn't know anything about it'. After three years of Brownies, she was due to 'fly up' to join the Girl Guides, but she declined. She thought it was too militaristic and joined the junior Red Cross instead. When I asked her how it felt to stop attending, she replied that she had not stopped being religious: 'I was never religious in the first place! I just played the game required of me in order to join the Brownies'.

The comment 'I was never religious in the first place' gave me pause. It fairly neatly summed up one of the emerging main findings of my research: Baby Boomers found it easy to give up performing religion because they were never religious in the first place. All those hours spent in Sunday school, all those carefully coloured exercise books, and all the Bible reading and hymns did not make any, presumably intended, religious impact.

Nevertheless, whether religious or not, the church was an important source of social contact. Kim, a retired British teacher born in 1941, grew up in a small English village where, she said, her family did 'the whole rigamarole', by which she meant joining in all the church's activities: 'the church was the centre of the village,' she said. The idea of 'centre' may be interpreted in at least two ways. It was the centre because social life revolved around it, and it was the centre because English villages are often constructed around the physical building of the church. As became evident from Canadian contributors to this study, small Canadian villages were also dominated by a central church building and the tradition of the church as organiser of social events in places where there were no alternatives.

Annabel, a retired British teacher born in 1946, recalled similar impressions: 'We lived in a village, so much of life centred on the church'. Even people who were not church attenders would come, she said, especially for music nights as the choir was good and quite well known. She sang in the choir and her mother directed it. In her small English village, she said, the Church and WI (Women's Institute) constituted all the entertainment in the village, from 'jumble sales' and village fêtes, to church picnics and outings.

The WI was founded in 1897 in Canada by a farming woman, Adelaide Hoodless, to help create a sense of community and provide skills-sharing amongst often geographically dispersed women in rural areas. Their meetings are organised around guest speakers and frequent outings to places of interest. The WI has also campaigned for the rights of women and girls worldwide, although this work of social action is usually ignored in popular discourse, which favours the softer gloss of 'jam-makers' or 'flower ladies', perhaps revealing a popular preference for women to be safely contained in a domestic sphere. The 1950s were the most successful for the WI, in terms of membership, with 467,000 in 1954. These were the mothers and often grandmothers of the Baby Boomers. Today there are half that amount, 220,000, with a typically older membership profile.

The village fêtes Annabel remembered are traditional outdoor parties, organised by the local church or resident associations to raise money for the church and other local causes. They typically have group games, like tug-of-wars, and pet shows, agricultural and food competitions (largest cucumber, best marmalade, tastiest cake, for example), and afternoon teas. Their heyday, like the WI, was also the 1950s, possibly due to the same demographic of Baby Boomer mothers. Their popularity declined over the next decades, although there is evidence that in some areas they may be making a comeback (https://www.britishheritage.com/art-culture/british-fete).

As an interesting update on her current irreligiosity, Annabel said towards the end of our interview that, after years living in a city she moved back to a village for her retirement. She finds it difficult to make friends, she said, as most of the social life is centred on the church, which she doesn't attend.

Helen, a retired British supervisor born in 1947, also emphasised several times during our interview the centrality of church-based social contact for her and her family: it was, she said, their 'whole social life, our whole being', particularly because her mother sang in the choir and also played the piano. This meant they would attend church three times on Sunday for the main services, and also for other events where music was involved. She said it 'was just something you had to do, like prayers at night, being sent to Sunday school'. She said she enjoyed learning the hymns because 'kids like stuff that's repetitious' and saying everything together.

Eleanor said her Church of England church was quite evangelical and that was probably why she and her friends at school created a Christian Union group. But, she added, the other reason was that there was nothing else to do.

Not everyone enjoyed the Sunday school experience, especially if their friends were absent. Annabel recalled that she was forced to attend Sunday school and was 'very cross about it' as she spent Sunday mornings indoors learning about missionaries while 'watching my friends outside on their bikes'.

Social Place

The Baby Boomer experience of their early religious activities show that the earliest memories of religious experiences took place in the social space of a Sunday School. A 'social space' in this context is perhaps tautological, following the concept of 'space' developed by geographer Doreen Massey

(2005) and others as a process (De Certeau1984; Lefebvre 1991), composed of a network of relations constituted through interactions. The main interactions studied here for the Baby Boomers were amongst other children; this was not a multi-generational space. The one or two adults present were the Sunday School teachers. Parents, and other adult members of the church, were separated into a different space of the church body.

Importantly, the Sunday school was the only space where religion appeared in the lives of most Boomers. It is striking that interviewees did not describe church or their homes as places where they encountered religion. I will discuss this more in the next chapter, when I discuss parental ambiguity, but I want to focus here first on the idea of the place where religion did occur—the Sunday school.

Anglican-based Sunday schools of the Baby Boomer generation were church-based and designed to provide instruction about Christianity. When the Boomers were young, the practice of separating children from adults at the main service was a fairly recent innovation. It was not something that their parents would have experienced as children; they would have attended the main church services with their parents and siblings. The Baby Boomer children only went into the main church for a few moments, either at the beginning or the end of the church service. The Sunday school was therefore set apart from the main church with its pews and altar. The idea of being 'set apart' will nudge most religion academics into a Durkheimian foray, however brief. Not only do the words 'set apart' echo the classic Durkheimian definition of religion, but it can also, I will argue, help to explain why the Boomers' Sunday school experience effectively guaranteed that they did not develop from it a strong, personal religiosity. Durkheim's (1915, 47) well-known definition of religion as 'a unified system of beliefs and practices relative to sacred things' puts belief and practice on an even footing, before moving on to the realm of performance, and separation: 'that is to say, things set apart and forbidden—beliefs and practice which unite into one single moral community called a Church, all those who adhere to them'. The Baby Boomer children became the separated, non-sacred profane.

Durkheim altered ideas about power, authority, and legitimacy by relocating belief to the social, produced through the performative engagement with others.[7] For the Baby Boomers, being set apart removed them from a main source of religion transmission: the church. Most did not attend the main church regularly until they were confirmed in their early teens and by then, as I will argue in later chapters, it was too late. The beliefs, practices, and habits Baby Boomers developed as children were therefore created in a specific social space that, they recalled, did not foster any sense of God, Jesus, or related religious or spiritual affect. Further, following a Durkheimian perspective, it is understandable that the Boomers do not recall anything particularly 'sacred' about that experience. As Wuthnow (2020) elucidates in his study of religious practice, setting a thing or a place apart does not in itself create a sacred space. The sacredness is created by the social assemblage and the manner in which people behave in line with their expectations that the space is already sacred and their experience will also be sacralised. While agreeing that the sacred is a social construction, Wuthnow (2020, 27) laments that there is a lack of studies to explain exactly how that construction takes place because 'there were ambiguities and weaknesses in how the sacred was theorized. While the main argument of these approaches was that the sacred was socially constructed, relatively little was said about how that happened.'

Examining the Sunday school as a non-sacred space may help to contribute to a wider understanding of how sacred space is, or is not, socially constructed. First, it was important for me to clarify exactly what was meant when Boomers told me about 'Sunday school'. The Anglican church-based Sunday morning Sunday school of the Boomer era was a different entity from what is usually described as the 'Sunday school movement' that began in the UK in the eighteenth century and was picked up in the USA and Canada. Many accounts suggest that it was started in the 1780s by an Anglican newspaper publisher, Robert Raikes, as a venue to educate poor children, more than a century before education became free and mandatory; others disagree and say that a more diffused working-class movement generated the schools pre-Raikes (for a more detailed discussion see Thompson 2017, 29–30). Scholars agree that such schools were an almost universal aspect of working-class life, providing children with basic, Christian-infused, education (Snape and Brown 2016). The movement was picked up in Canada, and the USA, with churches typically providing the service, often using the Bible to teach reading. While significantly diminished, Sunday schools lingered until the 1970s in some parts of Britain.

In their study of the American Sunday school movement, focusing in particular on the Southern Baptist Convention, the largest Protestant denomination in the USA, Penny Marler and Kirk Hadaway (2014, 19) suggest that the American Sunday school 'was more egalitarian and populist than the British model. In fact, it was a forerunner of the public-school movement. By 1860, the two were seen as separate but complementary.' The immediate post-war Baby Boom was the movement's most successful era, when Sunday school membership outstripped church membership. By 1963, Sunday school began to decline, bottoming out in the 1970s. In describing what happened, Marler and Hadaway say that (2014, 26): 'The most serious attrition was from 1963 to 1983 among children born from 1946 to 1971. Therefore, the greatest losses were among the cohorts that had flooded into the church during the Baby Boom, which ran from 1946 to 1964.' They cite Doreen Rosman (2007, 151) who studied the Sunday school movement in Great Britain, and found that its peak was 1888, but by the mid-twentieth century neither the parents, who sent their children to Sunday school, 'nor the children themselves regarded churchgoing as a logical corollary of Sunday School attendance'.

Those years match the exact period I have been researching in this current study, with all the interviews described here amongst people who attended, and left, Sunday school during those years. They are members of what Marler and Hadaway called 'the found and lost generation' and, as will be discussed in the final chapter, parents of the least religious generation of that last century, the Millennials. As Marler and Hadaway continue: 'They were aged 22 to 47 when adult Sunday school enrollment plateaued in 1993 (key years of family formation and family life), and 34 to 59 when adult Sunday school enrollment began to decline in 2005.'

Observing similar patterns across denominations in the USA, Canada, and the UK, what can we make of those statistics and the causal variables? A major influence was one outside the reach of evangelising Christians: demography. Marler and Hadaway (2014, 26–7) point to a pattern of falling birth rates and, consequently, a diminished potential Sunday school population:

In 1960 close to half of US households were made up of married couples with children; by 1990, that proportion fell to about 26%, and today barely 20% of all households consist of couples with children. As a result, denominations with family-oriented programs competed for an ever-shrinking proportion of the American populace.

In spite of demographic and institutional change, Marler and Hadaway (2014, 29–30) say that Southern Baptists held out longer than mainline Protestants by retaining 'an all-age Sunday school emphasis and curricular excellence as well as loyalty, investment, and committed older generations' before eventually experiencing similar decline. They discuss increasing university education and women's participation in the labour force as further reasons that the pool of young children shrunk, calling this 'a perfect cultural and demographic storm'. And yet, their argument does not help answer the question about why the Baby Boomers left Sunday school in hordes and did not resume a church-related religiosity. Nor does it provide reasons about why women discovered other priorities in their lives, beyond the usual, at least in religious sociology, suspects of the 'expansion of leisure and commercial opportunities on Sundays that interfered with regular church attendance' (Marler and Hadaway 2014, 27).

In her study of Sunday schools in the UK, Naomi Thompson (2017, 27) makes a similar observation: Sunday schools were popular in the early 1900s, and attendance declined significantly from the 1960s onwards. She, however, points to internal rather than external factors, arguing that the Sunday school became merged with churches and sought to achieve the church's objectives, rather than a more social objective, and ignored the needs, attitudes, and preference of the children. A more complicated story therefore needs to be narrated and understood: 'Churches may have alienated people rather than that people rejected Christianity outright' (Thompson 2017, 13).

Nevertheless, there was a strong tendency on the part of churches to jump on a bandwagon of trends to blame external factors such as leisure, labour, and welfare. Thompson (2017, 40–1) further discusses claims that the decline of church-based Sunday schools caused moral decay, described as smoking and alcohol abuse (and also noting that for many church-attenders, 'leisure' was counted as a vice), before concluding that churches failed to recognise children's needs by being rigidly structured and outdated. Children began to associate Sunday school with church and religion, although they were, in practice, two separate activities and institutions. When children outgrew Sunday school, Thompson continued, they outgrew religion. She concludes that the move to 'family church' sparked the decline, and, citing statistics showing church-based Sunday school decline since the 1960s, suggests that the shift to the practice of Sunday school attendance being composed of children of adult churchgoers was the last straw.

What Went Wrong? 'I Knew I Didn't Believe in It, So What Did It Matter?'

A trend within mainly theological literature links the decline of Sunday schools, as part of the Sunday school movement, to an increase in anti-social behaviour. Christie Davies (2017, 43), for example, is unequivocal, writing that Sunday schools were

> a great engine of respectability rooted in religion. During the time of its rise, deviant behaviour fell, and as religion decayed the Sunday schools declined: both religion and Sunday Schools collapsed together from the late 1950s, and as we have seen, a tide of deviance swept over the land. The trajectory of the Sunday Schools is that of respectable Britain.

Deviant behaviour, in Christie's study, referred to alcohol and drug abuse, and 'illegitimacy' and, as in most studies of Sunday schools, concentrated on the broader Sunday school movement of education on a Sunday aimed at the working classes, rather than the Sunday school as part of regular Anglican church attendance, as recalled by Baby Boomers here. Nevertheless, Christie links the decline of Sunday schools to the decline of religion more broadly, as does Christian activist Peter Brierley, whose detailed records of church attendance, furnished by clergy, have formed the bulk of the statistical record frequently used by scholars of religion.

Brierley (https://static1.squarespace.com/static/54228e0ce4b059910e19e44e/t/54353cfce4b05ee447c195df/1412775164001/CS4.pdf) cited, and generally agrees with, Christie that the decline of Sunday schools and religion led to a moral decline in the UK. He suggests another reason could be the decline of Christian missionaries and the fall of the British Empire. While noting that 'there are many cons as well as pros' linked to Empire, one pro was that it gave Britain a sense of purpose, to lead the world and to 'Christianise (civilise) the heathen'. Such language, he suggests, would not be acceptable today, but writes that it does not lessen the importance of the message. While in practice much of the Empire's power was abused, he argued, it did at least give people something to think about outside themselves and their social circles.

A less theological interpretation of what the Baby Boomer as children were experiencing, and why they chose to leave religion, may lie within the sociological theory of childhood. Unfortunately, there is a paucity of early research on childhood, a point that was made by Priscilla Alderson, writing in the British Sociological Association's online publication *Discover Society* (https://discoversociety.org/2016/02/02/the-missing-third-that-skews-sociology/) and see also Alderson 2016):

> Much mainstream 'adult' research in sociology, politics and economics ignores children and young people, while child-centred research tends to

ignore 'adult' concerns. Research thereby doubly excludes children from the mainstream world. Social analysis is then seriously skewed by biased sampling, when one fifth (in the UK), one third (globally), or nearly half of the groups being studied are routinely ignored. Childhood research is also distorted when it excludes the mainstream world, and the social and political structures which so greatly influence, infiltrate and explain children's daily lives.

As David Oswell writes (2012, 5–6), the sociology of childhood really only took off in the 1980s. Therefore, theories relating to Baby Boomers are necessarily retrospective, if not anachronistic, and explains why there is not a body of literature written in the 1950s and 1960s about Baby Boomer childhood. Further, Oswell says the main spaces where research on childhood exists is in schools, families, play, consumer culture, and health; he does not mention religion.

Oswell draws on the work of Phillipe Ariès (1962) whose understanding of childhood was imbued with historicity. His main assertions that influenced sociologists were that childhood is an historical invention and therefore a social institution, not a biological fact, and usually understood as a division or segregation from adults. Childhood was a case of quarantining children, institutionalising them, and keeping them separate from adults until they were deemed to be mature. Thus, most sociologists have followed Ariès in seeing childhood as a social construction.

Oswell is critical of those aspects, arguing that childhood is not, nor should it be, reducible to a social invention, category, or fixed location in some pure child-only space. He also says (2013, 14) that children should be understood not only through the social construction of the time but through 'a whole series of different kinds of affective and sensory relations'. Further, he writes that it is important to 'disclose children as social agents and not simply to see 'childhood' as constructed by adults alone' and see James and Prout 1997.

In the introduction to her edited handbook of methods for studying children and religion, Susan Ridgeley (2011) suggests there is a tendency to disregard children's own agency:

> In much of religious studies scholarship, as in most religious practice, children appear primarily as reflections of adult concerns about the present or as projections of adult concerns for the future. Until recently, the absence of children's voices in religion—and the widely shared

assumptions about childhood that inform this absence—led many scholars to view children as uncritically following the beliefs of their parents.

When people first wrote about the Baby Boomers, theories about childhood were just developing, and so it is unsurprising that they did not engage with such literature. My current study is one attempt to rectify that omission by more overtly engaging with ideas about power, agency, and authenticity as viewed through Baby Boomers' reflections of their childhoods.

Another problem some may raise is the veracity of historical accounts as they may be affected by lapses or revision in memory, as discussed in Chapter 1. While detail may be blurred, Boomers' recollections of their regular attendance, whether weekly or monthly, consistently relayed the lasting impression that they went because it was their family's habit.

Indeed, their accounts of Sunday school are remarkably devoid of detail. They consistently recall being separated from the main church, and, in many cases, of beginning to ask questions. But, beyond vague references to 'colouring in' or reading stories, the Sunday school experience seems to have been largely forgotten.

A source I frequently consulted has been Callum Brown's *Oral History of Humanism Compendium of Oral History (COT) Version E 18 September 2017*. These were interviews conducted as part of his 'History of Modern Humanism, 1945 to the Present' project to explore national and inter-national humanist development and loss of religion since 1945. Several of his questions concerned church attendances, such as: 'Did you go to church / Sunday school as a child? How often did you go? What kind of activities occurred? How did you perceive that experience at the time / since? At what juncture did you leave / drift away from church activities, and why? Do you regret doing so?'.

A key word search of the compendium revealed 191 matches to the search term 'Sunday school'. Reading the relevant sections revealed the same pattern found in my Baby Boomer interviews described here: no detailed accounts of what actually happened at Sunday school, apart from occasional references to feeling confused and sometimes aghast that what appeared to be illogical and far-fetched, even to children, was being presented as fact.

As I alluded to in the opening paragraphs on 'social space', the act of separating children from their parents and the wider church may have had several negative, unintended consequences. It consigned the children to an everyday, profane space that meant they did not experience the more religious atmosphere of a church and what that church community deemed sacred. For many Boomers, the Sunday school experience was just like their everyday school life: nothing much different, and certainly nothing to worship. As a social space composed of certain relations, it ingrained certain habits, or dispositions, that brought into being and reinforced behaviours that were not aligned more specifically to church or broader Christianity. This 'performative' aspect follows the ideas of Erving Goffman (1959) who argued that the way people enact their identities in relation to others helps to reinforce an identity and embeds a 'script' that can be read and relied upon for future interactions. Judith Butler (1990) emphasised in her theories on performativity that repeating such behaviours sediments the identity (gender, in her arguments). Arguably, acts of creating and maintaining church identity is performative, and brings into being a social reality which Butler referred to as the 'binding power' of the actions (Butler 1990). Besides church services, some churches offer a wide range of activities. As Anne-Marie Fortier (2000) discussed in her ethnography of St Peter's Italian Church in London, cultural identities were created, performed, and embedded through socially binding linguistic acts and events such as processions, weddings, newsletters, and first communions. Those 'performative belongings' were constitutive of cultural identities that were both simultaneously de-territorialised (from Italy) and re-territorialised (in London).

Durkheim's (1915, 475) ideas about religion stress the importance of repeated collective acts of effervescence to further bind the group and reinforce the group's feelings and beliefs. This reinforcement could not be achieved 'except by the means of reunions, assemblies and meetings where the individuals being closely united to one another, reaffirm in common their common sentiments'. Colouring pictures of camels and stars were not exactly generative of collective ecstasy and joy. What they did not receive at Sunday school was repeated experience or training in the habits of church behaviour. The behaviours and identities reinforced at Sunday school, according to most of my Boomer interviews, were secular, social, and subservient. Sunday school was something they had to do. Given a choice, which later they were, those were behaviours and identities they were keen to discard.

Apart from considering the acts of attending Sunday school, it is also appropriate to explore their beliefs, or lack thereof. I referred earlier to two significant statements two interviewees made: Philip described his Sunday school experience as 'more social than actually believing', and Robin reported that she did not mind reciting a Brownie promise that she did not agree with because 'I knew I didn't believe in it, so what did it matter?'.

The matter of belief is central for Anglicans and, other scholars argue, for Christianity in general. Webb Keane (2007) drew from his study of Calvinism the more general point that 'belief' is salient especially for Christians who follow the doctrine that when the word of God became 'flesh' in the body (or, as Keane reads, 'materiality') it became degraded. Calvinists thus associated belief 'with immaterial meaning over practices that threatened to subordinate belief to material form' (2007, 67).

And yet, while it tends to be taken for granted that religious people have beliefs, as Durkheim would argue, few scholars inspect what belief may mean to different people at different times. It certainly meant something particular for Philip and Robin. I will not detail here the long history of how 'belief' has been understood, often just implicitly, in disciplines such as anthropology, sociology, and religious studies,[8] but refer to two major theorists who influenced the direction belief took in anthropology, the discipline that has interrogated the term more than others, and whose conclusions bear most strongly on my interpretation of what Philip and Robin are likely to have meant.

When anthropologist Rodney Needham (1972) historicised from, primarily, the philosophical literature about how belief has been used by anthropologists and philosophers, he provided an exhaustive review and concluded that it was a mistake to universalise it. He argued that the broadly anthropological literature and, more specifically, ethnographic literature consistently fails to interrogate how scholars are using the term 'belief'. Further, he argued, there was nothing universal about belief. That, I suggest, introduced an idea of contingency that Philip and Robin mirror.

Following, and after much critique of, Needham, Malcolm Ruel accepted that belief was an unstable philosophical term, but even more important was the fact that it meant different things to different people at different times.[9]

It is difficult to generalise my conclusions beyond my study and a few theories, as above. As Ivan Reid (1977) noted, research about Sunday schools is scant, but studies that have been done show little impact of the Sunday school on future religiosity or moral beliefs. The lack of research will continue, I suggest, mainly because the numbers of children currently attending Sunday school has, in line with figures on church attendance more widely, declined significantly during the last decades. Reid concluded (1977, 8) from his research that any positive associations children held about Sunday school likely derived from a supportive family background and 'an association of like-minded individuals, rather than an effective religious or educational process'.

In other words, a social thing.

Notes

1. The reported figures are likely to be higher than actual. See Hadaway et al. 1993.
2. It was Meredith McGuire who first called sociologists of religion to attend to 'the body'. In her presidential address to the annual conference of the Society for the Social Scientific Study of Religion, Meredith McGuire (1990) delivered an argument which helped to shape the discipline's orientation. She urged social scientists of religion to take theories of the body, and embodiment, seriously because the body 'matters'.
3. I follow the UK spelling conventions here which differentiates between 'practise' as a verb and 'practice' as a noun.
4. He was the oldest of the Boomers I interviewed and, while outside the 1940s range usually accorded to the Baby Boomer generation, he insisted he felt strongly that he was a member.
5. I will return to the idea of 'actually believing' later in this chapter, and in more depth in Chapter 11.
6. It transpired that Robin was about 60 years ahead of her time. As I discuss more in Chapter 6 when exploring a clash of values, the Brownie and Guide promise was changed in 2013 to downplay God and country.
7. For more detailed discussions of performative belief, see Day 2011.
8. For more detail see Day 2011.
9. For more on the varied history of 'belief' see John Arnold (2005) and Talal Asad (1993).

3

Enabling Ambivalence

Introduction: 'We Went Along'

Religious transmission occurs primarily through families. That is, as Andrew Singleton (2017, 11) wrote, a 'sociologically established fact that mainline denominations are not built on switchers from other denomination or new converts, but on families, and the passing down of tradition within families (see Bengtson, Putney and Harris 2013)'.

As sociologists are generally loathe to claim anything as 'fact', apart from what Durkheim referred to as the social ones, Singleton's claim is one to take seriously, particularly as it has been corroborated by so many sociologists and demographers. Hadaway and Marler write (2005, 31): 'Research suggests that when a denomination loses its children, it loses successive generational sources of loyalty and investment. This is already occurring in Great Britain, where every generation is less religious than the one before.'

In later work, Marler and Hadaway (2014) concluded in their study of Sunday school decline that children's continued involvement depended on parents having a religious heritage and continuing with their own religious education. They cited Christian Smith (2005) who argued that keeping 'devoted' teens (about 8 per cent of all American adolescents) in church depended on both their attendance at the local church and Sunday school as well as the religious piety and involvement of their parents.

Marler and Hadaway (2014, 32) suggest that parents need to 'pray with a child, read the Bible with a child, share service to others out of religious conviction with a child, take a child to Sunday school, and take a child to worship' in order to ensure religious transmission. Further, they continue, parents need to demonstrate that they 'participate in Christian education and go to worship as a model for and with children. These things matter most for the identification and involvement of future generations in church and the continued viability of religious congregations and denominations.'

As Linda Woodhead (2016, 249) notes from her analysis of the British Social Attitudes survey: 'Children brought up Christian have a 45 per cent chance of ending up as "nones", whereas those brought up 'no religion' have

Why Baby Boomers Turned from Religion: Shaping Belief and Belonging, 1945–2021. Abby Day, Oxford University Press. © Abby Day 2022. DOI: 10.1093/oso/9780192866684.003.0003

a 95 per cent probability of retaining that identification.' How children are 'brought up' includes how parents talk to children about religion. In their study of Australian adolescents, Margaret Dudley and Roger Dudley (1986) found that children whose parents talked about their religion were more likely to continue with that religion themselves. They concluded that 'there is strong support for religious transmission in Australia. Both parents are involved, and there is evidence that supervision (either disciplinary, moral, or religious) during adolescent years has a strong impact on later adult religious belief' (Dudley and Dudley 1986, 765).

It therefore appears that something significant occurred between generations, from the older, more observant 'Generation A' through to their children, the Baby Boomer 'Generation B', and from the Boomers to their children and subsequently grandchildren, Generations X, Y, and Z. Little research has focused on the primary Generation A, those who were the most regular church attenders and church supporters of the last century (Day 2017). Although the 1950s is often presented stereotypically as one composed of happy families, with a male breadwinner, female housewife, and 2.4 well-adjusted children, there were more serious breaches in the background. This was the generation that began to unravel the formerly unquestionably respectable units of church and family, enabling their children's 1960s counterculture revolution of experimentation, 'free love', and secularisation. It was Generation A, the parents of the Boomers that liberalised divorce, made 'the pill' widely available, and decriminalised abortion and homosexuality.

The divorce rate, for example, rose faster in 1946 and 1947 than before or since in the 'west', those countries of the Global North's Anglican Communion. Various reasons for this are proposed by scholars (see, for example, Greenwood and Guner 2004; Pavalko and Elder 1990; Peters 1976) but due to lack of data, firm conclusions are rarely drawn: pressures of wartime, swift marriages, and psychologically damaged war veterans are three contenders for causality. As Eliza Pavalko and Glenn Elder write (1990, 1214), 'After World War II, the divorce rate soared to a new high, which many attributed to the fragility of hasty wartime marriages.' To complicate matters further, it is not feasible that a desire for divorce was only invented in the 1940s. As Jeremy Greenwood and Nezih Guner (2008, 236) found, 'except for a spike associated with World War II, the rate of divorce rose more or less continuously over the last century from about four per 1,000 women in 1900, to about 10 in 1941 (a doubling), to about 23 today (another doubling)'.

Another explanation for the post-war spike, and the one that is probably most relevant here, would be the reluctance of women to return to a home-based domesticity when many had led more independent and wage-earning lives during the war. Commentary from the UK Office for National Statistics advances that point, suggesting that changes in behaviour and attitudes are likely to explain the increase in divorces between 1930 and 1990. The large post-war increase in the late 1940s 'is considered to be attributable to women's increased participation in the labour force which meant couples were no longer as financially dependent on each other' (https://www.ons. gov.uk/peoplepopulationandcommunity/birthsdeathsandmarriages/articles/ victoryineuropedayhowworldwariichangedtheuk/2015-05-08).

Another, but more moderate, spike occurred in 1970 following the passing of the Divorce Reform Act 1969 in the UK and similar acts of liberalisation in other countries. But that spike was, once again, fuelled initially by the Boomers' parents' generation, Generation A. In 1969, even the oldest Boomer born in 1945 would have been only 24, which was 10 years younger than the average age at which people become divorced. It would have been the earlier generation, born in the 1920s and 1930s, who were campaigning for and taking advantage of those possibilities to more easily end their marriages. And, as in divorce behaviour in general, most of the divorce petitioners were women. I argue, therefore, that it is essential that scholars account for the influence of those older members in society, the Boomers' parents, their relatives, their friends, politicians, and activists. Even the church played an important role in liberalising divorce.

As Hadaway and Marler (2005, 30) observed: 'the key, which is often missed, is the adult, the parent: children's retention is closely tied to adults' participation and identity'. David Oswell (2012, 116) argued that most socialisation theory assumes that the family is the primary agent, construing 'family as the relay, or mediator, between society and the pre-individual, pre-social child', but he notes, this model does not accord women any agency, apart from, presumably, being part of the objectified 'relay'.

There is also sometimes a sense in the literature that 'the family' as prime agent of socialisation, was a single, unproblematic entity. Christopher Lasch (1979, 4) wrote:

If the reproduction of culture were simply a matter of formal instruction and discipline, it could be left to the schools. But it also requires that culture be embedded in personality. Socialization makes the individual want to do what he has to do; the family is the agency to which society entrusts this complex and delicate task.

Oswell (2012, 116) urges sociologists to think of the family as being more widely composed of different agents working in different ways, with shifting power dynamics: 'In this sense, socialisation is understood in the context of social interaction, inasmuch as social interaction is bounded within the familial and emotional relations of a particular household.'

If, therefore, religious transmission or 'the chain of memory', as Danielle Hervièu-Léger (2000) described it, broke between Generations A and B, then, I will argue, it was unlikely to be picked up in the future. Indeed, as I will review in the final chapter, this is exactly what happened: the failure of religious transmission continues.

While scholars generally focus on the Baby Boomers as the primary agents of change, I tend to disagree. The Baby Boomers were not hatched: they were born to women and raised by, mainly, two parents. If those parents were not transmitting religious beliefs and practice, I argue that it is essential to explore what was being transmitted instead that allowed, and in some cases encouraged, a turn from church and religion more generally. Taking a cue from social cognitive theories about learning (Bandura 1986), if young people learn through modelling behaviours, what non-religious behaviours of their parents were they modelling? Considering socialisation theory more broadly, work has generally stressed that the family is the most important source (Erikson 1950) and that both actions and words are necessary in successfully socialising children (Lanman and Buhrmester 2017).

In her pathbreaking work on modelling socialisation, Marie Cornwall (1989) summarised the four main factors thought to influence religious behaviour: group involvement, belief orthodoxy, religious socialisation, and socio-demographic variables. In her discussion, the influence of Peter Berger's (1967) work is relevant for this study, as he identified conversations with parents as a means of upholding plausibility structures that reinforce, or challenge, one's subjective reality. The effect of several factors Berger discussed, including plausibility structures and pluralism, will be further examined in the next chapter when changes in the Boomers' teen years are explored.

Cornwall (1989, 577) concludes, in her section on religious socialisation, that studies suggest 'that socialization processes influence the development of a world view, but perhaps more importantly, also channel individuals into personal communities which in turn help maintain a person's religious beliefs and commitment to religious norms'. As discussed in the previous chapter, parents of Baby Boomers channelled their children's religious activities into Sunday school, which seemed to have not had the effect of increasing religious belief or commitment, primarily because there was little within Sunday school to engage or inspire children to become more religiously committed.

In this chapter I hope to disentangle the various influences that contributed to generational religious transmission being severed as it passed from the As, to the Bs. I will argue that it was because of parental ambivalence, supported by rapid cultural change, that Boomers felt able to make the break from Anglicanism specifically and religion more generally. The main themes that influence my argument are what appeared to be a decline in the social compulsion to demonstrate 'respectability' through church attendance. This was likely linked to a decline in deference influenced by growing pluralism and tolerance, and disapproval of rigid class boundaries. A rise of feminism further produced disinclination to agree with patriarchal systems, including the church. Followers of scholarship concerned with that period of religious change may notice a few omissions from my list, such as neoliberalism, consumerism, the availability of 'time', the power of choice, and the so-called breakdown of the family. These were not factors raised by the Boomers I interviewed and, as I will argue, tend to mirror a normative, more theological than sociological set of beliefs.

Non-Religious Homes: 'She Had Done Her Duty'

As discussed in the last chapter, Baby Boomers were unequivocal that religion was something that happened at Sunday school and not at home. There were many opportunities in my interviews with Baby Boomers to discuss such things, beginning with my first question asking them to describe to me their earliest memories about religion. Invariably, they discussed Sunday school. To probe further the topic of religion at home, I eventually asked the direct question: 'Did you do anything at home that you might describe as religious or spiritual?' and, if nothing was recalled, by even further prompting 'such as, for example, discussing the content of Sunday school activity, or church event, perhaps reading the bible, saying prayers or maybe grace at dinner?' Those prompts were similar to, for example, Cornwall's (1989, 574) study when her surveys probed home religious observance consisting of 'family prayer, family religious discussions, family Bible or scripture reading, and family discussions of right and wrong'. She concluded (1989, 589) building on her earlier work (Cornwall 1987, 1988), that:

> parental attendance and home religious observance have a significant direct impact on adult belief and commitment. In addition, parental attendance and home religious observance also have a significant impact in that they channel individuals into friendship networks during the teen and young adult years which support and sustain the religious values taught in the home.

Baby Boomers sometimes recalled saying prayers before bed, in their bedrooms, in the company of a parent, usually their mother. The prayer they recalled, in Canada and the UK, was a pattern of what was commonly practised as the bedtime prayer: 'Now I lay me down to sleep'. In recalling this during our interviews, several would laugh, shake their heads, and express wonder that children were invited to contemplate their own deaths.[1] The words my interviewees recalled were:

> Now I lay me down to sleep,
> I pray the Lord my soul to keep;
> If I should die before I wake,
> I pray the Lord my soul to take.

They all also remembered that the next lines were theirs to ask God to protect, or 'bless' various family members and sometimes friends. It seemed significant that the routine of noting their care for others was something so many Boomers shared, and their mothers reinforced. Their nightly practice was, perhaps, a form of ritual that served to reinforce important social relations. Ana S. Itlis (2012) suggested, rituals create and maintain social reality by creating webs of social bonds that help maintain social cohesion, stability, and belonging.

Not all Boomers recalled prayers as markers of social stability. Kim said that her mother encouraged her to say prayers, but it felt 'a little like asking Father Christmas'. It seemed that even from an early age, a certain cynicism and doubt was creeping in. Her parents were not 'fervent' she said, and didn't discuss religion, apart from sometimes answering, if questions were asked, 'oh, well, yes, there is a God', and that would be the end of it. The parents went to church and the children went to Sunday school: 'We went along,' she said. Going 'along' seemed to be a common theme for the Baby Boomers and their parents.

The rare times that religion was a part of the Baby Boomer home life was also one that was met with ambivalence. Jennifer recalled of her abusive father and his impact on the family:

> When were we little at home, we did say grace. My father had some short of short grace, he sort of humoured mother, but then would get angry and say you should be thanking me, not someone else. We all had bibles. We were all given bibles, we sometimes read the bibles, but we didn't do any religious things at home.

As discussed in the previous chapter, Jennifer described her early experience as not 'a religious-based childhood, but it was a church-based childhood'.

Fran, a Canadian retired civil servant born in 1956, stressed that church seemed to be a social place, and no other 'religion related things at home, no grace'. Annabel said her childhood did not feature any religion. Religion was not, she said, 'being hammered home'. She was confirmed, but added that she did not 'remember my mother professing or talking about religion, though I remember once she said she thought the Church of England was the best'. The best for what, she couldn't say, but this may have had more to do with the church's 'social place' than its theology. Annabel felt that it was 'very powerfully drilled into me that Mother's religion was very much "this is correct", not a powerful faith, more like this is the thing to do'. Yvonne said she could not recall any religious behaviour at home: 'Maybe little pictures of Jesus on the wall but I think that was a souvenir from New York,' she said. 'I don't remember my mum even talking about theology.' Further, when Yvonne began to skip some of her confirmation classes her mother never intervened and when Yvonne stopped attending church altogether, her mother did not object: 'she had done her duty'. Stephanie, a Canadian social worker born in 1947, said she had a sense that her mother was 'drifting away' from the church.

There were, perhaps, specific values about tolerance and respect for others that were also being transmitted. Vikki, a British retired retail manager born in 1948, said she recalled that 'my mother and father allowed me, to a great extent, to find my mind'.

For example, she said, when her friends were listening to the Beatles and the Rolling Stones and she was listening to Johnny Mathis:

I didn't feel I was different because I was not in the mainstream, not a part of what was going on around me but just that I was finding my own mind, my own likes, and I could do that because of my parents, and I passed that onto my daughter as well.

Another Boomer spoke specifically about parental values becoming non-religious. Fraser, a Canadian retired magazine editor born in 1940, said he sensed as a child that his parents were becoming sceptical about the church: 'they could see the hypocrisy'. Although his mother 'retained a belief more than my dad' the church was definitely more conservative than his family. From the age of six, he said, he 'began to doubt that the stories and mythologies were true. For example, on one hand God was a vengeful god, then it was a forgiving god, but like Trump, he was telling you one thing one day and something different the next.'

One exception to the general pattern of a non-religious home was described by Michele who said that her childhood memories of religion showed that 'it was the fabric of my family'. It was their tradition to go to church on Sundays, although, she laughed, they were always late and, as discussed in Chapter 2, she felt that the Sunday school was more like a babysitting service. They always said grace before meals, and Michele had been both baptised and confirmed: 'Anglicanism was just the way the world was,' she said.

Michele's father had been a clergyman but died when she was two. Her mother, who also came from a family of clergy, died when Michele was 14. Michele went to boarding school after that and gave up religion. Her story will be picked up again in later chapters.

Social Expectations

Many Boomers felt a strong sense of social expectations from their parents to attend church that sometimes, they may theorise now, was related to social class. For a few, it was fear.

Samantha, a British retired college principal born in 1945, said that from about age 11 she was frightened by stories of the intensity of Christ's suffering at Easter and tied this to her own 'misdemeanours'. That guilt and fear 'would work against me' and force her to behave. She was, she explained, driven by fear and not by any love-based church belief or practice.

Robin said that in the Northeast of England, where she grew up, it was socially expected to have babies baptised because 'it was considered unlucky for an unbaptised baby to be in your house' and it was thought that if they died, they would be denied a Christian burial in their local churchyard. While this may have been folklore, she said, because of the effects of poverty, too many babies died in their first year. Some of those and related folk ideas died out in the 1950s, she said, but they did have a strong effect while they lasted on people's inclination to show a level of religiosity. David Clark's (1982) study of a fishing village in North Yorkshire in the 1970s corroborates her impressions: people's 'folk beliefs' (sometimes dismissed as 'superstition' by others) were often interwoven with conventionally religious beliefs and ideas.

Pam, a British retired engineer born in 1950, spoke along the same lines. She was baptised because, she said, it was 'something everybody did'. In time, people began to do things differently. That kind of social change and turn from religiosity could be understood by applying a different example, she said: 'It's like asking why people don't watch black and white TVs anymore like they did in the 50s. Colour came along and that was better.' She said she thought her father was relieved when she eventually said she did not believe in Christianity, as was her mother 'she was worried I'd become a nun,' she laughed. Her mother had not put pressure on her to continue with church attendance, she said, apart from the need to attend church to stay on with Brownies and Guides. Pam said she did continue with Brownies and Guides, even though she did not approve of the religious-based promise: 'We had to teach the promise to younger children. I justified my hypocrisy that it was a good organization.' Her mother admitted towards the end of her life, after Pam had left home, that she had also been a hypocrite going along with the promise. Pam was a little surprised to hear that because, as a child, 'I said my prayers every evening, and at that time I assumed my mother believed in it all'. In our interview, we discussed this maternal ambivalence in more detail. Pam wanted to tease out some of the pattern that had initially confused her. In retrospect, she said, she could see that as her mother got older and became busier with her career she only went to church 'on very significant occasions'. Her mother thought that, in principle, 'it was good to be in that community' and, even though she was a 'working mother', she was involved in church sales and Christmas bazaars: 'it was more of a social thing,' Pam added. She explained her lack of regular attendance to her daughter by saying 'if there was a god up there, surely he wouldn't judge a busy woman'. Other than with occasional comments,

Pam said she did not think her parents ever discussed religion: 'Their marriage was the classic case of man coming back from the war and marrying a local girl,' she said. Her mother later in life said that she was surprised her husband did not expect her to go to church more regularly. Although he didn't 'believe' his mother did, Pam said. Both of her grandmothers were 'very genuinely religious' she said, but, even as a child, she was not so sure about mother: 'I think she just went along,' Pam said, 'I think it was a society thing for her, an expectation and she just went along with it and when she didn't need to, she didn't'. Her mother later told her that a neighbour had said, 'you go to church, dear, and he will let you have a good coat'.

Peter, a retired British logistics manager born in 1951, also raised the difference between his parents' generation and his grandparents. His grandparents' generation, he said 'had to do as they were told' whereas the 'Baby Boomers are more like their parents, they ask "why"?' Peter thought the shift may have had something to do with World War II: 'the war changed them,' he said. At his school most of his teachers were retired army officers who 'had survived the war and a lot had lost their faith because of that they had seen. There was a colossal loss of human life.'

Simon, a retired British Human Resources manager born in 1950, also discussed the effect of war and how everything changed. His father was a distinguished air force pilot, he said, but never spoke about the war. He 'drew a line under it,' Simon explained and wanted to do other things, to look forward, not back. He discussed the 'massive sense of optimism' and how it affected people. They 'began to think in different ways for the future,' he continued: 'The religious component didn't seem to be as important—we kind of did it but mostly out of habit'.

Although most Baby Boomers did not report any memories of religiosity practised at home, one exception mirrored social expectations. Charlotte, a retired British bakery worker born in 1947, recalled that her family never said grace at dinner, unless 'people came over' for dinner or for Christmas. Having family in both Canada and the UK, Charlotte said she thought she could see differences where the UK's Church of England is more about 'social Christians' and more secular, whereas in Canada, Anglican Christianity is 'more evangelical, like Baptists'. On the West Coast of Canada, a multicultural demographic has tended to produce a more varied, nature-based spiritual milieu, she said, with sexism, racism, and homophobia seen as unwelcome characteristics of the established churches.

The sense that religion was 'the right thing to do', pervaded in her family, Kim recalled. She recalled her father often saying, 'the church wouldn't like it'. Her memories focused on a sense of the Anglican church being 'middle class, middle of the road'. Kim's family split their religious allegiances between Methodists and Anglicans, with Kim attending Church of England Sunday school and occasional services, and a Methodist youth group. She said that she preferred the Methodist version of Christianity, because at the Church of England so much seemed to be about conformity and respectability: wearing hats, and singing the hymns correctly, she recalled. One church even had incense: 'that seemed like worshipping an idol,' she remarked.

Charles, a British accountant born in 1948, recalled similar experiences. When I asked him if he had been baptised, he said:

> Yes, I was, but I think everybody was. I say everybody, but you know what I mean, everyone who was white English middle class, that's what happened, basically. I was born in 1948 and I was christened when I was a few weeks old. And I was confirmed as well, which looking back at it I find really bizarre, but I was. (*Laughs*)

His parents were not what he described as 'religious', and neither were his maternal grandparents. He father's parents were, on the other hand 'stalwarts' of their church. They were a farming family, and the church was the social centre of the community, he said. It was because of them, he recalled, that he and his parents were 'forced' to go to church: 'they were strong CofE, very strong indeed,' he said. His grandfather was a sidesman, and his grandmother was a member of the Mother's Union: 'a sort of militant faction of the CofE,' he added. Charles' father 'had no religion at all, he abandoned his original CofE affiliation,' Charles said. Charles organised a Humanist cremation for his father because 'he didn't want any religious elements in his funeral, basically'.

His mother, he said, 'didn't really have any strong religious beliefs, but she would say to me things like, "I think there's something there, you know, I can't dismiss it all, I think there's something there." But I wouldn't describe her as strongly religious at all.'

Jennifer recalled that social class and expectations permeated her childhood as her mother was 'High Anglican'. 'We went every Sunday, and I sang in the choir for years and years.' She was confirmed, she recalled, and

'Christmas and Easter were of course really special. We always wore our new clothes, a special dress, and there was a big deal made when you got confirmed. We got a special cross necklace.'

In his study of the Australian Anglican churches, Andrew Singleton (2017, 13) concluded that 'parents stopped sending their children to Sunday School because they no longer felt some social obligation to do so; moreover, shopping centres were open and junior football and netball matches had to be played'. I will discuss the impact of social class at more length in Chapter 6 where it became a salient variable for some Boomers and their decisions to leave religion.

Values Transmission

My analysis concurs with Andrew Singleton (2017, 14) who said sociological research 'suggests that it is deeper factors—personal, familiar and familial— that lead a person away from identification with the Anglican Church'.

When discussing the early period of their lives, Boomers introduced a number of topics related to values, and in particular the kind of values that their parents were transmitting and may have, I suggest, contributed to their leaving Anglicanism and religion more broadly. Several values seemed to relate to a turn from deference to more equal values of human rights and care.

During my interviews I always asked the Baby Boomers what sort of moral beliefs they had, and where they got those from. I discuss in future chapters how some of those values clashed with religion, but here I will stay with the theme of their parents' role in transmitting moral beliefs and values. Invariably, they said these came from their parents. I will argue that the choices the Baby Boomers made were partly possible because they had been raised to be more trusting, caring, respectful of others, and independent. The seeds of the 1960s' cultural revolution were sown and nurtured by the parents of Generation A who raised their Baby Boomer children in the 1950s, 1960s, and 1970s.

In his study of British families in the 1950s, David Kynaston (2009, 596–7) concludes that the Baby Boomers' 1950s parents were 'significantly less old school than the previous generation of parents... The overall sense is of parenthood on the cusp of fundamental change by the early to mid-1950s.'

I will discuss here some of the values and beliefs Boomers felt were handed down by their parents.

Social responsibility and human rights: 'it centred on kindness and equality'

It was not part of her 'church memory', but moral training was strongly part of her 'home memory', Virginia, a Canadian retail manager born in 1955, said. It centred on kindness and equality, values she said she learned from her mother and grandmother: 'I think I was well brought up, with right and wrong, being kind to others, treat others as you want to be treated.' She recalled her mother talking about those values and learning from her grandmother by watching her: 'a very kind, grounded soul'. Charlotte said she had learned her values of equality and human rights from her father, a strong socialist. Michele said that she had learned about morality from her parents, reinforced by her later career that emphasised 'humanistic' values of honesty and community.

Martin, a retired British plumber born in 1948, reflected that his child-hood coincided with a period of comparative peace: 'We had the UN, we had unprecedented peace, apart from the US, who has been at war at least every 10 years, but they also did police the world.'

Indeed, it was members of Generation A, parents of the Baby Boomers, who created the United Nations (UN) in 1945. Their aim was to prevent another world war and to agree international laws and conventions to protect human rights. The world was reeling not only from the global suffering and bloodshed of war, but more specifically from the emerging realisation of the Holocaust. The first treaty adopted by the UN in 1948 was the Convention on the Prevention and Punishment of the Crime of Genocide (known as the 'Genocide Convention'). It codified for the first time the crime of genocide, demonstrating the commitment of the international community to ensure that the horrors of the Holocaust would never happen again. Also in 1948, the UN issued the Universal Declaration of Human Rights (UDHR) (https://www.un.org/en/about-us/universal-declaration-of-human-rights):

> The Universal Declaration of Human Rights (UDHR) is a milestone document in the history of human rights. Drafted by representatives with different legal and cultural backgrounds from all regions of the world, the Declaration was proclaimed by the United Nations General Assembly in Paris on 10 December 1948 (General Assembly resolution 217 A) as a common standard of achievements for all peoples and all nations. It sets out, for the first time, fundamental human rights to be universally pro-tected and it has been translated into over 500 languages.

The UDHR has had it critics over the years, including the American Anthropological Association which argued that it was western-centric, Saudi Arabia which refused to sign up to it because it violated sharia law, and many Christian groups and sects which argued that it set secular rights over God-given rights and rules.[2]

Trust and freedom

Boomers frequently spoke of having freedoms when they were young, both by being allowed to question ideas and, to some extent, authority, and to explore towns and cities well beyond their own front gardens. I would argue that their Generation A parents were not being remiss, rebellious, or inattentive in their parenting, but they reflect a period where high levels of societal trust made such liberties more possible.

Virginia suggested that parents of the Boomers gave them more latitude: 'Things were being explored by kids in the 60s, whereas ten years earlier parents might have said you're not going there... there was a little more freedom, a little more trust.' She reflected that she was 'so grateful that I was allowed to explore that, some scary shit the first time, but then there's confidence building'.

The trend to show children more latitude may also have been influenced, at least in part, by Benjamin Spock, to date the most popular paediatrician, if numbers of books sold is a good measure. His book, *The Common Sense Book of Baby and Childcare*, published in 1946, was aimed at the new parents of the Baby Boomers, urging them to trust their instincts and allow their children more freedom and flexibility than their own parents had. Richard Gunderman (2019) writes:

> The book ignited a revolution, breaking free from conventional wisdom that said children required schedules, discipline and little affection. Instead, 'The Common Sense Book of Baby and Childcare,' written by Dr. Benjamin Spock and published in 1946, encouraged parents to think for themselves and to trust their instincts. Spock's book was a huge best-seller, second in the U.S. only to the Bible. It sold more than 50 million copies and was translated into more than 40 languages. It helped to usher in a fundamental shift in how Americans approached parenting.

The effect of Spock on Baby Boomers is difficult to measure, mainly because there are many different, and contested, interpretations of his work.

One that seems to have influenced a leading educator in the 1960s, is the claim that parents raised their children to be more permissive and rebellious as a consequence of Spock's book. In his survey of Spock's sources and influences, William Graebner (1980, 628) writes:

> In May of 1968, during protests against the Vietnam War, Columbia University vice-president David Truman charged Spock with having raised an entire generation of youth on an inadequate and harmful diet of permissiveness. In his defense, Spock has argued that moderate strictness and moderate permissiveness are both viable child-rearing methods and that the success of each is dependent upon the 'spirit' with which the parent manages the child and the attitude this spirit engenders. Poor results stem from 'strictness that comes from harsh feelings' or 'permissiveness that is timid or vacillating'.

Graebner (1980, 629) writes that the significance of Spock's views about permissiveness was not confined to childrearing but reflected wider cultural norms: 'The importance of Spock as an interpreter of American culture lies in the degree to which his ideas and methodology of child rearing were common to other aspects of that culture.' For Generation A, who became Baby Boomer parents, 'what came to be known as permissiveness in child rearing was part of a new democratic authority structure also being tailored for education, industrial relations, even the handling of the aged. Permissiveness was becoming a central characteristic of American life.'

The more trusting era of the 1960s and 1970s becomes particularly apparent when contrasted with more recent research on today's societies. Ryan Chae (2019) cites General Social Survey research that shows that levels of trust in society has decreased over the last two generations, leading to a trend in 'overprotective parenting', defined as: 'a collection of behaviors by parents toward their children that work together in an attempt to prevent children from taking on any risks to their emotional or physical health'. This is a worrying trend, he argues (2019), because:

> That is being reflected in policy-making and legal decisions, and that has left older generations shaking their heads. Generational gap notwithstanding, mounting evidence and research have begun to reveal a disturbing effect of this trend that should be cause for real concern. Overprotective parents, and the norms that prevail from an overprotective attitude toward children, are threatening to build a generation of young Americans that are

highly risk-averse, fearful, and unprepared to become engaged citizens and active leaders.

Research by Pew Research on trust confirms the pattern that shows contemporary young and less educated people are less trusting than older, better educated people, with considerable variation by region. In their 2020 survey (https://www.pewresearch.org/fact-tank/2020/12/03/social-trust-in-advanced-economies-is-lower-among-young-people-and-those-with-less-education/) of 14 countries with advanced economies, Canadians topped the list of most trusting, with the UK at the midpoint and Italy at the bottom.

Equality for women

Another important social trend of the Boomers' childhoods and teenage years was the more visible and widespread call for women's equal rights. Jennifer, for example, wondered aloud if her mother's generation were, inadvertently, raising their children to become feminists. It sometimes seemed, she said, that 'they were able to project onto their daughters what they couldn't have themselves'.

Detecting some ambivalence in her mother's engagement with church-based roles for women, Lesley, a retired British book editor born in 1948, said she was aware that while her mother had respect for the 'rota' at church (the schedule showing who was responsible for which tasks, such as arranging flowers or serving teas and coffees after the church service), 'she didn't really enjoy it'. Indeed, the rota was not just the schedule, it was also a document of public prominence, a list usually posted to be visible to anyone entering the church or pausing by its noticeboard. It is a fixture in most Anglican churches. As I reflected on my ethnography of elderly Anglican women (Day 2017), the 'rota' was both structural and emotional. It set out names and activities to help those who wanted to keep track of their schedule, but its position for all to see also created a strong sense of accountability and surveillance. The tasks themselves were not always, as Lesley's mother said, particularly enjoyable. Cleaning the church weekly was, for many, an added chore amongst so many that mainly fall on women in the home, the workplace, and the church. Providing biscuits or cakes for after-service refreshments might tax the domestic skills of those not accustomed to baking daily. Standing for an hour or so in a cold, draughty church handing out teas and coffees to people after a service was often physically uncomfortable and tedious. And, no matter what the activity or duty, that most people on the rota were women reinforced an assumed division of labour that would ruffle the emerging sensitivities of those leaning towards feminism.

In Lesley's case, both her father and mother were 'wonderful role models'. A convert to Christianity in his twenties, her father was a lay preacher who supported the ordination of women. This would have been unusual and controversial for that period, when the Anglican church was still vociferously opposed to having women priests. The possibilities for women to be ordained as priests in the Church of England began with a report in 1966 which opened the discussion. The General Synod, the governing body of the Church of England, reported nearly a decade later in 1975 that although there were no fundamental reasons that women should not be ordained, because there were objections amongst clergy and laypeople, the process derailed. In 1987, women 'deacons' (a ministerial role slightly lower than full priest) were admitted; in 1994, the first women priests were ordained. The first woman bishop in the Anglican Communion, Barbara Harris, became Bishop of Massachusetts in 1989: it took the Church of England nearly 30 years to catch up, with Libby Lane ordained as the first female bishop in 2015.

When Lesley eventually 'drifted away' from the church, her father was disappointed 'but he knew she wanted her freedom', she told me. He was likely acutely aware of the wider, social shift towards equality for women.

Boomers sometimes described their parents, particularly their mothers, as beginning to resist the rigid structures of the church. Martin picked up hints of ambivalence from his mother, who told him stories about how when she was young she was forced to go to church. It was very strict, she had told Martin. They had to sit still and couldn't talk during the service.

Paula, a Canadian finance manager born in 1955, described her mother not wanting to take the children to church anymore: 'Mom said she didn't want to take them anymore, that she didn't really believe anymore and felt the children could decide.' Many other Boomers recalled their parents, often their mothers, suggesting that the children 'could decide'. While that sentiment may reflect a wider cultural milieu of permissiveness and choice, it could also be, I suggest, a way for parents to side-step their own disbelief, particularly in an era when it was socially unacceptable to be an atheist.

Bruce, a retired British mechanic born in 1953, said that at age 16 he had begun to question his faith. He had been extensively involved in the church, including acting as a 'server'. Sometimes also known as altar boys (or, from the late 1960s, girls), servers assist the priest at the front of the church. Duties range from setting out the requirements for Holy Communion to opening the Bible at the right page for the priest. Bruce discussed his doubts with his mother and together they agreed that he could stop serving and attending church. He felt so strongly that he also resigned from the Boy Scouts, and religious education classes at school. It was the right decision, he said. At first, he said, he had described himself as an agnostic, but later felt 'atheist' applied better. It is a designation he has maintained for several decades.

Roger, a retired British trawlerman born in 1944, related a similar story. He 'started to have doubts' and questioned the rationality of religion in his teens. Once he discussed those concerns with his parents, he 'was never made to go and wasn't made to feel guilty about not doing'. He stopped attending church aged 15 and never returned.

Virginia's leaving story featured both her mother and grandmother. She had been very close to her grandmother and had always accompanied her to church, usually without her mother. When her grandmother died, both she and her mother stopped for good.

Betty Friedan's groundbreaking 1963 book, *The Feminine Mystique*, arguably began the strong 1960s feminist movements. Freidan, born in 1921, was a member of Generation A, the Baby Boomer parents' generation. Her readers would not have been primarily the Baby Boomers at first, but their mothers, the older women of Generation A. The book was addressed to 'house-wives' and sought to shatter the assumption that women were happiest in their homes, keeping busy with domestic duties. A Boomer born in, say, 1951, at the peak of the baby boom, would have been 13 when her mother read *The Feminine Mystique*. The opening words may have captured the sense of a maternal frustration that had, Freidan wrote, no name (1963, 15):

> The problem lay buried, unspoken, for many years in the minds of American women. It was a strange stirring, a sense of dissatisfaction, a yearning that women suffered in the middle of the twentieth century in the United States. Each suburban wife struggled with it alone. As she made the beds, shopped for groceries, matched slipcover material, ate peanut butter sandwiches with her children, chauffeured Cub Scouts and Brownies, lay beside her husband at night—she was afraid to ask even of herself the silent question—Is this all?

Freidan wrote magazine and newspaper articles in mainstream publications undoubtedly read by the mothers of Baby Boomers, including the *Ladies Home Journal*. The movement she began was, as has been critiqued, largely middle class, white, and heterosexual.

Germaine Greer, born in 1939 between the Generation A and Generation B birth waves, worked with Freidan to further the objectives of the new women's movement. Her book, *The Female Eunuch*, was published in 1970, catching the Baby Boomers as they matured into adults.

As I discussed in more detail earlier (Day 2017), Callum Brown argued that the sharp decline of Christianity occurred in the 1960s, particularly 1963, when two centuries of Christian tradition locating piety in femininity collapsed (Brown 2001, 195). That was when, he argued, women stopped subscribing to the discursive domain of Christianity. Simultaneously, the nature of femininity changed. Brown also focuses on the period pre-1960 when the Generation A women, those of the Baby Boomer parental generation, were returning to post-war domesticity. The shift in the following decade was, he argued, sudden and violent, with a quick series of major changes as the 'institutional structures of cultural traditionalism started to crumble in Britain' (Brown 2001, 176). Those changes affected culture, sexuality, and legislation, including a weakening of book and theatre censorship, legalisation of abortion and homosexuality in 1967, the liberalisation of divorce in 1969, the women's liberation movement since 1968, and waves of new styles of pop music, youth culture, the popularity of drugs, new fashions, and student rebellion.

It was a time, I concluded, that affected women's orientation to religion then and, subsequently, for generations to come.

Notes

1. The origins and purpose of this prayer are obscure, but most research cites its first publication in the early eighteenth century in the 'New England Primer', a textbook for the early Colonists in what would become the USA, and whose popularity spread to Canada and parts of the UK (https://www.britannica.com/topic/The-New-England-Primer). The prayer could have been both a means of embedding Protestant Christianity, and also reflected the high rate of infant and childhood mortality.

2. For further detail about the UN and its role in religious freedom, see Day 2020, 89–104.

4

Teen Angst

Confirming Doubts

Introduction

During my interviews, many Boomers identified confirmation as the single, pivotal event that prompted their withdrawal from church. Other researchers and religious professionals have noticed a similar pattern of church attendance ceasing abruptly following confirmation. Most of such studies are quantitative, and focus on more recent generations, with little insights provided about why young Baby Boomers stopped attending. I will explore here recollections from the Baby Boomers I interviewed that may illuminate further the effect of confirmation on Baby Boomer religiosity and declining attendance.

My findings thus far are primarily that Baby Boomers found it easy to leave because they never belonged. This was due partly to the segregationist practices of Sunday school, but also to the lack of home-based religious practice or beliefs and an increasing awareness of parental religious ambivalence. In this chapter I will explore how and why church attendance declined and, in many cases, abruptly ceased following confirmation. Having been confirmed, I suggest, Baby Boomers were seen by parents as mature Christians who had taken on the promises first made on their behalf by their godparents. The parents therefore did not overrule the young Boomers who wanted to leave. In this, they were theologically, or at least doctrinally, correct.

Confirmation: 'Tick that Box'

Within Anglicanism there are two main methods for people to become part of a church: 'baptism', also known as 'christening', and confirmation. According to the Church of England internet section on baptism: 'There is no difference between a christening service and a baptism service. Some churches will use the word "baptism" and some the word "christening". The moment when your child has water poured or wiped on their head is the actual baptism and is at the heart of the service' (https://www.churchofengland.org/life-events/christenings/christening-faqs#na).

Many Christians recognise two 'sacraments' they see as commanded by Christ: baptism and Holy Communion or Eucharist. A sacrament is something that Christians believe was specially instructed by Jesus and is an outward sign of divine grace. Apart from these Jesus-instructed sacraments, Anglicans also recognise other sacraments, including confirmation and marriage.

Although the child's name is spoken as part of the christening service, it is not simply a naming event. The purpose of the baptism sacrament is to be the point of entry into the church and to the Christian journey. Anglicans believe that Jesus was baptised by John (hence, 'John the Baptist') and instructed his followers to become baptised to show that they are his followers.

The second sacrament is the Eucharist, or Holy Communion, which refers back to the 'last supper' that Jesus ate with his apostles before he was crucified. He shared bread and wine at the table and told them to think of the bread as his body and the wine as his blood, and to repeat the ceremony with others in order to remember him. In the Anglican church, it was the case when the Boomers grew up that they could not 'take communion' until they had been confirmed. This is because they are not expected until they are older to understand the beliefs and 'duties' of being a Christian.

At the baptism ceremony for the child, two 'godparents' are appointed to look after the child's spiritual needs and ensure that they follow Christian teaching and practice. When a child is older, typically around 13, they are encouraged to study the core beliefs of Christianity and take on the godparents' promises for themselves. They are then able to participate with adults in the Eucharist.

In keeping with Anglican practice, the Boomers attended confirmation classes at around age 13 in order to discuss in detail points of theology and practice. The confirmation process followed by Baby Boomers in the 1950s, '60s, and '70s was based on instructions in the Book of Common Prayer, first written in 1549. Since 1980, the Alternative Service Book, with shorter, more up to date language has been used. In order to be confirmed in a ceremony conducted by a Bishop, the candidate must have memorised and understood the Lord's Prayer, The Apostles' Creed, and the Ten Commandments.

It is important here to review the context that existed for those children. As discussed in the last two chapters, unlike previous generations Boomers had been largely unsocialised into religion apart from being forced to attend a school on Sunday where they received basic ideas about their religion, often in the form of pictures and craft-like activities. They had not been attending church services where they would see adults and their parents repeating the lines of the Creed as they stood each week to affirm their faith. When they got home after Sunday school nothing about church or religion would be discussed or practised.

Into that religious vacuum, those children were asked to respond to questions about their faith and their intentions in a question-and-answer format known as the 'Catechism'. The first question was easy—just stating their name. The second question would likely be a little more difficult as it concerned their baptism and the role of their godparents. Like most people of their generation, the godparents would be a kindly aunt, uncle, or close family friend. The children were likely to have no idea that they would have to declare, as per the Catechism, that they understood that these genial figures had promised three things in the child's name, starting with renouncing the devil and his works. It was unlikely that the child had ever discussed such matters with their godparents or parents or had received any lengthy introduction to the nature of the devil, let alone his works. Nevertheless, the child would also need to agree that the godparents had, on their behalf, given up pomp and vanity and also 'sinful lusts of the flesh'. They next had to agree that the godparents had signed up to the articles of faith, and that the child would obey all the commandments.

The child then needed to memorise the articles of faith, to assert that they believed in a God who created heaven and earth, who had a son who was created by a ghost and a virgin (and a new concept of 'virginity' would likely also have to be explained), and that this Father had made his son, Jesus, suffer under Pontius Pilate, a Roman, and be nailed to a cross until he died, following which he would go to hell before coming alive again to go to heaven and be with his father judging everyone living and dead. Following that narrative, the child would also need to say they believed in the holy Catholic church, which was probably a bit confusing because by then they would probably know that they were Anglicans and others, whose church they didn't go to, were Catholics. They also had to believe in something called 'the Communion of Saints', and the forgiveness of sins, the resurrection of the body, and life everlasting.

They then had to recite the Ten Commandments, preferably in full form:

1. Thou shalt have none other gods but me.
2. Thou shalt not make to thyself any graven image, nor the likeness of any thing that is in heaven above, or in the earth beneath, or in the water under the earth. Thou shalt not bow down to them, nor worship them. For I the Lord thy God am a jealous God, and visit the sins of the fathers upon the children unto the third and fourth generation of them that hate me, and shew mercy unto thousands in them that love me and keep my commandments.
3. Thou shalt not take the Name of the Lord thy God in vain: for the Lord will not hold him guiltless, that taketh his Name in vain.
4. Remember that thou keep holy the Sabbath day. Six days shalt thou labour, and do all that thou hast to do; but the seventh day is the Sabbath of the Lord thy God. In it thou shalt do no manner of work, thou, and thy son, and thy daughter, thy man-servant, and thy maid-servant, thy cattle, and the stranger that is within thy gates. For in six days the Lord made heaven and earth, the sea, and all that in them is, and rested the seventh day: wherefore the Lord blessed the seventh day, and hallowed it.
5. Honour thy father and thy mother; that thy days may be long in the land which the Lord thy God giveth thee.
6. Thou shalt do no murder.
7. Thou shalt not commit adultery.
8. Thou shalt not steal.
9. Thou shalt not bear false witness against thy neighbour.
10. Thou shalt not covet thy neighbour's house, thou shalt not covet thy neighbour's wife, nor his servant, nor his maid, nor his ox, nor his ass, nor any thing that is his.

Several questions and answers then also needed to be memorised, along the lines of loving one's neighbour, but not his wife or ass, and promising to love and fear God, to honouring and obeying the Queen and everyone in authority including their teachers and spiritual pastors, while also keeping their bodies chaste.

The child would then be asked to recite the Lord's Prayer:

Our Father which art in heaven, hallowed be thy Name, thy kingdom come, thy will be done, in earth as it is in heaven. Give us this day our daily bread, and forgive us our trespasses, as we forgive them that trespass against us; And lead us not into temptation, but deliver us from evil. Amen.

They were next quizzed on how many 'sacraments' there were in the church which were 'necessary to salvation': Baptism, and the Supper of the Lord, otherwise known as the Eucharist, or Holy Communion. Further questions and answers concerned the detail of baptisms and the Eucharist. Finally, the Bishop (a more senior cleric than the parish priests they had known) would put his hands on their heads to transmit the Holy Spirit. They would have been told in confirmation classes that this was a holy, sacred moment where they would receive God's 'grace'.

All of this instruction and the eventual ceremony would have been unfamiliar to the children who had never been acculturated into religion but had merely gone along to Sunday school or a similar youth group in the spirit of it being 'a social thing'. It is probably unsurprising that they recalled, years later, that they had asked questions and often been frustrated with inadequate answers. It was also perhaps unsurprising that they did not remember the detail of the Catechism that they had to memorise: unless memories are 'made' they are likely to be forgotten. Anyone who has crammed at the last moment for an exam will be familiar with the result. A few weeks, or even days later, the memory of what was hastily memorised will have faded. It was also interesting to note that the Baby Boomers who agreed to my interview knew we would be discussing their lifetime experiences, and had therefore been primed to think about them, with some even telling me that they had telephoned a parent or, considering their age, most often a sibling to compare notes. Even after such discussions and jostling, the memories did not flow back. They were, I suggest, never there.

What they do remember, however, is the feeling of the event—like the anxiety of sitting an exam and the relief following. The Baby Boomers I interviewed spoke of the memory of being frustrated with the content of what was being told to them, and then the relief that, having now been admitted as a full and nearly adult member of the church, they had loosened themselves from the bonds of their godparents and, to a large extent, their own parents, and were considered mature enough to make their own choices. For most, that left only one reasonable option: exodus.

Charles said that looking back on confirmation classes there seemed to be a quality of a routine, or of a checklist that they were going through until, for someone's ledger or book of accounts, they could 'tick that box':

[I]t was something you had to do, and you might as well get it over with, a bit like going to the dentist in a way, you had to do it. I just assumed that everyone did it so I might as well get on with it. Once a week we stayed an hour after school and the local vicar came. I can't remember what was said. Yes. Confirmation service. Tick that box.

It didn't seem to boys like Charles that the religious part of his education held the same interest as other ideas he was beginning to think about. 'I got interested in other things,' he said, describing himself as a 'voracious reader', interested in political issues, and 'in the world around me'. He had a strong sense of morality, although that did not relate to what he had learned specifically at church. When some family members went to live in South Africa when he was 14, he recalled having a big argument with them as he could not understand why they were, implicitly at least, supporting the apartheid regime: 'I was branching out, away from what you might call religious, becoming more political. This was not for lack of exposure,' he stressed. He had attended a boys' grammar school run by the Church of England. The school had its own chapel and all boys, 'apart from a few Roman Catholic boys' attended a religious service each morning, including 'one Jewish boy who was the only person in the school who could play the organ, so he played for every service'. The school had a 'CofE' flavour, he said. The teachers all seemed to be Anglican: 'It just seemed to be how things were done, it was the natural thing of the time. We all did religious knowledge, and I got the highest grade. There was something ironic about that.' And yet, despite the intense Church of England confirmation instruction, when Charles became confirmed he felt that he had 'ticked that box', and shortly after ceased attending church.

In our conversations, Baby Boomers reflected on their impressions of confirmation and suggested answers to my questions about why they left so soon thereafter. The main reason may have been, as I have alluded to above, was simply that they could. For many, this was not a rebellion against a religion of their youth. It was not so much that they left religion as that they had never had it in the first place. Through confirmation instruction, they were receiving an intense introduction to the essence of Anglican belief and practice and to Christianity and religion more widely. For most, what they learned made neither logical nor moral sense.

In as much as it could be assumed that such instruction and training would lead to sedimenting the key beliefs of their religion, I suggest that would have only occurred if the beliefs had been produced in the first place.

As I have discussed in earlier chapters, particularly Chapter 2, and more fully in an earlier work (Day 2011), belief is 'performative'. It is produced socially through interaction and repetition over time, not through simply memorising key phrases or attending a few classes. And so, onto the Boomers' fragile and delicate religious ground, discussions about core tenets of Christian faith did not, I suggest, bed in.

Doctrines and Tenets: 'Load of Tosh, Load of Rubbish'

Although its origins are unclear, most dictionaries agree that the centuries-old British slang 'tosh' means 'nonsense' or 'rubbish'. It was a term Boomers sometimes used to describe Christianity, particularly the rote-form they learned at confirmation class.

Reaching that moment had a profound effect on many Baby Boomer adolescents. Ben, a retired British computer programmer born in 1950, described being involved in music as a teenager and, through a group, he and his brother had the opportunity to play at several churches. That was when he was able to hear how different churches stressed, and their congregants believed, much the same thing. He began to think that what he was hearing in the service were not statements he could believe in: 'this is a load of tosh,' he concluded. But, significantly for Ben, it was not just that he could not believe in such things, he could not believe in anyone who did.

In analysing interviews such as mine with Ben, it was sometimes difficult to unravel the 'logic' from the 'moral' and the 'meaning' in many of these conversations because, for many people, they were all part of the same thing. As Ben said, reflecting on the 'tosh' he had heard, he wondered why people in the USA were averse to atheists, insisting that presidents were Christians. He said he did not understand how people could possibly vote for someone who based most of their ideas on religion:

> I would find it difficult to vote for someone who believes 95 impossible things before breakfast. How many other rubbishy things is he going to hoover up and spit out for the benefit of the country? I know it's the case in the United States that you wouldn't vote for someone who's an atheist, but for me it's the other way around. I would have to think very hard about it and look very closely at their record. I wouldn't trust somebody who believes all that sort of rubbish.

Believing '95 impossible things' is, I suggest, only possible if we understand 'belief' as more faith-based than logical or 'propositional'. Particularly for religious people who take a literalist approach to their sacred texts, their faith is based on what they may describe as grace or revelation. Without such religious emotion, it was unlikely that young people could confirm such religious affirmations. For many, such beliefs were simply not plausible and were unsupported by either history or their experience. I will explore more about 'plausibility structures' following Peter Berger's (1967) work, and his and Thomas Luckmann's (Berger and Luckmann 1966) theories about the social production of knowledge, in the next chapter.

In conversation with the other Boomers I interviewed, the same sentiment, or lack of it, prevailed. In response to my questions about whether they had ever felt emotional during any of their Sunday school, church, or confirmation experiences, the answer was always negative. When, for example, I asked Charles if he had ever felt any religious or spiritual emotion, he said no. He did, he added, say his prayers every night—'the Lord's Prayer, and a couple of other things as well, but I think I stopped doing that around being confirmed'. There had never been, he said, any 'sense of spiritual awakening'.

Even when I phrased the questions most generally in my interviews, such as 'Did you ever feel close to Jesus, or God?', and therefore not demanding any kind of major, overwhelming conversion-like experience, the answer was the same. No. I wondered if this was because the Boomers had felt forced to attend Sunday school and church or expected to simply engage in activities without ever feeling part of the whole. It was, I suggest, the absence of a link to the wider religious body of the church that may have partly caused emotional distance.

Olie Riis and Linda Woodhead (2010, 144) called attention to the ways in which religious emotion is created, felt, and regulated, pointing out that a Durkheimian version of collective, effervescent emotional experience cannot simply be imposed on people, as 'each individual is likely to have personal standards for what they ought to feel in a situation and how their feelings may be expressed'.

I doubt members of any generation would dispute the idea that people have, and even should have, their own personal standards for their feelings and actions, but some sociologists of religion have, I argue, mistakenly blamed the Baby Boomer generation for exercising a degree of personal choice that forced Christianity's decline. Bryan Wilson (2001, 44–5) refers to the modern family being 'split apart', with parents insufficiently present to take a role in the moral inculcation of their children. This, he says, is not only because family structures have changed but also because individuals are being encouraged today to 'discover their own identities', to 'be themselves', to 'do their own thing'. Wilson is overstating the impact of those ideas. After all, 'to thine own self be true' was the injunction of Polonius to Hamlet back in Shakespeare's day. The injunction to 'know thyself' was carved into the pediment of the temple of Apollo, c. 500 BCE. Probably the most famous quote to support that reason for Christian decline is that attributed by Bellah et al. (1985) to a woman they interviewed, Sheila Larson. 'I believe in God,' Sheila told them. 'I am not a religious fanatic. I can't remember the last time I went to church. My faith has carried me a long way. It's Sheilaism. Just my own little voice.' Barely an undergraduate dissertation on contemporary religion is written without reference to a style of hyper-individualism based on that quote. In my own doctoral thesis (Day 2011, 205) I mentioned her in relation to 'Tom', a 15-year-old student who told me he had his own religion:

> It's like my own religion, it's like I believe in stuff like, I just believe in being good, stuff like that, be grateful for what you get. Others can't get, other people in other countries may not be able to get that. Stuff like that.

I reflected then that it would be a mistake to move from Tom's reference to his 'own religion' to ideas about self-orientation. People who believe in their inner voices or their capability of working out meaning, destiny, and morality are not necessarily, I suggest, highly individualistic, but reflexive in a socialized way. Feelings are, as Riis and Woodhead (2010, 144) discuss, socially created and embedded through interaction with other people:

> In order to form a correspondence between the communal programme and the individual standards a link must be formed between the community and its members. For the latter simply to 'go through the motions' and feign feelings is not sufficient to sustain the regime. Feelings are social acts as well as personal ones.

Robert Wuthnow (2020, 145) makes the same point, discussing how feelings are never situated wholly within individuals, but rather 'from social interaction governed by feeling rules'.

With those theories in mind, I will explore further the relationship, or lack of, between Baby Boomers and the religious communities of which they were never fully part. The lack of any faith-like beliefs or emotion made it nearly impossible for Baby Boomers to simply accede to the list of promises, beliefs, and ideas presented at confirmation. Wendy, a retired British teacher born in 1946, said she was so appalled at what she was expected to believe during school assemblies when there were hymns and Bible reading, that she, and a few friends, resisted by refusing to stand during hymns or prayers. She thought to herself, 'These are intelligent people—how can they believe in this rubbish?'. One day, she said, a vicar came to speak to the class and, in protest, she ignored him and sat ostentatiously reading a well-known communist newspaper.

The repetitive rote of memorising articles of faith, prayers, and commandments seemed to bring back some of the most negative feelings of formal schooling, such as the practice of memorising timetables. As Virginia described it, she had a 'run-in' with a priest who said it was important to memorise the prayers, as he tried to avoid discussing the content in more detail. Virginia recalled that she had told him 'it was more important for me to understand them, but he was an old guy who knew how things needed to be done. I was more curious. I wanted to know more; it wasn't like times tables!'

Her comments reflect a wider educational change that was occurring in the 1950s and 1960s, where teachers (with, presumably, parental consent) were following a more 'child-centred' approach. It was widely becoming more the norm that children were being invited to explore and think more for themselves, as the previous rote style learning was swiftly falling out of fashion. Teachers were provoking questions and students felt more freedom to question. Carl, a retired British travel agent born in 1945, said that, despite his school being strongly Anglican:

> there were one or two teachers who, intentionally or otherwise, made me question my beliefs, and by the time I left school, outside term-time I was attending church, if at all, simply to accompany my mother and keep her happy. Although I sang in the chapel choir at university, I counted myself an agnostic.

The 'tosh' and 'rubbish' Ben and others referred to was not only the kinds of so-called 'propositional' beliefs that could be safely debated in class or common rooms: these were often trust-based, value-driven beliefs about how the world should be and how people ought to be treated. Robin said that about the time of confirmation was the idea that teenagers should have the 'freedom to think for oneself'. In so doing, she 'realised there was a lot of hypocrisy in religion, women of my generation were going out into the world and told we could do anything, but religions don't do that'. There were no women priests at the time, she recalled, and she had had an aunt who had been 'churched'. This was a practice where women who had given birth were instructed to stay away from church for a period of four to six weeks, after which she could return and participate with the priest in prayers thanking God for her safety: 'Think of that tight hold on women's behaviour at a community level, not just a household,' Robin exclaimed. As discussed in the previous chapter, ideas about women's equality were beginning to circulate and even teenagers were becoming aware of them.

When I asked Baby Boomers where they thought they derived their moral values from, they emphasised the home and their parents. This is not surprising, as most theories of moral development identify the family as a primary source. Once again, I will emphasise that these Boomers were not hatched or created in a pristine petri dish but raised by parents who would be transmitting some kind of values. What the Boomers were finding was that those values did not always correspond with what they were hearing from the church or from confirmation classes.

Apart from what seemed to many to be illogical impossible things to believe, there was also the beginning of an important clash of morals. Kim said she went to the classes, but they did not seem to have 'anything about other human beings'. She asked questions during confirmation classes 'about pestilence' and about wars, but these were largely ignored and did not seem to have anything to do with Christ's teachings: 'I tried hard to believe it because it seemed like the right thing to do', but ultimately, she could not:

> ...in that it didn't seem to be looking forward. I didn't see how an all-loving God could allow those things. It's less to do with helping your fellow man, and more to do with belonging to the club, or you could be ostracized. I worried that a lot of my friends went along with it. The vicar wouldn't answer questions, he had almost a telephone voice.

I am aware that I am opposing here certain scholars of religion who argue that because people are not being raised with church-based, religious values they will, as Smith and Denton (2005, 156–8) suggest, live in a 'morally insignificant universe' where decisions are not guided by or grounded in larger, invisible sources of either religion, philosophy, or other supra-mundane moral forces. Bryan Wilson (1966) wrote about what he saw as non-regulated, laissez faire collections of changing beliefs leading to an inevitable relaxing of moral standards. This would create a level of moral freedom 'enjoyed by man individually, but is costly to society as a whole' (Wilson 1966, 63). Keith Ward (1992, 21) wrote, in a similar vein:

> Our whole understanding of morality really does depend upon the existence of God, upon seeing human conduct in the context of a wider spiritual realm, if it is to make sense.

For many Baby Boomers, and possibly their parents, a God-based view of morality evidently did not make sense. As will be discussed further here and was elaborated also in earlier work (Day 2011), young people draw on their relationships with family, friends, and other loved ones to provide them with faith and love. If the church was not offering them that, for many, the decision to leave was straightforward: confirmation, being the acceptance of their status as full members, was the trigger that gave them permission to fire their parting shot.

Another reason a Baby Boomer gave me for quitting church was more disquieting. Ben had a deep concern about some of the 'pretty dodgy experiences with some of the people at the church' by which he was referring to encounters bordering on sexual misconduct. He began to get uncomfortable, as did his brother. They then refused to take part in attending any churches. I return to this theme of abuse and institutional complicity in Chapter 6.

Another 'Social Thing': 'Me and My Friends Would Bunk off . . .'

In a way that resonated with conversations about Sunday school, the Boomers' recollections of confirmation classes strongly featured the importance of their friends in both attending, and not attending. Kim said that she had not been christened, but when other friends were joining confirmation classes, she became christened so she could become confirmed and join them.

Harry, a British television producer born in 1955, was like Kim and so many of the other Boomers who joined confirmation classes because a friend wanted him to, 'he was a bit of wimp and wouldn't go on his own,' Harry explained. Fiona, a retired Canadian university lecturer born in 1947, said that after confirmation her church attendance 'petered out'. She joined Job's

Daughters, a women's group affiliated to the Masons, because a friend wanted her to. Once they arrived and signed in, Fiona used to 'hang outside and smoke' and often meet her boyfriend. Vikki, a retired British retail manager born in 1948, reflected that she was confirmed at age 13 because 'at that time in my life, I wanted to conform, and for quite some while I went every week and took communion, especially if it was a Brownie thing'. The effect of peers and church attendance was noted in an American study that found the usual pattern of declining church attendance in teenagers 'disappears with the addition of friends' who attend church (Regnerus et al. 2004, 31). Unless, of course, those same friends decide not to attend church, as seemed to have occurred with Charles. Charles described what happened after confirmation, when the expected pattern of church attendance never caught on: 'Looking back it now seems funny, we were expected to go to church every week, but me and my friends would bunk off and go smoke cigarettes by the river.'

The significance of belonging or not to certain peer groups was indicated by Kati Niemelä's (2008a) longitudinal study of confirmation training in Finland. Respondents were asked several questions about God-belief, one of which was designed to probe respondents' sense of both belief and belonging—'I believe in God, but I am not a "believer"' (Niemelä 2008a, 48). Forty-six per cent of those who had completed the confirmation training programme chose that answer, far outweighing those (9 per cent) who chose 'I am a believer' or those (7 per cent) who said, 'I do not believe that there is a God'. I asked Kati Niemelä if that meant the respondents did not feel they belonged to a group of religious people yet wanted to express their belief in God. In reply, she (Niemelä 2008b) said:

> When the youngsters in Finland talk about 'believers' they tend to refer to that small group of very religious and often also morally strict. So, when one agrees to this item, she/he is most likely saying something like (and our open questions in the survey also reveal this): 'Yes, I do believe in God and have a faith in Him, but I do not I belong to that small group of active ones nor do I totally live according to my faith.'

Church, or What?: 'I Didn't Really Give It a Thought'

It was apparent from my interviews that the young people did not meet with resistance from their parents when they decided to stop attending church.

As I suggested in the previous two chapters, the children had already been segregated from the main church and not made to feel part of it, and their parental ambivalence probably only reinforced that sense of alienation. For the most part, it did not seem that they had felt any wrench or even an inclination to rebel. As their childhood experiences had not made any significant impression on them thus far, there was nothing really to turn from, or rebel against. While some felt drawn to other activities besides church, it did not seem to have given them much pause for thought. No one, I have concluded, woke up on Sunday mornings seized with an overwhelming existential question: worship, or Walmart?

From age 16, Harry did not attend church anymore, he said. He played tennis and field hockey on both Saturdays and Sundays. Ending his church-attending practice did not require deep reflection: 'I had no inclination to go. I didn't really give it a thought.' Shortly after confirmation, Harry decided he would not continue with church, and met no resistance from his parents. 'My father never commented on religion anyway, and my mother's attitude was—"fair enough", I was a perfectly normal well-behaved boy.' Rolf, a retired British army officer born in 1954, said that he went to boarding school in his early teens, before he had been confirmed. His parents had stopped attending church as regularly by then, but said they hoped he would be confirmed. He promised them that he would at school, but he didn't. Further, he added, 'I told them I had, so I'm doubly bad'. It was never, he added, a topic his parents pursued and so it was easy to let the matter lie.

Most theories of child development agree that a child's moral development grows through stages, from being generally a mirror of their parents, to one of increasing moral autonomy. It seems, following my Baby Boomer interviews and subsequent research, that while the adolescent Boomer may have rejected church and Christianity on the basis of their morality, it was a morality characterised by a wider familial and social context. The outliers, I argue, were not the defecting teenagers, but the churches. Following Michel De Certeau (1984), this would be typical of actions within different realms of power: those with institutional power are in the position to conduct themselves strategically; those without power typically act tactically in ways that may not appear to be obvious or groundbreaking but which, over time, may affect institutional patterns. I am suggesting that these small acts of Baby Boomers withdrawing from simple activities such as attending church had a cumulative effect. David Oswell (2012) explored how sociologists need to understand the agency of children relative to power and generational divides over time and space. Recognising the different agencies of children, Oswell (2012, 75) suggests:

> Children and young people, who so often are denied access to resources and to the means of accumulating resources, find strength through their creative bricolage, through their make-shift mash-ups, and their making do. Adults, in contrast, so often control the resources, the means of reproduction; they control the space; they make the environment; they build the schools, the homes, the television sets and computer networks; they people the police, the teachers, the parents, and the social workers. This is a schema which sites two camps, the strong and the weak, the structural form of the one is the inversion of the other.

I am suggesting that the small acts of Baby Boomers withdrawing from simple activities such as attending church were acts of agency with a cumulative effect of subverting the institutional power of the church, beginning with the withdrawal of children and young people's participation after confirmation, subtly supported by parental collusion, as discussed in Chapter 3.

A minister in a western Canadian town, Reverend Christine Conkin, reflected on the post-confirmation exodus in a sermon she delivered in 2017, and later posted on the church website. She was speaking about the practice in the 1950s and 1960s of children going through Sunday school, confirmation, and then leaving the church. As I was writing about the unusual practice of separating children from the main church for Sunday school, her comments seemed to resonate with my impression and emerging argument about how that particular segregated Sunday school practice may have begun the eventual Baby Boomer alienation. In correspondence with Reverend Conkin, I expressed my view that such a practice may have had negative consequences. Interestingly, before she became an organised minister, she had studied sociology at university. She agreed with my emerging theory and, with her permission, I reproduce here extracts from that sermon (https://www.st-andrews-anglican-calgary.ca/we-moved-a-pew/):

> We don't have to look far for examples. Earlier this week I asked our own... about her experience of church as a child. When I asked if I could share what she told me, she agreed. She described: 'Oh, I've been going to church my whole life! When I was a kid, every Sunday I went to Sunday School at 10am, church at 11am, and then because my sister was running

a Sunday school at another church, I went there at 1pm.' The church she attended was one of our sister denominations and what she described was a common traditional pattern: everyone attended an age-appropriate Sunday School either before or after common worship all together.

. . .

Conkin then reflects on the ministry practice that had been adopted since the 1960s:

The difference in ministry model also happens to correspond to a significant drop-out rate from church among younger generations. We have long noticed, for decades, that children who attend nursery and Sunday School and then become confirmed as young teenagers are often never seen in church again. We jokingly refer to confirmation as 'graduation from church'.

. . .

I remember a seminary colleague saying in class one day that her experience as a child and teen, was that she and her contemporaries were only allowed in church on Christmas and Easter. 'And then we grew up,' she reflected, 'and the adults were surprised that we only came to church on Christmas and Easter.'

In good sociological style, Conkin adds that there were other, wider cultural forces at work that would also have influenced long-term attendance, but in any case, she advocated the change to a ministry model that incorporated, rather than excluded, young people and children.

In conclusion, I have reviewed in this chapter the subtle shifts that were operating within and around the teenage Boomers. Personal, institutional, cultural, intellectual, embodied, emotional—sociologists may look at one or more of those influences when trying to understand the small and large movements in society. What was becoming more clear to me as I discussed their early lives with Baby Boomers is their own appreciation of all, and more, of those factors. It was a complicated period, but one that offered more clarity as they matured. Their reflections, and mine, increasingly suggest almost an inevitability of their final and permanent moves away from religion.

PART II
BELIEVING IN LEAVING

5

Drifting Away, Fading Away

Introduction: 'Like a Vaccination that Never Took'

The vast 1960s' turn to higher education, often involving moving away from home, appeared to cement the Boomers' growing withdrawal from church. While much research links atheism to education, I am increasingly wary of establishing education, in terms of intellectualist or rational thinking, as the main causal variable to explain the Boomers' increased disassociation from religion. Other factors, such as their already established non-religiosity, and the effects of peers and pluralism were, I will argue, far more important. Indeed, an apparently dichotomous, yet mutually constitutive, relationship between rationality and belief has been of particular interest to anthropology and, to a lesser extent, the sociology of religion and will be discussed in more detail (and see Day 2018).

Many Boomers described this as inevitable, given that they had already experienced and facilitated their own religious decline, which seemed to have only been accelerated by leaving home. Apart from university, Boomers also often experienced travel, the workplace and other cultural exposures to different ways of being, believing, and belonging. Those experiences perhaps reflected what Peter Berger (1967) described as the effect of pluralism weakening the 'plausibility structures' that had, for many Boomers, already decayed. Their early exposure to religion had not inclined them to continue in religiosity: Stephanie said 'It was like a vaccination that never took'.

The effect of larger workplaces, economic developments, university education, travel, and media all contributed to values changes within industrialised societies, wrote Ronald Inglehart (1977, 7), one of the first academics to reflect on the dramatic changes occurring at the time. The Baby Boomer cohort was raised in what he described as 'a quite different world from the one which shaped their parents or grandparents. They have grown up in a relatively affluent, communications-rich societies. It was a world that seemed both exciting and yet, for many Boomers, a comfortable and welcome fit' (Inglehart 1977, 11).

Why Baby Boomers Turned from Religion: Shaping Belief and Belonging, 1945–2021. Abby Day, Oxford University Press. © Abby Day 2022. DOI: 10.1093/oso/9780192866684.003.0005

As described in Chapters 2, 3, and 4, the young Boomers did not have a strong belief or spiritual, emotional sense of a god or other deity: consequently, there was nothing significant to leave. Indeed, the word most often used by them was 'drifting'. Despite their reputation of being revolutionary radicals, as they matured into adulthood many Baby Boomers did not engage in a revolt against religion, although those who did, through experiencing a significant 'clash', will be discussed in the next chapter. The words mostly used by the Boomers I interviewed were those evoking a gentle, almost inevitable, transition from a lightly held habit of church attendance to a life where the idea of religion or church simply did not matter.

They 'drifted away', they told me. Their beliefs, some added, 'ebbed' away. Religion, for many, simply 'faded'. As George, a retired British surveyor born in 1943, put it, 'I think I sort of drifted, more than anything else.' The 'anything else' could have been strong feelings about the church's teachings, or practices, but that is not what happened most of the time. Their 'drifting away', as many phrased it, was spatial, temporal, and ontological, often facilitated or provoked by physically moving away from home to pursue education, work, and travel.

Who, or What, 'Drifts'?

In analysing the interviews, and writing this book, there was something about the word 'drift' that intrigued me. Although they used it often, the term 'drift' has complications if used to describe a person. I could not, in fairness, describe the Baby Boomers as 'drifters'. This would be to apply a normative, negative term that did not match their stories. For example, those who sometimes join religious congregations but do not participate in their activities or financially contribute are often called 'free riders' by, most commonly, social scientists in the USA. The term, first used in political policy discussions in the 1940s, is applied by some sociologists of religion to describe those who apparently use other people's resources or goodwill for their own benefit, without giving anything in return. This is not, however, a complimentary or neutral term. It is normative, with negative connotations, similar to 'freeloader'. Rather than affix a pejorative label, such as 'free rider' or 'drifter', I would prefer to see scholars try to explore exactly why some people do not want to contribute to a congregation or to remain in it. One reason, as I have discussed in earlier chapters, may be because they feel alienated from church, its people, or its religion.

Calling someone a 'drifter' is to imply that they move aimlessly from place to place, picking up occasional work opportunities before moving on, eschewing ties, and commitments. Boomers are often associated with periods of economic growth and comparative wealth. The Boomers I interviewed were articulate about their lives and described their long careers, involvements in a variety of organisations, and commitment to their families. The term 'drifter' did not match either my sample or those of others who have studied Boomers: Wade Clark Roof (1993) for example, described a 'generation of seekers', not a 'generation of drifters'.

Most dictionary definitions etymologically locate 'drift' in nautical parlance. Boats drift downstream, onshore, or offshore, moved by outside forces such as tides, currents, or winds. They might get thrown onto a beach, a rocky headline, a bank, or be swept out to sea. Importantly, and for the purpose of this study, boats drift because they are not anchored, moored, or tightly bound to a dock. It is unlikely that a sailor would stop to sleep at night close to shore and simply forget to try to anchor the boat; in practice the only way that an anchored boat can drift is if the anchor becomes 'unset'. This is usually because it was never set properly in the first place. An improper setting may have occurred either because the seabed was too rocky or because the sailor had not caused the anchor to dig into the seabed. Anchoring technique depends on the skipper reversing the boat and applying sufficient resistance against the anchor to force it to bed in. It is only through pulling hard against it that the anchor sets safely and maintains its position.

As I have discussed thus far, the Boomers' religiosity was frequently not bedded into firm ground, such as through active participation in church or a religious household. The anchor did not set. Further, when the Boomers began to make moves to leave, they were not resisted. As discussed in earlier chapters, parents usually told their Baby Boomer children that, having been confirmed, they were now old enough to make their own choice. The Boomer therefore easily drifts away from the church with, using another nautical analogy mentioned by a Boomer, an ebbing belief. If they turned to look for the lighthouse's beam, they would see that it had 'faded'.[1]

Having further untied the hold that religion had on them so loosely, the Boomers experienced new ways of being that further set their emerging convictions in non-religious sites of believing and belonging. I will explore here two themes that arose most frequently: the effects of university and of travel.

University: 'I Lost God and Found Marx'

The number of people in UK full-time higher education doubled in the 1960s. While most often this is attributed to the Robbins Committee on Education report of 1963, Harold Perkins (1972) pointed out that the report mainly put into action recommendations and policies that arose in the 1950s, both because it was evident that there was a significant bulge in the population and also because it was felt that the population in Britain lagged behind other countries in terms of productivity and prosperity. Education was seen as a way to improve both an individual's prospects and the country's chance of increased health and wealth.

Perkins (1972, 113) quotes an impassioned speech given in 1955 by Lord Simon, a Stockport industrialist, Labour peer, and Chairman of Council of Manchester University:

> He declared that the projected targets were 'totally and almost fantastically inadequate', that Britain had both the smallest proportion of the age group at university of any civilized country and a desperate shortage of scientists and technologists, and that the trend to stay on at school was increasing at the rate of 5% year. This, together with the bulge, would mean a doubling of existing student numbers by 1965.   (He was to prove exactly right.)

To meet the forecast demand entailed building new universities, a move opposed by some of the older universities who were worried about competition. The general public however, the 'electorate', were the Generation A parents of the Baby Boomers. They were overwhelmingly in support. Perkins (1972, 117) reported that 'Ultimately, I suppose, it was the electorate which decided-or, rather, it was the conviction on the part of the politicians that any party which did not accept the need for expansion would be punished at the polls.' The impetus behind the mass education of the Boomers was not a fringe fashion of a political party, but the design of those whose ethics and values drove them to demand new opportunities for education and experience for their Boomer children and for wider society. Once again, as argued in Chapter 3, the seeds of Boomers' values were sown by the older generation.

University expansion was not, however, simply a feature of UK society: it occurred in all countries included in my study and further. Canada's university student population, for example, tripled in the 1960s. In the USA, it doubled in the same period. Indeed, the global expansion of university education in the 1960s was a reflection of a worldwide phenomenon that could be called a global culture, consistent with effects of globalisation and emergence of a 'world polity' after World War II, argued Evan Schofer and John W. Meyer (2005, 900) when 'a new model of society became institutionalized in that period, reflected in trends toward increasing democratization, human rights, scientization, and development planning'.

They researched university activity globally and found that growth occurred after roughly 1960 in every type of country they studied. Although, they showed, many African countries lagged behind the Global North, in proportional terms growth was still high: 'We also find extremely similar patterns when nations are broken out by other criteria, such as level of development, and in plots of individual countries' (Schofer and Meyer 2005, 908).

Schofer and Meyer argued that a new model of society was being institutionalised (2005, 917):

> Indeed, universities reflect the themes and the contradictions of world culture. They produce individuals who study neoclassical economics and wish to work for the WTO (World Trade Organization), just as they produce sociologists who decry the WTO's evils. Yet, such people are linked by a (mostly) common cultural frame.

Concerns were arising worldwide about discriminations by gender, race and class, write Schofer and Meyer (2005, 916), showing a move towards enabling equality and 'human rights in general'.

While I discussed briefly the turn to human rights in Chapter 3 as a feature of the Generation A ethos, the material in this chapter shows how those aspirations were operationalised through university education and, therefore, affected Baby Boomers in particular.

The impact of further education did not emerge as a 'Damascene anti-conversion', as Paul, a retired British marketing manager born in 1947, described it. It seemed part of what was happening already in Baby Boomer lives as they moved into the 1960s. Paul had already begun to question religion and the existence of God in his early teens. Encouraged by an 'inspirational' science teacher at school, he went to university to study physics. 'That turned me into a humanist, scientific thinker,' he said. Continuing with the science theme, Paul said that at university he could, at more of a distance, 'look back down the telescope at my parents', who were 'still locked into a hide bound structure, whereas I was at the university'. I infer here that his reference to 'hide-bound' (originally a term to describe malnourished cattle whose hides had become stiff and inelastic) means they were not shifting positions or attitudes. University, on the other hand, provided more space and possibilities for change. The reasons, I suggest, were broader than simply the syllabus.

While some academics discuss whether there is a conflict between science and religion (see, for example, Jones et al. 2019; Dawkins 2006; Brown 2003; Roof 1993, 1999) the more interesting question, as Lois Lee proposed (2019), is what does such an idea of conflict mean to those who hold it? It is important, she suggests, not simply to see religion as something that can be understood in terms of ideology and mythology, but to recognise that science can also be understood in the same ways. She argues that the nature of the relations between religion, non-religion, and science are more cultural and historical rather than intellectual and epistemic. As she discussed in earlier work (Lee 2015, 57–67) religious professionals often disdainfully refer to the 'enquiring mind' as a main reason people become non-religious, while non-religious people often claim they have a more rational or scientific outlook on life than religious people.

In practice, both religious and non-religious people usually accept science as a reliable source of knowledge about empirical matters. Elaine Eckland and Jerry Park's (2009) survey amongst academics at 21 American elite universities from both natural and social sciences is particularly relevant for this work as it considers the same generation, as they explain (Eckland and Park 2009, 280), because many academic scientists are 'part of the baby-boomer generation, a generation that sociologist Wade Clark Roof describes as the harbingers of syncretistic forms of spirituality (Roof 1993, 1999)'. The main objective of their project was to address the kinds of research that considers the religion–science conflict paradigm and argues that more education leads to less religiosity.

The question they asked in their survey was (Eckland and Park 2009, 281):

[T]hinking now about your faith or spiritual perspective and your professional life, please indicate if you 'strongly agree,' 'somewhat agree,' 'have no opinion,' 'somewhat disagree,' or 'strongly disagree' with the statement, 'there is an irreconcilable conflict between religious knowledge and scientific knowledge.'

Other questions asked about how respondents were raised in religious or non-religious households, what their own religious orientation was, and if they engaged in certain religious or spiritual practices, such as Bible reading, church attendance, or yoga. They found that of the scientists they studied, most either lacked religion or were religiously liberal, with only a few involved in spiritual practices and with a slight majority being raised in religious homes. Only a minority of those surveyed thought that a conflict exists between religion and science; the slight majority who did not perceive a conflict were raised in homes where religion was important. Being raised in a home where religion was not important increased the likelihood of adopting the conflict paradigm. That may be, as the authors noted, somewhat counterintuitive were we to believe that science and religion is somehow essentially opposed. People who were raised in religious homes and attend church may have unique ways of reconciling that possible conflict, they suggest, such as believing that religion and science are in separate spheres and therefore cannot be compared. There was no significant variation between those in either natural or social sciences. They also found that scientists who thought their peers had a positive view of religion were significantly less likely to agree there was a conflict between science and religion.

One of the most relevant of their findings for my study here is their conclusion that plausibility structures tend to be upheld when linked to a religious community (Eckland and Park 2009, 289). It is therefore belonging, not religious identity, that is the most significant predictor of attitudes towards science and religion:

> Participation in religious services requires being part of a community of others who uphold the plausibility framework both of a given religion as well as the possibility that there is not a conflict between religion and science. Lack of attendance then may be the most important religiously based threat to the plausibility structure of religion, particularly if an individual previously attended (although these data do not allow us to test whether scientists attended and then switched to not attending). Those people who actively switched out of religion to a non-religious affiliation— 'a pronounced weakening of the religious plausibility structure'—are the most likely to adopt the view that there is a conflict.

I will now explore the idea of 'plausibility structures' in more detail. Plausibility structures are, as they imply, socially structured, drawing on social locations and relationships, and thus, for Peter Berger and Thomas Luckmann (1966), part of what they described as a wider sociology of knowledge. Their formulation was clear—'Society is a human product. Society is an objective reality. Man is a social product' (Berger and Luckmann 1966, 79).

The origins of such an idea arose in early philosophy and sociology. Aristotle discussed categories being human generated, and Durkheim and Mauss expressed it thus: 'The first logical categories were social categories; the first classes of things were classes of men into which these things were integrated' (1963, 93). But, importantly for sociologists of religion, Berger and Luckmann argued that knowledge is constructed socially through a tripartite, dialectic relationship between so-called objective and internal realities. An apparently objective reality, such as an institution like a church, is experienced as an independent reality through processes of externalisation. This supposed reality is produced and then 'internalized' through 'habitualization' (Berger and Luckmann 1966, 70–1):

> All human activity is subject to habitualization. Any action that is repeated frequently becomes cast into a pattern, which can then be reproduced with an economy of effort and which, ipso facto, is apprehended by its performer as that pattern. Habitualization further implies that the action in question may be performed again in the future in the same manner and with the same economical effort.

These processes relate to the performative production of belief as discussed here and in earlier chapters (and see Day 2011).

Paul, however, was not just discussing in our interviews the theoretical process of knowledge formation. He included 'humanist' in his description of his style of thinking, which adds a normative dimension. He was a member of the national humanist society, although he said he did not pay a particularly active part. Like many of my research participants, he had joined the organisation or similar groups because he heard about them and felt that their definitions of humanism matched the way he thought about himself and the world (the importance of 'belonging' to such, and other, groups is discussed in more detail in Chapter 10).

Many Baby Boomers I interviewed described themselves as 'humanist', and seemed to at least mostly echo the definition of a humanist posted on the Humanist UK website (https://www.humanists.uk/), although some expressed variations related to what they understood as the 'here and now' as I will discuss in Chapter 9:

Humanists are people who shape their own lives in the here and now, because we believe it's the only life we have. We make sense of the world through logic, reason, and evidence, and always seek to treat those around us with warmth, understanding, and respect.

Pam also defined herself as a humanist, and said it was a term she first came across at university. She discussed it amongst her new friends and joined a humanist society for a period. The acts of Boomers such as Paul and Pam were typical of those I interviewed: their ideas and sense of identity were embedded in new, non-religious social structures and relationships, thus further weakening the plausibility of religion.

The Baby Boomers I studied who attended university were not all scientists, of course. The disciplinary effect of studying non-science subjects also had an impact on the Boomers. Fran said that in her late teens and early twenties she studied history at university. It was then she concluded that religion was a form of social control. Pam also stressed the point about social control and community cohesion, made clear for her as she moved away to university where, she said, she became convinced that 'there was nothing to it, apart from keeping communities together'. There might be something to the dietary rules laid down in the Bible, she added, 'if pork goes off in a hot climate it may be better not to eat it,' she said, but it was also, for her, 'a way of keeping the patriarchy'.

Jack, a British lawyer born in 1958, said he first started to withdraw from religion at school when he studied Classics, and then again at university, where he specialised in it. It made him realise, he said, that every civilisation, or historical period, has its own gods. He began to ask himself what happened to those Greek or Roman gods when Jesus came along. Greeks and Romans were not stupid people, he knew from his studies at school and later at university. Indeed, they were responsible for some of the most groundbreaking philosophical and scientific findings and theories. And so, he told himself, they must have had good reasons to hold their beliefs. He felt it was illogical to assume their false gods just died out and were replaced with something true and everlasting. He found himself wondering if the god of Judaism, Christianity, and Islam would also die out and be replaced, and if so, by whom or what? And, if not, why not? Why, given the comparatively short period of western civilisation, would some gods be the 'right' ones and others not? Jack's questions and experiences may be understood as a further example of the weakening of plausibility structures.

Certain ideas and beliefs maintain plausibility, Berger (1967) had argued, because they are supported by institutions which reinforce them. Applied to the example of the Baby Boomers I have studied, it seems likely that as the Boomers did not typically strongly belong to church institutions, and religion was rarely discussed or practised at home, then there were no institutions or frameworks to ensure the plausibility of a monotheistic God was sustained.

What Berger (1967) refers to as pluralism, and posited as a causal variable of religious decline, may be particularly accentuated in the Boomer university experience. Baby Boomers were not the first generation to realise that there were other cultures or other religions in the world, but they were the first generation to move away from home *en masse* and to live, eat, study, and party with others who shared their age and, in many cases, aspirations. The residential aspect of university life required students to live everyday in an environment where they were encouraged to explore options and other ways of being.

As Berger (1967) suggested, there were other institutions and frameworks that may have actively weakened such structures in an increasingly postmodern world. I suggest that leaving home to partake in a university secular education and forming friendships amongst non-religious fellow students and friends may be examples of those alternative institutions and frameworks. Indeed, friendships are so important they can both strengthen and weaken institutional loyalties, as (Regnerus et al. 2004) argued as they found that maintaining close friendships with church-attending friends can ensure that young people retain their church-attending practices.

As Viv told me about her university experience: 'Households didn't stay together the whole time next door to mothers. We moved around, those who went to university moved around.' Laura, a British chemist born in 1951, described both her and her future husband she met at university as having the same experience. As soon as she left home and went to university she stopped going to church and never returned. Simon described his experience in similar terms. Initially, he said, he felt he had 'drifted' away from religion partly because 'there was less of a sense you had to follow in family's footsteps, you move away, the cultural mix was changing'. He added that by the time he got to university, he and his friends led lives where religion 'didn't really play a part. I don't think any of my cohort at university are religious.'

Charles also stressed that impact of moving away 'from convention, and the assumptions we'd grown up with post 1945'. Charles reflected on his studies in economics and political theory when he began to question capitalism: 'I started reading Marx at the time,' he said. 'I lost god and found Marx.' His comment, although wryly put with a laugh, echoed the trend of the Baby Boomer generation to revisit and in many places help re-invent academic disciplines such as sociology, philosophy, and linguistics. I will return to this in more depth in Chapter 7 but will make the point now that Charles was hinting at a component of university life that created a new philosophy of, perhaps, neo-Marxism and countercultural ideals that affected the Baby Boomers intellectually and emotionally.

Radical Rationalists

One of the themes that arose in my interviews was a preference for 'rational' thinking. As Viv said, when we were discussing paranormal possibilities, 'there is a rational explanation for everything'. Lois Lee (2015) described one of her interviewees specifically drawing attention to the idea that rationality was a comforting place to be. Matthew said:

> I believe in science as a frame of reference I think that in the sense of finding one's place in the universe... the method and the whole perspective of a scientific age is one that I find very comforting... I don't need supernatural explanations because... nature in itself is impressive enough.

As discussed in the introduction to this chapter, 'rationality' has a rich and contested history, particularly within the discipline of anthropology.[2] Edward Burnett Tylor (1958 [1871]) thought that religion originated from incorrect, although not irrational, belief in ancestor worship. Defining religion as a 'belief in spirits', Tylor argued that the root of all religion could be found in animism, or a faith in an immortal soul. While its origins were not irrational, he argued, adhering to those beliefs would indicate only the survival of an earlier, mistaken idea which would be relinquished, he thoughts as societies, like people, grew up. Many of the Baby Boomers I interviewed would agree with him even while, sometimes admitting with embarrassment, that they had experienced a connection with spirits. This is the subject of two later chapters—9 and 11. Within the wider discipline of anthropology, over time, and with much debate and soul-searching, anthropologists changed those questions and moved to reflect more on the relationships between rationality and 'belief' and the manners in which the anthropologist is implicated. As their considerations continued, it became apparent that there was not one acceptable definition of 'rational', but that in practice it mostly seemed to involve either 'reason' or, through 'rationalisation', a means to achieve ends. Roger expressed this in terms of his attraction to books about science: 'There's no place in believing in something, like faith, with no evidence, I want facts and a hypothesis to be proven.' A preference for rational thinking did not obscure, for some Boomers, moments of insight or even transcendence, as I will discuss more in Chapter 9. As Annabel explained, some of her experiences were 'hard to explain because I consider myself a rationalist', and yet she recalled sudden moments when 'everything seemed to come together as perfect'.

In philosophy, René Descartes' assertion that we think therefore we are links personhood to a process of self-conscious thinking. It is that, I suggest, more than cognitive processes that makes the idea of rationality so important for Boomers: it provides a way to assess and assert the self, particularly in relation to an 'Other', often depicted in the person of their parents to whom, as Paul expressed, they could now look from afar, down the telescope as he suggested.

This is therefore a marker not only of propositional or cognitive belief but also of personhood and separation. As psychologists argue, the process of individuation means a satisfactory and permanent break with parental dominance. It does not necessarily entail, as I have argued throughout, a turn to a mean, self-centred individualism, but possibly to a more mature, equal, and adult relationship between parents and former child, and to a shift in values.

Inglehart (1977) argued that the significant value changes that occurred during the 1950s and 1960s happened partly because of greater university education, which not only helped people become more adept at analysis, but they also became more aware of the possibilities and importance of political participation. Both rational thinking and radical participation may therefore be part of a collective generational identity that many Boomers feel was forged then and replicated throughout their lives. As Helen Horowitz (1986, 25) argued:

> Cultural change divided young from old and created a new sense of connectedness among youth. Political rebels banded together to create the New Left, ground it in statements of philosophy and tactics, and extend it on campus. The Movement offered to sympathetic college youth a radical community with a sense of collective meaning and a plan of purposeful action.

And yet, as she points out, the Boomers did not invent radicalism but tended to be 'stimulated by adult mentors' (Horowitz 1986, 25). These older people, members of Generation A, provided inspiration and encouragement, demonstrating again a central point in my book here: Baby Boomer identity was in many ways forged by their parents' generation. Studies of Boomers who formed part of protest movements against, for example, the Vietnam War do not reach a consensus about the Boomers' psychological profile or motivations. Much, Horowitz observes, 'depends on the politics of the questioner' (1986, 26). Researchers who sympathised with the protestors' actions and goals tended to describe them as 'living out their parents' ideals, healthy, more highly developed morally, and in the avant garde'. On the other hand, those researchers who opposed the protestors' actions and ideals tended to describe them as rebellious, unwilling to accept authority, even 'sick, unwilling to face adulthood'. A further reason it may be difficult to reach a definite conclusion is because, she says, 'the pressures were less personal than cultural'.

As discussed earlier, not only did Boomers often share political and cultural ideals, but they were also the first generation, in large numbers, to live together in congenial circumstances for several years, being able therefore to converse, party, protest, and study with others of their same age and, in many cases, dispositions.

Travel: 'I Found People Who Didn't Think Like Me'

Baby Boomers participated in a 1960s and 1970s' revolution in travel. Inglehart (1977, 9) showed that before World War II, 'only a tiny minority of native-born Americans had ever visited Europe; in the last twenty years higher incomes and charter flights have enabled millions of Americans to cross the Atlantic. Similarly, by 1970 most Western Europeans had visited at least one foreign country; indeed proportionately more Germans visited Italy than Americans visited Florida.'

Leaving home and travelling, or working in other places, had a similar effect as university in introducing the young Boomers to other people and other cultures. Anita, a retired British social worker born in 1946, described that after three years working, she began to drift away from religion as she travelled to several European countries. But, she said, the biggest change occurred when she lived in the Middle East.

I was very aware of the Muslim call to prayer and the way that dominates the day. Muslims are reminded of their God, and although there is a lot of hypocrisy—I'm aware of that—I think it must have a lot of influence in keeping people in touch with their faith. Seeing them spread out their mats on the pavement—it's a ritual, it keeps them in touch.

Observing that did not make her more religious, but less so as it seemed to present, in contrast, Anglicanism as something shallow and inconsequential.

Carol, a British retired teacher born in 1952, said she was able to travel between secondary school and university because she worked as an *au pair* at the same time. An *au pair* is a young person, usually female, who lives with a family in a different country for a few months, receiving free room and board and a small amount of spending money in exchange for helping with childcare. The movement began in 1969 to assist predominantly middle-class Baby Boomers between the ages of 18 and 26 who wanted to live in a different European country, and also to assist families who found that a steady supply of 'servants' had dried up post-war. Unlike servants, the *au pair* would not earn a formal wage or wear a uniform but live as part of the family. The main purpose of the scheme was to facilitate inter-cultural exchanges and help young people to learn a different language, often by attending a language school as well as conversing with the host family. The scheme then spread to other countries and generally operates with similar frameworks and visa restrictions. In Carol's case, the effect was both to help her perfect her French but also, as an unintended consequence, to move her more quickly through her process of withdrawing from religion. The family she lived with was non-religious, which was a novelty for her, coming from an Anglican church-attending family: 'I saw a model of a family who were doing perfectly well without religion,' she said. Her already weak attachments to religion then 'slowly ebbed away from me', with the matter finally settled a year later when she went to university and decided that all the Christians she met there 'were all desperately dull'. As an indication of the parochialism of the small UK country town where she had been raised, it was also at university where she first met a Jew, she said; it would be a few years yet before she met a Muslim or a Sikh.

Small English towns could be, and to a large extent still are, overwhelmingly white and nominally Christian. Roger said he felt the impact of travel, even within one country. Raised in a small town in northern England, he said he drifted away from religion when he left home: 'I Went to London. Met other people, other cultures.'

Even a language degree prompted more movements away from religion: Eleanor described how her withdrawal from religion became stronger at university where, studying for a French degree, she went to France and 'found people who didn't think like me'. That was, as she described it 'a bit unsettling'. One of the religious puzzles about France is its large Catholic population coupled with a discourse of secularity. The constitutional secularity in France is known as laïcité, which, loosely translated means 'secularism'. The word reflects a long history of struggle between the church and state, brought to a climax in 1905 when they were legally separated. In 1946 the separation was enshrined in the Constitution. France may seem to have a stricter form of secularity than, for example the UK, where about a third of schools are run by the Church of England, the head of state is also head of the church, and bishops sit in the House of Lords. And yet, the French state financially supports religious buildings and funds Catholic schools.[3]

Charles said he travelled around France not long after the 1968 student uprisings. These were, as I discuss further in Chapter 7, extraordinary times affecting large sectors of the country and population, not just Paris where the main riots took place. The country was infused with debates about politics, workers' rights, and questions about legitimate authority.

In conclusion, I suggest that the effects of leaving home for education and travel had significant effects on the Boomers' non-religious identities. The practice of living together and of experiencing other people's beliefs and cultures both created new forms of belonging that made the ideas of church and religion increasingly implausible.

Notes

1. Fitting as it is, I will resist overworking the metaphor, although it does seem to be apt. See, for example, Peter Brierley (2000) who discusses contemporary religious in terms of a tide running out.

2. See, for example, Day 2018. Unfortunately, much of the impetus for that exploration in anthropology stems from the discipline's involvement in nineteenth- and early twentieth-century colonial projects focused on establishing whether people, the so-called 'primitives' being encountered for the first time by white men of the Global North, had rational, reasoned, evidence-based thinking systems or were clinging to 'false' beliefs and 'superstitions'. These were not idle questions. The white people engaged in such endeavours, whether sent by churches or by states, all shared the same questions: Were 'they' like 'us'? Can we trade with them? Convert them? Conquer them? Western colonial masters and missionaries came from places they thought were more civilised, and more 'evolved', according to

their Victorian-era style of thinking. An important attempt to correct such assumptions can be found in Evans-Pritchard 1976 [1937].

3. It may be that the more vociferous opposition to religion was, suggested Michael Kelly (https://theconversation.com/frances-la-cite-why-the-rest-of-the-world-struggles-to-understand-it-149,943) in fact an opposition to: 'the large-scale migration from North Africa after decolonisation in the 1960s, and the emergence of new generations of French-born Muslims. In 1989, disputes began over whether Muslim girls should be allowed to wear headscarves in state schools.'

6

Blinding Light on the Road from Damascus

Climbing the Moral High Ground

Introduction: 'I Think God Is a False Idol'

For some Boomers, a profound shock or revelation was a pivotal moment that accelerated their withdrawal from religion. Those experiences and values helped to promote their desire for social equalities, such as feminism, and for many, clarified the virtue of people being able to decide for themselves what they did with their bodies, and with whom. Many Boomers were also part of the first generation to experience the worldwide new phenomenon of university education, as discussed in Chapter 5, and many referenced this move as they discussed their deepening non-religiosity. What they discussed, and I inferred, was the influence of meeting and in many cases living with other people, often from other social strata or groups, and also from their own backgrounds. This provided, I suggest, a dialectic between known and unknown which combined to create a new, stronger ethos of accepting and even encouraging diversity. For some Boomers, this provoked a sudden, dramatic sense of the need to forcefully reject the religious tenets they had been told to believe as younger people.

As Vikki put it:

> I treat everyone the same because I think God is a false idol. Religion is different for everybody, but the world is not different for everybody. We are all living on it and we should take care of it and each other. I always treat everybody with the same attitude, the same thought. That's my philosophy, should we I say, but I come to that through seeing all different religions, all different churches, and how they're not together, they're not working together like they should be.

Why Baby Boomers Turned from Religion: Shaping Belief and Belonging, 1945–2021. Abby Day, Oxford University Press. © Abby Day 2022. DOI: 10.1093/oso/9780192866684.003.0006

Much has been made of Peter Berger's theories of pluralism helping to weaken if not shatter the plausibility structures that allowed religion to maintain its 'sacred canopy'. While some of those ideas have explanatory value here, I will argue that the effect of pluralism was not the most significant influence. As discussed in Chapter 5, the increased awareness of other religions did not provoke people to switch their religious identity to a new one, nor to acquire or espouse another belief system at random. They did not become members of 'flat earth' societies or start worshipping fairies at the bottom of the garden. While some explored varieties of spirituality, most did not. What they did do, in concert with others, was question and reject specific forms of religion and religious ideas, mainly those with which they were raised and which rested on ideas of a fixed and often unequal social structure, hierarchy, and patriarchy. The realisation that churches were being more publicly implicated in sex scandals and accounts of abuse furthered the Boomers' desire to separate from the institution and much of its teaching. Boomers did not, I argue, experience a vague, generalised dismissal of religion or have a deep urge to shop rather than attend Sunday service. The church itself, and for many, Christianity and religion, represented key beliefs and behaviours the Boomers found unethical and incompatible with their own values.

For some, they felt that the influence of religion had permeated the public sphere where it did not belong. Several of my interviewees joined campaigning organisations in the UK and Canada in order to influence a stronger church/state separation. While most of my interviewees described, as discussed in the previous chapter, a gentle drifting away from religion, others wanted to stress, during our discussions, a 'pivotal' moment. When Paul described, as discussed in Chapter 5, his final move away from Christianity as 'not a *Damascene* anti conversion moment' he was indexing the biblical story of Saul's conversion to Christianity on the road from Jerusalem to Damascus. Few biblical stories have retained such a hold on popular discourse: from here we have references to the 'blinding light' of revelation, the moment when we see clearly. The invocation of the 'road to Damascus' represents a critical journey towards some important realisation or personal conversion to another idea or way of living.

But what is less discussed is the social experience of Saul's journey. Saul was not alone on the road to Damascus. Known then as the Pharisee Saul, he was on his way with a band of men to arrest Christians, members of a new and illegal sect, and return them to Jerusalem for trial. When he saw a blinding light and heard the voice of Jesus, his companions were also stunned by the light and, according to some variations,[1] heard but did not understand what the voice was saying. Blinded and temporarily helpless, Saul's companions led him by the hand into Damascus where his sight was restored when he was baptised by Ananias and received his new name of Paul. He was later canonised by the Catholic church and became known as St. Paul.

In this chapter I will discuss how Baby Boomers often experienced a sudden rupture, separating them sharply and finally from their childhood and teenage involvement in religion, mainly accompanied and assisted by new friends and associations. The mood here was one of confidence and certainty in their sense of morality. What may be mistaken for a turn to individualism was, I argue, more of a turn from a certain kind of believing and belonging that had stressed convention, conformity, inequality, and individual salvation. That they told their stories of rejection and repulsion with often vivid, detailed examples speaks to a neglected area of scholarship I hope to contribute to here: the texture of lived non-religion.

A Time to Reject 'the Socially Correct Thing to Do'

Discussing the impact of forms of individualism on politics, Florence Sutcliffe-Braithwaite (2016, 132) argued that:

> individualism shouldn't be simply linked to Thatcherism, though, and nor should it be equated with selfishness. Individualism—in the sense in which it is closely related to the decline of deference—is not simply a 'me first' attitude. Rather, it is an insistence on the individual's right to respect, to make their own choices, to define their own goals. No society is ever entirely individualistic: we are all shaped by social norms. However, across the postwar period, Britain has become less bound by tradition and convention; people are more keen to make up their own minds, less willing to accede to the rightness of hierarchies and snobbishness.

The idea of individualism cannot, I suggest, be linked simplistically to the decline of religion. It does not alone have sufficient explanatory power to account for a rise in secularity: religions such as Christianity have also been construed as individualistic through its emphasis on seeking one's salvation through a personal relationship with Jesus Christ. The idea that Christianity 'in many if not all of its forms promoted various kinds of individualism became a staple of the literature in the anthropology of Christianity,' wrote Joel Robbins (2012, 2015).[2]

Being moral beings presumes an association within society. It is, argued Durkheim (1992, 74), a societal phenomenon:...since we know that morals are the product of the society, that they permeate the individual from without and that in some respects they do violence to his physical nature and his natural temperament, we can understand...that morals are what the society is and that they have force only so far as the society is organised.

An apparent decline in collective morality and turn to individualism has contributed to a decline in religion, argued Charles Taylor (2007, 299). The latter part of the twentieth century had 'a generalised culture of "authenticity" or expressive individualism, in which people are encouraged to find their own way, discover their own fulfilment, "do their own thing"'. Taylor claims this 'ethic of authenticity' began in the romantic period and has 'utterly penetrated popular culture'. His tone resonates with how Bryan Wilson (2001, 44–5) described changes in family structure and the move for people 'do their own thing'.

Noting wider cultural shifts away from fixed structures and hierarchies, Grace Davie (2002, 18) argued that church attendance declined at a time when participation in other organisations, such as political parties and trade unions was also reducing as they were 'losing their appeal, mainly because they offer hierarchically organized pre-defined roles into which members are expected to fit'.

I will explore more of why Boomers may have preferred their, and their friends', 'own things' to an institution they found lacking in moral legitimacy, and what specifically they rejected about the church's social structures and hierarchies. Terry, a retired Canadian doctor born in 1953, said that he had noticed that his mother and other church-attending women wore hats to church when he was growing up. One of the main reasons that he recoiled against religion, he explained, was because he later understood the social significance and class-based nature of hat-wearing.

Terry's remarks resonate with theories about how 'display' represents something deeper than just a fad or fashion. Everyone in a given society is confronted with 'signs', which do not have intrinsic meaning, but must be understood and de-coded to see what they mean. Signs, for Ferdinand de Saussure (1961), consists of the signifier, such as a word, and the signified, being the meaning the signifier represents. Although his work was based in linguistics, other theorists in the social sciences have taken the concept further to apply to objects, and even sounds and smells. The same idea, however, prevails: the culturally specific meaning of the sign needs to be decoded and interpreted according to the social and historical context in which it is set.

Roland Barthes (1967) distinguished between levels of 'denotation' and 'connotation' to differentiate between what we may see, and what we may culturally know. Hats, for example, were signs connoted differently in the 1950s in England or the USA than they would be in, say, contemporary North American and European contexts. Stuart Hall (1997, 24) described these within his wider theories of representation as 'completed signs in terms of the wider realms of social ideology—the general beliefs, conceptual frameworks and value systems of society'. His reference to 'social ideology' flags important moves in the work around representation made within disciplines of cultural studies, sociology, and anthropology in the twentieth century: that which is signified forms part of an ideology. Hall drew also on Michel Foucault (1977, 27) to show that fields of representation are also fields of knowledge, and therefore power: 'There is no power relation without the correlative constitution of a field of knowledge, nor any knowledge that does not presuppose and constitute at the same time, power relations.' Therefore, what one wears and how we relate to and display our bodies are not individualistic decisions, but part of wider social relationships. Both Taylor and Wilson were mistaken: there was no individual self nor possibility for anyone to do their 'own thing'. Importantly, we need to consider, following theorists such as Bourdieu and McGuire, more about the social constructs and ideals that were helping to form the Boomers' social identities.

Pierre Bourdieu (1977, 124) described the 'socially informed body' as being formed through processes of socialisation that determine the tastes, likes, and dislikes that people tend to think, erroneously, are highly individualised. Therefore, he argued, people's bodies become a site of competition and struggle: 'The specifically symbolic power to impose [such] principles of the construction of reality...is a major dimension of political power' (Bourdieu 1977, 165).

Meredith McGuire described (1990, 284) why 'the body' is an important area of study for sociologists. She argued: 'Part of the reason our bodies matter to us is that we strongly identify our very selves with our bodies. We experience things done to our bodies as done to ourselves.' Further, she continued, bodies are matter: 'The human body is material, and society inscribes itself on the body' and as such as bodies are both biological and cultural products, both physical and symbolic, and always social.

Returning to the specific example of the women's hats, it can be argued that some women may have felt that they were following a religious instruction to cover their heads, as articulated by scripture: 'Any woman who prays or prophesies with her head unveiled disgraces her head' (1 Corinthians 11:5). And yet, the twentieth-century Anglican church did not require the practice; the Catholic church abandoned its insistence in the 1960s. (Other religions have equally varied practices relating to women's hair and head covering in history and contemporary society.[3]) But what drove Terry away, he said, was not the religious instruction but the meanings of the social practice which the church was representing and reproducing. These helped to form and sustain unequal social class distinctions with strong messages about social superiority and exclusion. He said that once he realised that the apparent 'religious' practice of hat-wearing was mainly performed because 'it was the socially correct thing to do', he decided to have nothing to do with it.

Paul also recalled feeling angry at the class-based nature of church as he was growing up. His family was far from being a part of a comfortable or affluent middle class, but members, he said, of a communist working class. During our interview he paused as if to warn me of the unpleasant nature of what he was about to say: 'Here is an awful story,' he began, before describing his childhood home that did not have an indoor toilet. As a child, he had to 'stand on a brick to pee in the toilet' which was on a raised piece of land at the end of their back garden. A friend came over once and couldn't believe it, he recalled. He became acutely aware that there were differences in society, and he didn't like seeing 'all these upper-class snobs practising religion on Sundays and not during the rest of the week'.

Like Terry, Paul was rejecting not simply 'church' but an institution that signified inequality, class, and hypocrisy. Social class is a human invention, but no less real for that. Drawing on Aristotle, the sociologists Durkheim and Mauss (1963 [1902]) argued that all classifications are social classifications, not biological or immovable: 'The first logical categories were social categories; the first classes of things were classes of men into which these things were integrated.'

According to academic and clergyman Adrian Stringer (2015), while there has never been a systematic study of socio-economic classes and the Church of England, he discussed American research that showed how Episcopalians,   part   of   the   Anglican   Communion,   have   been disproportionately drawn from the upper echelons of society from the colonial era (Finke and Stark 2005; Roof and McKinney 1987, 110) through to the mid-twentieth century. Stringer cites further studies that continue the link between class and Episcopalians in the twentieth and twenty-first centuries. Constance Buchanan (1992, 310–11) wrote: 'The Episcopal tradition has always been small, exercising social and cultural influence vastly disproportionate to its size. More than any other Protestant denomination it has been identified with the national power structure and destiny.' The popular description of the Church of England today as 'the Conservative Party at prayer' is only partly tongue in cheek. Although smaller numerically than the Nonconformist and Evangelical churches, members of the Anglican/Episcopal Churches have historically been disproportionately represented in society's establishment.

Sean McCloud (2007) argues that class-related religious culture is transmitted through personal networks, thereby creating a stratification of religion mirroring the stratification of material resources in the wider society. Jay Demerath (1965) analysed Lutherans according to whether they were 'church-like' or 'sect-like'. Those who were church-like not only attended church but also participated in a variety of church-related organisations in the church and parish, unlike the 'sect-like' people, who attended less and participated less, leading him to conclude that people from different social classes seek different outcomes from religion.

A significant finding about the studies into social class is the connection with families, and with religious transmission. Johnson's (1978) investigations into nineteenth-century Rochester, New York, found that religious congregations were built upon extensive family networks, together with associated networks of friends and colleagues. David Kynaston (2009, 53) wrote of the UK in the 1950s: 'Women accounted for almost two-thirds of church attendances, with a bias towards the Family and Community. The elderly, and a middle-class person was at least twice as likely to go to church each Sunday than a working-class person.' Those were mothers of the Baby Boomers: partly religious, partly classed, and wholly gendered.

Sex: 'No one Tells You How Great It Is, and then You're Supposed to Ask for Forgiveness!'

As I noted in the introduction, Charles Taylor (2007, 299), had described the latter part of the twentieth century as a period characterised by 'a generalised culture of "authenticity"'. Aspirations towards authenticity, combined with rejecting what they perceived to be hypocrisy, seemed sometimes to provoke the Boomers I studied to break off with religion. Apart from class, discussed above, another specific form of inauthentic behaviour that bothered Boomers was the structure of the church that promoted forms of dominance by male figures. The Boomers did not express a general aversion to structure or authority but to the specific form of male hierarchy that dominated: patriarchy.

They, and to some degree their parents (as I discussed in Chapter 3), were engaged in processes Anthony Giddens (1991) would recognise as reflexive. Conditions of late modernity, argued Giddens, require an active approach to social structures which he defined as consisting of rules and resources. In a dialectic, reflexive manner individuals may use resources (such as university education, friends, and money) to challenge and often change structures that no longer allow them to behave and flourish in ways they feel are authentic, beneficial, and ethical. Giddens argued that uncertain conditions of late modernity present historically specific challenges concerning equality and global emancipation. It is this condition of late modernity to which the Boomers were responding. Some did so through quick and sharp rejections of religion; others drifted. Most created or joined less hierarchal and less patriarchal organisations, as will be discussed more in Chapter 10.

Paul said he moved to London to attend university and made what he described as the 'classic break' from the church and its 'structures'. Since then, he said, he only attends church for occasions such as weddings or funerals and does not miss it. The inauthenticity of the church was felt by Sally, a British retired secretary born in 1954, on an occasion when she attended a concert with a Pentecostal choir. That was a 'pivotal moment,' she said. The experience felt like emotional manipulation—'it freaked me out!' she said, and right then she turned firmly away from religion.

Jennifer described the moment she decided abruptly to stop going to church. She was in grade nine, she said, aged 14, and had been out for the evening with her boyfriend who was slightly older than she. When they entered her house, she said, they encountered her alcoholic, abusive father drinking with the local minister. 'The reverend laid into my boyfriend about being out with a young woman. We weren't even late,' Jennifer said, her voice beginning to rise in anger with the memory of it. 'And that's what used to drive me mental, when the minister starts coming over and is drinking with your alcoholic father and then says you're the one that's bad! Bugger that.'

Jennifer described in more detail another aspect of the church that she found alienated her and, she suggested, others of her generation. She described the church as being structured around patriarchy: 'I hated it, absolutely, I could never understand why god always had to be a man. The patriarchy really got to me.' Jennifer had attended an all-girls school for most of her education and said during our interview that it was the Headmistress of the school 'who really impressed upon us, to me, that girls could do anything'. She contrasted that message with that of the church minister 'who was saying girls can't do this'.

Put into the social context of the time, she suggested, would explain why people of her generation 'didn't necessarily bring up their next generation in the church. We started questioning in ways that other generations before us hadn't, or hadn't been able to question, at least not overtly.'

Charles also spoke strongly against what he saw as patriarchy, lying at the root of 'my criticism of organised religion'. He elaborated with an example of attending the funeral of his wife's aunt. They had been very close, he explained, and therefore his wife wanted to do a reading at the funeral. The priest, he said, 'was really opposed. That's an example of patriarchal control.'

Lesley said she had already been 'drifting away' as a teenager, mainly because she could not reconcile the church's attitude to sex with how much she enjoyed it. 'No one tells you how great it is, and then you're supposed to ask for forgiveness!' When she arrived at university to study English literature, she made a final break from religion, she said. She found that all the students she met (and, in our interview, she repeated and stressed the word 'all') 'were ditching their religion. Religion was associated with a very traditional and hierarchal past,' she explained.

Allison, a British retired teacher born in 1949, also raised the issue of sexuality and how Christian teaching on the subject finally turned her away for good. The Christian Union group at university was very strict, she recalled: 'Holding hands was tantamount to a proposal of marriage.' She met a man in her first term who had rejected his Christian upbringing and together they formed a strong emotional and sexual bond. She suddenly realised that she wanted to be 'in the world and of the world, embrace it entirely', including the 'sexual mores of the time'. Allison also had her 'anti-Damascene' moment when she realised that although she believed in many of Jesus' moral teachings as expressed in the Sermon on the Mount, she felt after that 'it got messed up by Paul and then the church'. She is referring to St. Paul's (after his conversion) instruction to the early Christian church to keep women in submission. His writings on the topic were often used by those who oppose the ordination of women who tend to quote a few passages such as Paul's first letter to the Corinthians: 'Let your women keep silence in the churches: for it is not permitted unto them to speak; but they are commanded to be under obedience, as also saith the law' (1 Corinthians 14:34) and to a young new Christian minister called Timothy (1 Timothy 2:11–15):

> Let a woman learn quietly with all submissiveness. I do not permit a woman to teach or to exercise authority over a man; rather she is to remain quiet. For Adam was formed first, then Eve; and Adam was not deceived, but the woman was deceived and became a transgressor. Yet she will be saved through childbearing—if they continue in faith and love and holiness, with self-control.

Allison said she recalled when growing up that a pervasive patriarchy influenced her: 'The only female thing in the church was one statue of Mary, and I couldn't join the choir because I was a girl!' She contrasted St. Paul's vision of a church with the teachings of Jesus as presented in the Sermon on the Mount where he, amongst other directives, seemed to have subverted traditional authority by saying, for example, that 'the meek shall inherit the earth', and 'blessed are the peacemakers', and inviting people to 'turn the other cheek' rather than fight one's enemies.

The effect of resisting patriarchy had a long-term effect on Yvonne, for example. She divorced her first husband, a staunch Christian, because he insisted that he was 'head of the household'. Nevertheless, it still took her 'years to get the big thing out of my head, that male authority thing'.

Declining to Defer: 'If There Was a God, Wouldn't He Be Kinder?'

While the turn from the authority of the church is sometimes described as a 'decline of deference' it has not, I suggest, been sufficiently explored to whom or to what people declined to defer. There are, I found, specific qualities of the church, God, and Christianity that sufficiently repelled the Boomers I spoke with to effect a final, permanent alienation.

Florence Sutcliffe-Braithwaite (2018) makes the point, contra to theorists such as Charles Taylor and Bryan Wilson, that a decline of deference to pre-existing hierarchies was ethical, not selfish. It showed a part of a society where people would no longer accept that they or other people were inferior to elites and hierarchies but demanded control over their own lives.

She observed that in the 1950s and 1960s a decline of deference was met with a rise in new social movements that served to democratise policy-making, devolve power, and increase worker participation. All of this was driven, she argued, by a shift which 'lay in the triumph of authenticity and ordinariness, which implied that deference to older class hierarchies and traditions was wrong' (Sutcliffe-Braithwaite 2018, 206).

For example, Helen told me about what she described as a pivotal moment, beginning with a need to rebel against her parents, 'they were very controlling,' she said. She had studied science at school and wanted to be a doctor, and by the time she reached her last year of school she had acquired all but one of the courses necessary to enter medical school. She could have stayed at home another year to re-take the final course, she said, but she could not bear to stay any longer: 'I had to escape my parents.' At university she went once or twice to church, and then got engaged to a man who was not a Christian. The first question her mother asked her was: 'Is he a Christian'? The two moved in together, which enraged her parents who cut her off financially. That was fine with Helen, she told me. In most mean-ingful ways her relationship with her parents, Christianity, and the tradi-tions they represented held no moral authority.

Sherry, a British graphic designer born in 1950, described that when she was just 13 and her mother, in her early forties, had a major stroke that left her physically and emotionally vulnerable, Sherry prayed frequently to God, asking first of all if her mother could be healed. When that didn't work, she asked only that her mother might be 'ok'. Without any apparent change happening, she got to the point, she said, of asking God to give her some of her mother's pain instead. Finally, when she saw that her prayers were not being answered she suddenly had to ask herself the uncomfortable question about 'how God could have allowed that to happen to my mum, who had done nothing wrong. That triggered my rebellion from God. How could he allow that to happen?' She stopped praying and going to church. I asked her if she thought this was a case of turning from a 'bad god' or losing her faith in the existence of a god at all.

'I lost my faith in the existence of God,' she said. 'One or two times as an adult when I felt in desperate times, saying oh God please make things right, but logically I don't believe in him.' Roger expressed a similar sentiment when he said he stopped believing in the 'fairy tale' of God's existence because he could not believe in the existence of such a deity: 'If there was a god, wouldn't he be kinder?' he asked.

Theologians and philosophers refer to that moment of disbelief as the confrontation of the problem of evil, or the problem of meaning. Max Weber (1922) analysed this to show how its reconciliation is necessary, but impossible, within monotheistic religions. The problem proposes that it is inconsistent to believe that an all-good, all-powerful god would allow bad things to happen to good people. All monotheistic religions wrestle with this problem, he said, and try to resolve it through 'theodicy'. Originating in Greek, and theorised by the philosopher Leibnitz, the word derives from 'theos' for God and 'dike' for justice. The religious adherent needs to rationalise the problem, and may do so through various means, typically by pointing out that most problems are caused by humans who are granted free will to behave as they choose, and having granted them such power, God will not intervene. Another response may be that God is, indeed, allowing such pain or terrible events to happen but this is only because he is testing someone's faith. The prime example of being tested is often told through the biblical book of Job, whereby someone who appears to be good and godly, is tested through a rivalry between God and Satan. When Satan suggests that Job only believes in God because God offers him protection, God disagrees and bets with Satan that Job will be devout even if God withdraws his protection and Satan causes bad things to happen to Job. Satan takes this on, and causes Job to lose his children, his health, and his wealth. Job, as God predicted, remains faithful and loyal and is rewarded through more wealth and children (for more discussion of how the problem, and examples of how religious women work through the problem, see Day 2005).

Ben described an event when he was younger that seemed to him to be an unreasonable test of faith. His best friend's parents were Irish Catholics, 'good people' of whom he was very fond. After having five children, with the last being a difficult birth, a doctor told the mother not to have any more children 'as it could kill her,' Ben said. The couple decided to use contraception and, 'being an honest woman, she told her priest,' Ben continued. The priest was horrified and forbade her to come to church or receive communion.[4] That was the final turning point for him, he said: 'That was not a value system I wanted to have anything to do with.'

Several Boomers specifically mentioned the scandals of Catholic priests abusing young boys, and the church colluding in cover-ups. Philip's experience is particularly memorable for the sudden emotional impact it had on him. In 2008, he went from England to the USA for a conference, he said.

When it was over, on the Friday, he went to the hotel restaurant for breakfast. He had time to spare before his flight and looked forward to having a leisurely read of the paper and something to eat. He picked up the free newspaper provided by the restaurant and settled in at a table. It was the week before the 2008 American election, he recalled, with Barak Obama and John McCain in the running. In the newspaper he saw a full-page advertisement taken out by the Catholic church comparing the two candidates in order to advise Catholics. The advert drew attention to the fact that neither candidate had spoken out about contraception or genocide. Philip said that reading those words stunned him: 'They were equating both as equally bad.' He suddenly realised, in what he described to me as his 'anti-damascene moment' that 'the Roman Catholic church had completely lost its moral compass'.

'The scales fell from my eyes,' he said. How, he asked himself at that moment, could the church equate using a condom to prevent having a baby to the mass killing of people? 'From that moment, I became a humanist,' he said. He never regretted his decision, particularly when a few years later it became obvious that 'the Catholic church had been systematically protecting priests who had abused children'.

The refusal of the church to help women and children suffering abuse has been well documented. For 20 years, Canadian researchers Nancy Nason-Clark and Catherine Holtmann (2015) have studied how churches have helped or ignored women experiencing domestic abuse. They concluded that while laywomen often gave practical and emotional support, the response from the typically male church hierarchy was pitiful. They note that domestic abuse is a worldwide problem, documented by international institutions such as the World Health Organization (WHO), the United Nations (UN), national governments, and charities. Between one in three and one in four women from across all socio-economic, ethnic, and religious categories have experienced domestic violence, and the response from their churches of whatever denomination has been broadly similar.

One detailed account they give is that of 'Carrie' who finally managed to escape and take refuge in a women's shelter, leaving her abusive husband, a priest, who had beaten and humiliated her for years. One day while out walking near the shelter, she happened to see the diocesan Bishop, the man to whom her husband reported—effectively, his line manager. When she approached him, he tried to avoid a conversation with her, but she persisted, asking why he had not intervened or even visited her now that she was in her refuge. His answers shocked and saddened her: he denied any knowledge of her husband's abuse, refused to believe that the priest could have been violent, and said he did not personally intend to ever be seen in a shelter. That example was similar to others found in Nason-Clark's and Holtmann's studies, leading them to conclude that religious leaders systematically ignore domestic abuse, refusing to see that the issue is often rooted in men's attempts to gain power and control over women.

The church's neglect of abused women sometimes emanated further than a single institution. As I discussed in earlier work on Anglican women (Day 2017, 44), the Anglican charity, the Mothers' Union, was implicated by Esther Mombo (1998, 219–24). She wrote that the largest women's group in Kenya is the Mothers' Union which, with its emphasis on the family, marginalises single mothers and even ignores domestic abuse. In discussing violence against women in Kenya, she argued that abuse is rooted in 'a tradition reinforced by Judeo-Christian religion' (Mombo 1998, 220). She also described the structural unfairness that means women, although numerically in the majority, are kept outside decision-making processes that affect them.

Sometimes, it was not neglectful church behaviour that drove women away, but the contradiction between being an active Christian and an active abuser. Samantha dutifully went to church well into her twenties, had her children christened, and took them to Sunday school, just as her parents had before her. Her husband shared her faith and was at times, she recalls, even more religious than she was. And yet, he could not control his temper and frequently punched and slapped her. One day, she asked herself why, if he believed in what he described as the one true religion, he could behave like that. 'That was out of my realm of understanding,' she said.

It was the sense that people worshipped in a religion that somehow incorporated pain and punishment that, Paul said, 'completely unglued' him. 'It's a medieval con,' he said, 'that there's something like an afterlife punishment'. It was that, he explained, that led him to reject religion entirely: 'no god, no easter bunny'.

In this chapter, I have argued that some Boomers experienced shocks by suddenly seeing that religious ideas and practices seemed contrary to their set of morals, particularly concerning what they saw as a lack of consistency, with regular churchgoers only paying lip service to ideals of love, compassion and generosity. In the next chapter, Boomers reflect further on the social milieu in which they were raised, and which seemed to have made a generational impact across borders: the often turbulent, sometimes peaceful, always fascinating 1960s.

Notes

1. The theological debates about the extent to which St. Paul's companions also heard or understood the voice, and the implications for Christianity, are discussed at more detail by Richard N. Longenecker (1997).
2. See also his earlier discussion (Robbins 2004) about how salvation was centred on the idea of the individual being saved by his or her personal saviour, and Robbins 2015 for related discussions stemming from the work of Louis Dumont 1980.
3. See, for example, research on contemporary 'modesty' fashion (Lewis 2013; Cameron 2013; Tarlo 2017).
4. Although the Catholic church had forbidden contraception since 1930, with the advent of the contraceptive pill the church redoubled its opposition to any method of 'artificial' birth control with Pope Paul V1's *Humanae Vitae* issued in 1968.

7

1960s' Cultural Revolution

Sex and Sensibilities

Introduction: 'I Had Already Started Losing My Faith Pre-Beatles'

The Anglican Baby Boomers didn't lose their religion in the 1960s; most of them never had it long before that decade began. By the time the Boomers experienced the 1960s, the older members, born in 1945, were in their late teens and early twenties; those born in the mid- to late 1950s were in their early and mid-teens. Although some academics take the Baby Boomer generation to include those born into and including the early 1960s, none of that age group was in my study.

I suggest that looking for a reason for irreligiosity in the 1960s is a little like looking for the key to lock the stable door: a pointless task when the proverbial horse has long bolted. As Carl told me when I asked if he thought the 1960s had an influence on him in terms of religion, 'I had already started losing my faith pre-Beatles'.

As I have discussed in the previous chapters, the annexing practice of Sunday school cut the Boomers off from the collective worship experience. The lack of any religious reinforcement at home, combined with parental ambivalence towards religion, pushed them further away from mainstream Christianity, and confirmation training where they were expected to memorise strange and, to them, irrational belief statements, only confirmed their confusion and doubts. As I explored in more depth in Chapter 3, the parents of the Boomers enabled many of their attitudes and changes they brought into their childhood and teenage years: more latitude, more room to explore, more doubt. The parents had already prepared the ground and began many of the movements and institutions the Boomers adopted and adapted in the 1960s.

As I have argued thus far, as the teenaged Boomers matured and affirmed their moral sentiments, they rejected further what they saw as a hypocritical and unkind religion. The effect of leaving home for university or jobs

Why Baby Boomers Turned from Religion: Shaping Belief and Belonging, 1945–2021. Abby Day,
Oxford University Press. © Abby Day 2022. DOI: 10.1093/oso/9780192866684.003.0007

completed their usually gradual, but sometimes more sudden (see Chapter 6), separation from Christianity specifically and from religion more generally. As they formed new friendships and joined new groups and movements, their sense of a collective identity became strengthened. In the 1960s, they solidified those identities and beliefs and experienced moments of collective recognition and, at times, celebration and despair. The 1960s was for some a transformative decade, for others it was a time for affirming, enriching, and consolidating their values and collaborating with others in their non-religious beliefs.

If there was one phrase that described their strongest moral stance at that time it would have been the 1960s mantra: 'make love not war', and yet it would be incorrect to refer to all Boomers as peaceniks or protestors—many were some, none, and all of those things. Speaking about the shared sense of identity, Mary, a retired British doctor born in 1941, said 'you didn't have to be an out and out rebel to enjoy life'. Twenty years earlier, she said, their behaviour would have resulted in them being cast out as 'a black sheep in family'. In the 1960s, she said, their behaviours (for the most part) were more tolerated.

There was, of course, considerable internal variation within the Baby Boomer generation. Rebecca Klatch (1999) looked at the wide range of identities and experiences in the 1960s and explores in particular the accounts of young people who grew up as young conservatives in that decade alongside the hippies and radicals. While a time of noted anti-establishment, countercultural thinking, the 1960s was also, as she shows, a period of anti-communism and mobilisation of the 'new right'.

While other members of their cohort were smoking marijuana and agreeing with Dylan that the 'times they are a-changing', young conservative Boomers were sticking to soft drinks and reading conservative books and magazines (see also Riggs and Turner 2000; Cornman and Kingston 1996 for further discussion of variations).

Those Boomers I interviewed were not reflecting far-right sentiments but were also not wanting to tear down the establishment for the sake of it. They were not protesting against everything and anything, but against what they saw as specific misuses of power and illegitimate authority. Their sound-track, as many mentioned, consisted of the protest songs of Bob Dylan and Joan Baez. As I will discuss later in this chapter, 1968 was the most significant year for many Boomers.

My discussions here seek to further expand the discussion I began in Chapter 1 and to move into operationalising the concept of 'generation' as suggested by Karl Mannheim (1952). The 1960s, due to the decade's memorable events and lasting cultural resonance, will be, I suggest, a potentially fruitful case example to be analysed here. Following Mannheim, I argue that a generation is not simply a cohort of people sharing similar birth years, but a collection of people born at a time of historical note and even trauma that has shaped their identity. I will suggest that the Boomers' non-religious identities studied here were, in their eyes, powerfully shaped by that 1960s era.

Belonging to a generation, Mannheim argued, requires a self-awareness of that cohort's location in a certain time and place. Drawing on that concept, June Edmunds and Bryan S. Turner (2002, 7), stress the importance of self-identity being formed by a shared cultural conscience, not just by a series of events:

> But the social processes that shaped the generation of the trenches, the depression and the post-war boom are not simply determined factually by a specific time. In a general sense, we may define a generation as an age cohort that comes to have social significance by virtue of constructing itself as a cultural identity.

There is a widespread cultural resonance in the term '1960s', and one usually related to upheaval, anti-establishment protests, and a counterculture 'underground', as described in a *Guardian* article (https://www.theguardian.com/culture/2011/jan/30/underground-arts-60s-rebel-counterculture):

> The underground was a catch-all sobriquet for a community of like-minded anti-establishment, anti-war, pro-rock'n'roll individuals, most of whom had a common interest in recreational drugs. They saw peace, exploring a widened area of consciousness, love and sexual experimentation as more worthy of their attention than entering the rat race. The straight, consumerist lifestyle was not to their liking, but they did not object to others living it.

To explore the degree to which they felt as if they shared a common 'Boomer' and a 1960s identity, I did not ask interviewees if they had belonged to an underground, or similar anti-establishment, countercultural movement. I asked them instead if the term 'Baby Boomer' resonated with them, and if they felt they belonged to that generation. I also asked them if they felt the 1960s played an important part in their identity formation. In answer to both questions, most said, emphatically, 'yes'.

'Absolutely,' said Michele, 'We are the pig in the python.' Michele was using a phrase commonly adopted in demography and marketing circles to describe the large bulge in the population caused by the high post-war birth rate and subsequent influence on society. The size of the bulge was not the only defining feature, however. Referring to the 1960s, Michele continued: 'It was a golden era, it defined who we are.'

Martin said that the 1960s was the best decade, having a 'free, easy, heady mix'. Although studying and working part-time, he had a full social life: 'I had a wonderful misspent youth in the 1960s and feel very privileged to have lived through what I consider the best of times,' he said. It was a 'premium time for music' when he and his friends would go to pubs, not for the drink but for the music.

Young people also went to record shops and clubs to be with their friends, recalled Victoria, a retired British Human Resources manager born in 1952:

Teenagers would meet in record shops and talk about music and about life. The shops used to have listening booths where an individual could step inside, close the door, and listen to music on their own, but soon the booths changed so that the walls came down and people could stand, under a helmet-like object and listen to music and talk at the same time.

Other Boomers also spoke about the importance of music, ranging from the advent of Motown to the Beatles. Peter said 'one of my biggest drivers was the Beatles. Sergeant Pepper! We sat around wondering what it meant.' Trevor, a retired British town planner born in 1944, recalled that his parents had mixed feelings about the music: 'The Rolling Stones! Parents did not like them, yet they liked or at least tolerated the Beatles. Probably because they wore suits!'

In discussing the impact of the 1960s on their generation, most of my interviewees agreed that it had a significant impact in terms both of their good fortune in being able to reap economic, cultural, and political benefits, but also through being affected by specific events and influences. Affluence was a word mentioned in several interviews. Terry told me that his son is now a doctor, but the cost of university and related living costs means 'he is hundreds of thousands dollars in debt. I could go virtually for free' and have money left over for travel and other pursuits.

The importance of affluence applies not only to consumerism, or the ability to pay for goods and thus influence markets, but also the ability to take actions that have a longer and deeper impact. This impact means that a particular generation may have strategic importance for future generations, both through providing and consuming resources, as Edmunds and Turner noted (2005, 562): 'They can act strategically within a field to influence significantly the opportunities for collective action of future cohorts.'

The affluence afforded to the Baby Boomers allowed them to participate sometimes globally in ways unavailable to previous generations, thereby shaping, in this case, their non-religious identities. Edmunds and Turner (2005, 562) argued that Baby Boomers could afford to create the activism of the 1960s because they already had both social and economic capital:

> . . . and solidarity formed as a result of having something to protest against, that is, the Vietnam War with its prolonged threat of nuclear escalation, and the 'warfare state' diverting resources from the 'welfare state'. These, together with full employment and well-defined career structures, gave this generation the security to drop out or speak out without risking their long-term economic future and enabled links to develop across national borders.

The formation of this, first, 'global generation' occurred both because the media allowed the simultaneous transmission of global news events, and more. Pam said she thought the 1960s was a major influence on her and the wider culture, with much of that occurring through television, including advertising. Children and teenagers were recognised by the early 1960s as a major target market for advertisers, who quickly capitalised on the audience through after-school and weekend programmes (O'Barr 2008; Alexander et al. 1998).

Media do not only communicate with their target audience, but they also shape how people interpret events (see, for example, Lövheim 2013; Lynch et al. 2012; Hjarvard 2008). The Baby Boomers were forming a 'global conscience' (Edmunds and Turner 2002, 565). Indeed, as the Boomers I interviewed expressed, the events inspiring their protests and solidarities in the 1960s often had little to do with their immediate surroundings, as I discuss below.

In his study of the 1960s, and its impact on religion, Hugh McLeod (2007, 15) notes that while there was a number of factors influencing this 'explosive' period, the most important was 'the impact of affluence because the changing economic climate affected so many other aspects of people's lives and opened up new possibilities'. Those new possibilities included travel and the ability to see other places and other people. A consequence, as I've discussed thus far, was a more diverse outlook and appreciation of others' viewpoints.

Peter, for example, said he thought the movements of the 1960s resulted from a trend to wider education and a different educational style. Students were encouraged at school and at university 'to question things... there was an openness'. It was the 'first time young voices were being heard,' he said. As he 'grew up very much in the swinging sixties' and was involved in student politics, it felt like there was an 'immense change in society'. He added that he thinks there is a 'current conservative, right-wing press' that criticises the 1960s, but he thought 'it was fantastic, a golden era'. Yvonne voiced similar thoughts: 'In the 1960s the door opened to new ideas, everyone I knew had something different up their sleeve.'

Carl also drew attention to a period of questioning and doubt, epitomised by books and 'philosophical movements' ranging from the popularisation of the existential writings of Jean Paul Sartre to the publication in 1963 of *Honest to God*, a book by Anglican bishop John Robinson (1963). Robinson argued that a conception of God as an authoritarian, external, distant entity was outdated and should be replaced by the idea of a god 'within' and a more flexible moral code. Response was immediate and, for the most part, outraged.[1] As Carl noted, 'people one admired at the time were questioning'. He paused for a moment in our interview to recall the words of a poem: Philip Larkin's *Aubade*, in which religion was referred to as a 'vast moth-eaten musical brocade' designed to stave off fears of death. Carl said he could not 'see how people envisage an after-life. Maybe I did,' he said, adding, 'I can't remember'. Nicola, a British retired teacher born in 1947, also referred to changes in church and clergy during that period where 'the early beginnings of clerical mischief were beginning to seep through'.

Although most Boomers I interviewed were no longer attending church and would therefore not have experienced such 'mischief' first-hand, the theological controversies caused such divisions that they were widely reported in mainstream media.

Viv agreed that the 1960s resonated with her Baby Boomer identity. Their generation was lucky, she said, with accessible education, good lives as teenagers, and eventually the ability to buy houses. There were vibrant cities, festivals, and 'the pill', she said, describing that period as having a 'shared zeitgeist'. It was, as Naomi Woodspring (2018) suggested in her study of Baby Boomers ageing, a 'state of mind'.

One part of that state of mind was their consolidation of non-religious beliefs. Sally said the tempo of the time was immediate, a here and now rather than an ever-after: 'Never mind the pie in the sky, you don't have to wait to be dead to have fun.' Ben also suggested religion was fading from society in the 1960s. He drew connections between religion and the growing anti-establishment, counterculture movement of the 1960s. Religion, he said, was 'a social power phenomenon. It was one of the ways the establishment keeps the plebs in control.'

Sophie, a Canadian restaurant owner born in 1950, recalled the 1960s as 'a powerful cultural time' in Canada with waves of socialism, feminism, the anti-Vietnam movement, and the foundation of environmental campaigners, Greenpeace.

A significant aspect arising in my interviews was the similarity amongst the interviews despite their relative ages or even locations in the UK and Canada. Due to television and travel, the 1960s produced, for the first time, a sense of a transnational generation. Many of the events they describe were the first examples of how television broadcast to and influenced audiences with the media shaping what people see and to some extent how they feel about it. I will now address some of those key events: the first moon landing; waves of student street protests and a brutal police response; an existential threat prompted by the Kennedy assassinations and the Cold War; and campaigns for sexual and gender equality. Tying the themes together was the influence of an international media further shaping and communicating a strong sense of a global identity.

Moon Landing and Earth Rising: 'Like We Can Accomplish Anything We Want'

It seemed that the American approaches to and eventual landing on the moon in the 1960s affected the Boomers in several significant ways. There was, as Virginia put it, a sudden sense of confidence that occurred with NASA's moon landing on 20 July 1969: 'The man on the moon was pretty spectacular, it was like we can accomplish anything we want.' Simon expressed similar thoughts: 'The first men on the moon, those were massive breakthroughs and gave a big sense of optimism that everything was possible.' Terry expressed a similar sentiment of excitement and achievement and added another thought: 'Man landed on the moon in 1969—my 16th birthday! The world had changed so quickly, and religion moves too slowly. Religion depends on keeping things the same.'

The moon landing was presented as wholly secular by NASA and most accompanying media. Anyone watching it live on television would have seen the image of the module landing, and later of Neil Armstrong stepping down the ladder placing his foot on the lunar surface and speaking the words (written for him by the NASA public relations department): 'That's one small step for a man, one giant leap for mankind'. There were no prayers, no mention of God. The other astronaut who walked on the moon that day, Buzz Aldrin, admitted later that he had engaged alone in an act of communion on board the module, but no one watching the event would have been aware of that. Communion is a regular rite practised at Christian churches where people participate together, and are given a sip of wine and a wafer, by the presiding priest, to commemorate what is described in the Christian Bible as the Last Supper amongst Jesus Christ and his disciples. The liturgy is formed around the idea of the community of followers, coming together as 'one body', not as an individual partaking alone. Aldrin was an elder at Webster Presbyterian Church, and received their, and NASA's, permission to take some bread and wine with him into space in order to have his private communion. Later, he reflected that this may not have been a wise choice as it was too Christian-specific:

> Perhaps, if I had it to do over again, I would not choose to celebrate communion. Although it was a deeply meaningful experience for me, it was a Christian sacrament, and we had come to the moon in the name of all mankind—be they Christians, Jews, Muslims, animists, agnostics, or atheists. (https://www.theguardian.com/commentisfree/belief/2012/sep/13/buzz-aldrin-communion-moon)

Due to a religion-focused controversy on the previous space mission, NASA did not want to publicise Aldrin's private ritual. One year earlier, on the Apollo 8 mission, astronauts Frank Borman, Jim Lovell, and Bill Anders were the first humans to orbit the moon and to see the dark side. On Christmas Eve, they read from the King James version of the Bible the first chapters of Genesis describing how God created the earth ('In the Beginning, God created the heavens and the Earth...'). NASA explained how that occurred:

> 'We were told that on Christmas Eve we would have the largest audience that had ever listened to a human voice,' recalled Borman during 40th anniversary celebrations in 2008. 'And the only instructions that we got from NASA was to do something appropriate. The first ten verses of Genesis are the foundation of many of the world's religions, not just the Christian religion,' added Lovell. 'There are more people in other religions

than the Christian religion around the world, and so this would be appropriate to that and so that's how it came to pass.' (https://www.nasa.gov/topics/history/features/apollo_8.html)

NASA also reports (https://www.nasa.gov/topics/history/features/apollo_8.html) that on Christmas morning, scientists at the mission control 'waited anxiously for word that Apollo 8's engine burn to leave lunar orbit had worked. They soon got confirmation when Lovell radioed, "Roger, please be informed there is a Santa Claus".'

Although the President of the American Atheists Association, Madalyn Murray O'Hair sued NASA (following her successful lawsuit in 1964 to ban prayers and Bible reading in schools) and lost, on various technicalities, the Bible reading did not seem to have caused widespread controversy. Nor, apparently, did the quip about Santa Claus.

One of the more lasting impressions from Apollo 8 was their photo of the earth rising, becoming one of the most iconic photos of the decade, as NASA explained: 'The mission was also famous for the iconic "Earthrise" image, snapped by Anders, which would give humankind a new perspective on their home planet. Anders has said that despite all the training and preparation for an exploration of the moon, the astronauts ended up discovering Earth' (https://www.nasa.gov/topics/history/features/apollo_8.html).

That picture was what gave Vikki her idea that the Christian God was a false god. As mentioned in the previous chapter, she was moved by the idea that people all inhabit the same world, and should take care of it.

1968: Murders and Protests: 'Everyone Mourning at the Same Time'

Boomers I interviewed sometimes referred to the Kennedys' and Martin Luther King's assassination in the USA as critical events defining, for them, the 1960s. President John F. Kennedy was assassinated in November 1963 and his brother, then presidential candidate Robert F. Kennedy was murdered in June 1968. In April 1968 civil rights activist Martin Luther King was assassinated.

Both Kennedys and Luther King had captured the mood of the 1960s towards a more centrist/leftist politics and ongoing demands for human and civil rights. As Virginia described it: 'The death of the Kennedys, so stark in your face, one of the first times something like it was practically live on tv, everyone mourning at the same time.' There had briefly been, she said 'a world of possibilities' and connection that seemed to shatter with the deaths. Sally recalled the moment she heard about John F. Kennedy's assassination, saying 'JFK was a ray of light, and we were watching "Take Your Pick" on the telly and the screen went black and then there were the announcements'. She also recalled the civil rights movement where 'they were trying to get things changed and all the churches were divisive'. Sally was referencing the differing ways churches, particularly in the southern states of the USA, reacted to demands for more racial equality. Julia Blackwelder (1979) shows, for example, how Southern Presbyterians lobbied extensively against desegregating congregations and demanded that churches withdraw from organisations such as the National Council of Churches who were campaigning for racial equality. Blackwelder (1979, 335) quotes the founder of the *Southern Presbyterian Journal* L. Nelson Bell who argued that not all Christians agreed with desegregation:

> There are others—and they are as Christian in their thinking and practice as any in this world—who believe that it is un-Christian, unrealistic and utterly foolish to force those barriers of race which have been established by God and which when destroyed by man are destroyed to his own loss.

Blackwelder (1979, 338) describes how the Southern Presbyterians claimed that 'voluntary' rather than enforced desegregation was their preference, and during the foment of the 1960s they criticised civil rights movements. She writes: 'White Southern fundamentalists had shown little concern over the violence of whites against civil rights demonstrators in the early sixties, but they expressed fear and outrage over the seizure and destruction of property during the ghetto riots of 1967 and 1968.'

Other church movements, however, were actively campaigning for increased civil rights, writes James Findlay (1990), with the National Council of Churches formed in 1950 to act as a unified voice for more liberal and politically engaged forms of social activism. Findlay points out the divisiveness amongst churches that may have captured Sally's attention: in particular, the pro-civil rights activities of Presbyterians in the northern states of the USA which were at odds with the views expressed by Presbyterians in the south.

When the Boomers mentioned 'Vietnam War' and 'Paris Riots' they were mainly discussing, for them, the events they felt both marked the 1960s and influenced them. Nobody I interviewed physically participated in either the war or the riots but were citing the protests and anger they felt they shared as a generation. The Boomers were the first generation of non-combatant youth to be able to see, via televised accounts and images, the horror of war nearly in real time. It has been argued that the media coverage of the Vietnam War affected public opinion for two main reasons: for the first time, *in situ* war correspondents often contradicted the government's official statements and, also for the first time, the sight and sounds of war, unfiltered by government agencies, were brought into people's homes on a daily basis. The public's realisation of the realities of war, and the increasingly contested, often by media commentators, justification of American involvement turned public opinion against it. Daniel Hallin (1986, 3), wrote:

> [I]t has come to be widely accepted across the political spectrum that the relation between the media and the government during Vietnam was in fact one of conflict: the media contradicted the more positive view of the war officials sought to project, and for better or for worse it was the journalists' view that prevailed with the public, whose disenchantment forced an end to American involvement.

Further, the American practice of forcing young male Baby Boomers to fight in Vietnam caused a backlash in the USA and elsewhere. The riots and disruptions for seven weeks in 1968 throughout France brought the country to an effective halt through general strikes and occupations of universities and factories. They were precipitated by Baby Boomer student street protests, occupations, and street battles with the police. The police response was one some Boomers remembered in anger, as Sally said when discussing those events: 'In France 1968, the student protests—you see how the police reacted so brutally.' The effects were profound, not only on French civil life, but also on academe. The influential philosopher and member of Generation A, Michel Foucault, born in 1926, was angered by the police response to the riots and wrote his classic book, *Discipline and Punish* (1977) in response. The riots were, he argued, an example of a protest against what he saw as an illegitimate authority of the state and an unquestioning acceptance of the primacy of Enlightenment era adherence to principles of reason.

A *New York Times* article reflecting on the riots drew attention to the wider effect beyond education and worker rights (https://www.nytimes.com/2018/05/05/world/europe/france-may-1968-revolution.html). The mass strikes and protests 'upended social norms—the authority of the father of the family and of the leader of the country', and forced France to confront its identity in the modern world.

In another retrospective article, Kate Keller (2018), writing in the magazine of the American Smithsonian Museum, asked 'What were the protests about?' (https://www.smithsonianmag.com/history/fifty-years-later-france-still-debating-legacy-its-1968-protests-180968963/). While many Americans remember the summer of 1968 as one 'of nationwide turmoil, with political assassinations, anti-war protests, racial unrest and highly publicized clashes with police', it was not, she wrote, a season of protests only felt in the USA, but a reaction more widely against war and 'a tightening of law-and-order efforts'.

Students in Paris were partly demanding more participation and representation in how their universities were being governed but also, she wrote, more broadly: 'they were protesting capitalism, American imperialism, and Gaullism', and, due to 'daily horrific images of the Vietnam War' the students and others created or joined anti-war movements, leading to violent clashes between students and police in May 1968, followed by a nationwide general strike.

Keller (2018) quoted Chris Reynolds, 'a British scholar of modern French history', saying that for activists, the Vietnam War 'represented everything they believed needed to change' such as a younger generation's embrace of modernity, anti-Catholicism, and opposition to capitalism.

Indeed, several Boomers mentioned specifically positive effects of the riots. Charles said he had travelled around France 'not long after 1968 student uprisings' and was struck by people's messages of determination and commitment to change. Bruce spoke about the 1960s and the 1968 student riots in particular as 'being a time of change and hope'. Roger said the riots and the 1960s in general showed that:

[W]e had been expected to respect people regardless of whether they had earned it, or not, or because they were older or in a position of trust, and that changed. People lost respect for authority—especially if they weren't nice people.

Roger said that he thought much of what happened in the 1960s, even the changing musical styles, were because attitudes changed. There was unrest, he said, because people were 'having to do things that they weren't happy to do'.

Although for the purpose of this book I am exploring the beliefs and behaviours of non-religious Boomers, there was also, in the late 1960s, a surge towards liberation theology in the Global South and Christian evangelicalism in the Global North that partly represented a protest against illegitimate authority. Historian Philip Jenkins (https://www.abc.net.au/religion/the-religious-world-changed-in-1968-but-not-in-the-ways-we-think/10214328) noted that:

> The secular developments of 1968 have received plenty of attention in recent months: the assassinations and racial unrest in the United States; the popular youth movements around the world; violence in Paris and Mexico City; the continuing war in Vietnam; the Chinese Cultural Revolution; the first stirrings of global terrorism; and so on. The world seemed to be in a period of grave crisis, even on an apocalyptic scale. Each of these events, in different ways, discredited some long-accepted source of authority.

As Jenkins pointed out, the much-discussed turn from Christianity to more varied, often Easternised, religions was not sustained: 'Particularly off-base were any claims about esoteric and occult sects and cult movements. They created a media sensation throughout the 1970s, but were wildly over-estimated and largely vanished by the early 1980s.'

The student protests also strengthened global alliances, as Edmunds and Turner discuss (2002, 565). The student protests first felt on the streets of Paris spread to Soviet bloc countries and sparked, they argue, 'the 1968 Czechoslovakian "Prague Spring" and the government change in Poland in the early 1970s'. They also stress the point that the links between European and North American intellectuals and those in Eastern Europe were made amongst universities (implicitly, I suggest, the Baby Boomers) 'rather than workplace-based dissidents in East Europe who led uprisings in East Germany and Poland in the 1960s and 1970s'. Further, the leaders of the student movements left Paris and travelled the world, as did feminists and socialists in the west who travelled to and created alliances with African liberation movements.

Just as one of my Baby Boomer interviewees said that the poster of Che Guevara was standard on many Baby Boomer university or bedroom walls, Edmunds and Turner discuss how he inspired activists throughout the Americas and Europe (2002, 565). Their observations are important to highlight the key role of individuals who became iconic figures and leaders who helped give personality and pressure during periods of generational change (see also Alexander 2004).

Cold War and Bomb Threats: 'I Was Scared, My Mum Was Scared'

Several of my Baby Boomer interviewees mentioned the overwhelming nature of certain events in the 1960s that represented not just a problem or protest, but the real possibility of global annihilation. For some, this was first personally realised by the widespread civil defence air raid drills in the 1950s sparked by the Soviet Union testing its atomic bomb in 1949 and the USA realising it was not alone in having such a devastating weapon. School children were shown how to hide under desks to evade the effects of a bomb, causing widespread anxiety and often panic: 'The now-infamous duck-and-cover drills simulated what should be done in case of an atomic attack—and channeled a growing panic over an escalating arms race' (https://www. history.com/news/duck-cover-drills-cold-war-arms-race).

The fear of mass nuclear war was perhaps most acutely felt during the Cuban missile crisis of October 1962. The stand-off between the USA and the Soviet Union was played out in detail over radio, television, and through newspapers. It is probably not an exaggeration to say that many young Boomers were traumatised by the possibility that the two superpowers could exchange nuclear bombs and trigger widespread, if not global, civilian deaths in both Europe and North America.

A BBC archive (http://news.bbc.co.uk/1/hi/world/europe/6906777.stm) containing statements from people who were children at the time of the Cold War shows a global spread of contributions, with most speaking to the fear and confusion of the time. One woman, for example, recalled how she used her bed sheets to practise protection in case of a bomb during the Cuban missile crisis. A man described being 'born in the last week of official "war" in 1945. I remember the entire Cold War very well. The Cuban Missile Crisis forced us all to "grow up" in ways not intended by either our parents or our teachers.'

A personal recollection for me comes from being a child in the Canadian capital city of Ottawa in the early 1960s. We were alerted to potential danger by an air raid siren whose wail was our signal, in drills, to file quickly to the cloakroom to fetch our coats and then to run home as quickly as possible. It was terrifying. We were also aware of what was known as the 'six-minute warning' (four in the UK), which was the siren warning us that a missile had been tracked heading towards us from the Soviet Union and would impact in those few minutes.

Wendy's memory of the 1960s, for example, included what she describes as a 'life-changing' moment in an otherwise 'sheltered life'. At age 15, she said, she read *On the Beach* by Nevil Shute (1957). The post-apocalyptic story concerns a group of Australians who are awaiting their inevitable death following nuclear war in the northern hemisphere and the radiation's spread southwards. It affected her deeply, she said, and prompted her in 1963 to join the annual Aldermaston anti-nuclear march organised by the Campaign for Nuclear Disarmament (CND). This was a pivotal organisation for her and, I found, several other Boomers I interviewed who, like Wendy, told me about not only supporting the campaign through membership but also meeting other like-mind people.

While Boomers could experience those threats as a global as well as local problem, their sense of imminent annihilation was visceral. They did not, however, turn back towards the church for comfort. In one case, it was precisely a connection between religion and war that was, in Joan's opinion, responsible for Christianity's decline from the 1960s. A British potter born in 1947, she said that when she was a teenager the Irish Republican Army (IRA) was becoming active in the UK. 'That set me against religion and what it could do. I was scared, my mum was scared every time I went outdoors.' I will return to this topic in Chapter 10 as there is more to be examined in the context of the Boomers' later lives, beliefs, and sites of belonging.

Gender Equality and Sexual Freedom: 'Let's Enjoy Ourselves'

When the Boomers in my study spoke about sexuality, they were not focusing simply on the possibility of sex without pregnancy. Their stories usually stressed that this represented a new, and better, period in history. Sally described wartime as a phase when people were repressed, illustrated for her by the example of an unmarried aunt who had a child. The matter was deeply shameful for the religious parents, she said, who 'hushed it up': 'Then things got so much freer with swinging 60s, people were back from the war and there was a sudden burst of "let's enjoy yourselves",' she said.

Roger makes a similar point about post-war conditions, saying more women went to work in wartime and, when war ended, they didn't want to stop going to work (and see Chapter 6 for more on women's post-war identities in relation to work and divorce).

Fiona said that the 1960s influenced her to reject stereotypical norms, and particularly those imposed by religion: 'As a kid I liked Barbie dolls but not white weddings. They just repulsed me. I was with a man for ten years but didn't want to get married and take his name. I admired Gloria Steinem and the whole anti-patriarchy movement, anti- church.' Lesley's views were similar. She said the 1960s decade was 'a period of increasing cultural change' with more people rejecting the framework of patriarchy.

Sally made a direct link between the church and sexual guilt. Because of 'the Pill, we don't have to be guilty about sex. The Church isn't going to find out because they won't see us pregnant,' she said. It was the church's judgement, therefore, not the sex that caused guilt. Allison recalled the 1960s as a time of 'peace, love, the pill and all the rest of it' and an opportunity to question conventional ideas and practices.

Jennifer felt that the 1960s was transformative for women. 'Historically,' she said, 'all religions suppress women, so they finally got their voice and started hitting back. Maybe the 60s was the beginning of the end for western Christianity—they clearly were unhealthy for religion.' The 1960s were important for people, she said, because 'they gave people choice'. Allison provided other examples, saying 'It wasn't just music, but fashion as well was liberalised and a means to show preferences, autonomy. Twiggy, Dior, there was a choice over length, from mini to midi to long. And cosmetics, Mary Quant!'

Nicola spoke about religion's negative impact on sex and women in the 1960s when the horrific practices of Irish nuns running slave-labour laundries became more widely known, although not publicly discussed until mass graves of babies and women were uncovered in the 1990s. This two-century old practice enabled the incarceration and abuse of thousands of women deemed to be 'fallen' through sex work, unmarried pregnancy, or other apparent moral transgressions (see, for example, Rebecca McCarthy 2010). Although the growing record of these institutions focuses mainly on Ireland, similar institutions ran elsewhere in Australia, Canada, the UK, and the USA (Jones and Record 2014).

When she visited Dublin during the 1960s, Nicola saw what she described as 'gangs of children completely out of control, their mothers clearly couldn't control them. This opened my eyes to one of the great harms of the Catholic church—you'll have 13 children whether your body can cope or not.' She was angered by the church's statement against methods of artificial birth control which she said, rightly, was a response to the more liberal moves of the 1960s. She had read the declaration, known as *Humane Vitae*

(https://www.vatican.va/content/paul-vi/en/encyclicals/documents/hf_p-vi_
enc_25071968_humanae-vitae.html) which outlined the reasons for the
statement as a response to changes in population and 'a new understanding
of the dignity of woman and her place in society, of the value of conjugal
love in marriage and the relationship of conjugal acts to this love'. The
statement also re-established the doctrine that procreation is 'inherent to the
marriage act', and 'man' could not alter this connection, established by God.
The statement also included an 'appeal' to public authorities not to allow
morals to be undermined, particularly if they affected the family:

> The family is the primary unit in the state; do not tolerate any legislation
> which would introduce into the family those practices which are opposed
> to the natural law of God. For there are other ways by which a government
> can and should solve the population problem—that is to say by enacting
> laws which will assist families and by educating the people wisely so that
> the moral law and the freedom of the citizens are both safeguarded.

Nicola described her response in more detail:

> I read Humane Vitae. Before the 60s the church didn't say anything about
> contraception, But then these Encyclicals came around—so no more
> contraception! We need more souls for Jesus! Women must have thought,
> who does this ancient bachelor think he is? With greater freedom of
> women, it made them question what business is it of his? He's an old
> bachelor.

Nicola said she thought that people began to turn from the church as they
became better educated and 'things dawned slowly and then it was—what??'
Global communication and travel also played a part, she said, because 'it
helps, if you don't know what's going on in the next city or country but then,
with communication, you can say, . . . oh, it's different in that country!'

The differences in countries outside Ireland increased significantly during
the 1960s when many countries, including Canada, the USA, and the UK,
decriminalised abortion and homosexuality. Although the government in
Westminster ordered Northern Ireland to allow abortions by March 2022, at
the time of writing a legal challenge has not been resolved.

Samantha also felt the 1960s affected countries differently, with Ireland
retaining its hard line against abortion and same-sex relationships until
recently. She had been to the Republic of Ireland shortly before our

interview in 2020, two years after abortion had been legalised. People talked to her, she said, about 'religion downgrading because they want to think for themselves'.

Victoria pinpointed reproductive control as pivotal for women: 'It all changed with the Abortion Act and availability of the contraceptive pill in 62 or 63. That was massive for women,' she said.

The contraceptive pill was made available and legal, at first for 'therapeutic' rather than birth control purposes, in the 1960s in the countries being studied here: mainly the UK, Canada, and to a lesser extent, the USA. The contraceptive pill was important for the Baby Boomer generation, not just for the effect of the pill on reproduction, but its symbolic, empowering value.

In the *New York Times*' 50-year retrospective special section, they quoted a Baby Boomer saying that everything was 'enlarged' in the 1960s: 'In religion, in sexual things, what it meant to be a woman—that it did not mean only to serve a man or to submit to men. These are questions you think about your whole life,' she said. The article further stated that the 1968 'upheaval' and the intellectual 'ferment' caused both the women's liberation and gay rights movements (https://www.nytimes.com/2018/05/05/world/europe/france-may-1968-revolution.html).

All of these movements tend, I suggest, to cluster around ideas of legitimacy. The idea that young people did not want to abide by authority because it was not, in their eyes, legitimate tends to be overlooked. Callum Brown (2001) focused on a deeply held value, women's equality, to explain why so many women (and, hence, their children) turned from the patriarchy of Christianity. In general, as summarised in Chapter 1, the root causes of the Baby Boomers' turn from existing authoritative structures, particularly religion, tends to be attributed by scholars to rebelliousness, consumerism, selfish individualism, or hedonism. For an excellent summary and critique, particularly of the misguided quest amongst scholars for a single causal variable or master narrative, see Hugh McLleod (2007). McLeod (2000) also provides an important historical perspective on the issue by pointing out that the early stages of more liberal, egalitarian movements began in the late nineteenth century, not the mid-twentieth century (and see, in this book, Chapters 3–5).

In summary, I have explored in this chapter reasons why Boomers were rejecting traditional hierarchies and authorities. Their turn to more authentic, equal, and respectful relationships and structures helped to solidify the moves they had already made from a religion they found to be at best inauthentic and, at worst, offensive and unethical. As a further contribution to the work of Mannheim on generation, I conclude that the 1960s provides a good case example of how particular events and their interpretations shaped a shared non-religious identity.

Note

1. Colin Slee's (2004) edited collection of a symposium reflecting on the book 50 years on provides a good overview of the reaction and its legacy.

8

Adulthood and Acceptance, with Lingering Trails

Introduction: 'For a Humanist Household We Have a Surprising Number of Bibles'

As the Boomers created their adult lives, often with partners, they carried through their non-religious identities, occasionally interwoven with lingering trails of church-based experiences. As explored in previous chapters, as the Boomers were largely non-religious throughout their childhood and teens, there was nothing specifically 'religious' to miss as they matured into adulthood. And yet, I will explore here, some of them expressed nostalgia for church-related experiences which were, I suggest, more related to fond memories of family and friends than God.

Although a few briefly explored different religions and spiritual movements, there does not appear to have been any lasting, significant generational move towards those options: as discussed in more detail in Chapter 10, secular forms of belonging and behaving favoured by Boomers are morally and socially significant to them, while markedly non-religious.

They were careful, in our conversations, to mark differences between churches as buildings and 'the church' as an institution. These were spatial, material, and ontological distinctions delineating differences between enjoying the physical building of a church or, more commonly, a cathedral, and some of their events, such as Christmas midnight mass, but not the institution for which those buildings stood. Even the most non-religious of the Boomers I interviewed expressed a fondness for certain types of church-based experiences. Attending Christmas carol services, for example, was a significant annual ritual for many—sacred, and secular, I will argue, having deeply relational, non-religious, nostalgic trails for many, linked to familial, rather than religious, memories. Even getting married in a church, or having their own children baptised, were explained as decisions made to satisfy their parents, the more religious Generation A. They did not, as will be described in more detail in the final chapter, raise their own children to be religious.

Why Baby Boomers Turned from Religion: Shaping Belief and Belonging, 1945–2021. Abby Day, Oxford University Press. © Abby Day 2022. DOI: 10.1093/oso/9780192866684.003.0008

Several described enjoying the physical presence of a church with its architectural and historical periods and not, they stressed, as a symbol of the people who populate them nor of the religious or spiritual beliefs those people represented. While many Boomers, particularly those who had sung in choirs as children, said they missed the music of church, they were not talking about the hymns, whose lyrics made many recoil in distaste, but largely the 'early music' revival period of medieval, Renaissance, or Baroque choral music typified by Bach, Byrd, Purcell, or Tallis. Those composers' works enjoyed more mass appeal during the 'early music revival' which peaked in the 1960s and was characterised by one of the characteristics Boomers valued most: authenticity. As well as helping to instigate and sustain the early music revival, Boomers were also key to the revival of handbell playing in the 1960s, as discussed more in Chapter 10.

The attachment to early music is perhaps one reason why cathedrals, capitalising on that trend, have noted an upsurge in attendance from that generation even while there is a downward trend in the parishes. A report commissioned by the Church of England (ECOTEC 2004, 52) on the economic and social benefits of cathedrals noted that 'cathedrals have strong links to music with all reporting having at least one choir. cathedrals are noted for the quality of the music performed there and are recognised as having an important role in upholding the English choral tradition'.

Contemporary Cathedral Attendance: The Non-Religious Alternative

Annabel said she was drawn to the beauty of churches, but more specifically, to cathedrals. She liked their architecture, she said, and their music. Despite Jennifer's strongly expressed antipathy towards Christianity and the church as an institution during our interview, she added towards the end of the interview that 'I actually like churches'. Jennifer explained that she was fascinated by the 'garish gold and wealth' of St. Peter's in Rome, but added that 'I would never, ever go back to organised religion, no. But I love going to midnight mass' particularly at cathedrals.

Charlotte described wistfully her visits to cathedrals, and in particular for Evensong. 'The vicar had a beautiful voice, and said the words beautifully, modulated, and I would sit and listen and really want to believe in what the words meant, but I never did.' She was disappointed, she said, that she could not find an emotional or spiritual connection. Her last trip to a cathedral was around 1980 when she went to Evensong. 'There were only three of us,' she said. She felt, stressing the words: 'absolutely nothing'.

Charlotte's experience might have been different had she attended 'sung' Evensong, as it appears that this, more popular church service, has qualities that attract even the most non-religious. What seemed to me at first to be a contradiction in my interviews, with non-religious Baby Boomers claiming a deep affection for 'church music' may be explained by the particular form relating to an 'early music revival' corresponding to the Boomer value held in high esteem: authenticity.

In the UK, there are 42 Anglican cathedrals that differ in size and historic importance. A report commissioned by the Church of England in 2004 (ECOTEC 2004) provided a short typology of cathedrals, from the large cathedrals of international importance through to those lesser in size and historic significance to some doubling as both cathedral and parish church.

It has been well-documented by both the Church of England and academic researchers that visits to cathedrals have increased during the last decade. An increase in Anglican cathedral attendance has also been noticed in Canada, the USA, and Australia. There are many reasons given for that increase, ranging from better marketing by cathedrals, to a growing variety of non-religious activities being offered. For example, a Canadian marketing study in 2013 showed that 96 per cent of cathedral visitors come for 'culture, heritage, music and other non-religious factors' (https://www.anglicanjournal.com/more-visitors-seek-cathedrals-historic-churches/).

A 2018 article in a popular online Christian magazine mused that this non-religious style may be going too far. Cathedral tour guides receive training about, for example, how the general public should be treated but, the article laments: 'Many who volunteer to be guides have no faith, but just an interest in the history, the architecture and the art. Arguably these are important aspects but result in no appetite for God's mission to reveal himself.' The article described the experience of two guides, both Christians, who said that their training had been devoid of anything about faith: 'The guide at Norwich cathedral had been so disaffected that he was now conducting historic guided tours for the City of Norwich instead' (https://www.premierchristianity.com/home/guided-tours-of-cathedrals-are-a-huge-opportunity-for-mission-why-are-we-wasting-them/575.article).

It appears that it is mainly the cathedrals' move to more secular, less religiously demanding activities that has driven most of the attendance surge. Grace Davie (2012, 486) observing the rise in cathedral attendances, remarked that only a few decades ago they 'were frequently referred to as dinosaurs—with the strong implication that they were excessively large and increasingly useless.' And yet, they are currently growing in numbers of regular and infrequent 'worshippers'. In considering why this might be so, she suggests that a strong appeal of cathedrals is how they engage the senses, as well as the mind, paying attention as they do to the 'aesthetics of worship: to music, to art, to architecture and to liturgy'. Another reason, she continues, is that they are spaces for reflection for those 'who appreciate the relative anonymity of cathedral worship as opposed to the warm, sometimes too warm, embrace of the parish or the evangelical church'. Applying Davie's (2007) concept of 'vicarious religion' may also help us to understand the role of cathedrals. She argued that the non-religious general public may approve of the tiny group of regular worshippers who maintain a religious presence on behalf of the wider society.

Following through Davies' suggestion above that cathedrals may provide pleasure through anonymity, Leslie Francis and Susan H. Jones (2020) suggest that through interviewing participants they were able to discern their motivations, revealing a depth of bonding and bridging of social capital. They also found, through psychological tests, that such participation enhanced the psychological health and well-being of those who attended the Sunday service.

Andrew Brown and Linda Woodhead (2017) also noticed the trend towards cathedral attendance and attributed much of it to the cathedral's ability to act more or less autonomously and therefore being able to offer a wider range of activities independently of the broader Church of England. Cathedrals are, they noted, 'fiercely independent' (2017, 97). The cathedrals are 'mother churches' of a diocese, and historically did not compete with the parish churches for numbers. As Simon Coleman (2019, 20) observed, cathedrals have a 'double identity' as both places of worship and also 'locations of heritage'.

Part of that identity, as a place of worship, may becoming more important to cathedrals as competition for a dwindling regular congregation grows.

In my earlier research into the religious lives of older laywomen, the mothers of the Boomers (Day 2017, 207), I noticed a regular core of older people who travelled in from other areas just to attend a cathedral service on a Sunday. This seemed, I thought, as though the cathedral was performing more of the role of a parish church. When I raised this with a cathedral priest he agreed. Historically, the cathedrals had respected their places as sites for history and ceremony but more recently, faced with falling numbers of regular worshippers everywhere, the cathedral was moving into the parish church territory. I asked him if this meant that with a shrinking market, everyone was doing what they could to survive. He nodded. 'Gloves off?' I suggested. 'Yes,' he replied. 'Gloves off.'

It may also be possible, I suggest, that those who travel to city cathedrals for services come because their local parish church has closed. As discussed in my earlier research (Day 2017), Christians are fiercely loyal to their church where they regularly worship, and even in areas where there is more than one Anglican church, they tend to resist ideas of mergers or sharing buildings or clergy. I termed this a 'liability of loyalty' (Day 2017, 204–5) where it appeared that sometimes a congregation's loyalty to their church may work against them. It seemed logical, to an outsider, that a church under threat of closure due to falling numbers would join with other small churches nearby, but in practice I found that people were not in favour. Church attenders, I soon discovered, are so loyal to their own church that most will not even attend a coffee morning, let alone a major fundraising event at other churches: these are the competition. As the success of churches is measured by numbers, of those congregating and the income they generate, it is unsurprising that they are not willing to co-operate with others competing in what is a dwindling market.

Research conducted by Carol Roberts and Leslie Francis (2006, 54) observed that 'in rural areas the core members are reluctant to transfer their membership when their local church closes'. If they are right, the future for churches looks grim as closures are increasing. In research for the Church of England on church closures, Andrea Mulkeen (2019) noted that in the decade ending 2019, 209 churches had closed. For the most part, this is due to 'small or dwindling (often ageing) congregations struggling with caring for buildings which may be in poor condition, or need significant expenditure, or are no longer deemed fit for purpose'. Although the Church of England has not collected quantitative data to corroborate my claim that at least some members of those dwindling congregations may travel to cathedrals instead, I think it is a reasonable suggestion.

The above arguments, while convincing, notably apply to those who attend to 'worship'. They form only part, and are probably the minority, of the growing numbers who visit cathedrals. The most popular service is, as I will discuss, the weekday 'Evensong', rather than the Sunday main service or the weekday Holy Communion or Morning Prayer services. 'Evensong' occurs at a time convenient for people as they leave their workplaces, and is a shorter service than on a Sunday, typically 45 minutes. It centres on music sung by a choir rather than on lengthy prayers spoken by the priest and congregants, or on Bible readings or sermons. As an event, it is closer to a concert, with occasional audience participation, than a religious service. For those in the know, it is also the only way to enter a cathedral without paying the hefty admission fees charged by many. To preserve its 'religious' standing, and the financial benefits thus incurred from government and charities, cathedrals need to allow open, free access to its regular services.

Writing in the *Spectator* magazine (<https://www.spectator.co.uk/article/why-cathedrals-are-soaring>) Simon Jenkins (2016) showed that the number of cathedral visits has risen, even accounting separately from tourists. He suggested that the phenomenon was odd, considering that church attendance has declined by two-thirds since the 1960s, and only about 50 per cent of the UK population self-identifies as Christian and 'just 1.4 per cent regularly worship as Anglicans, and many of those do so for a privileged place in a church school'. His comment about schools refers to the condition applied by many popular Church of England schools that families are church attenders in order that their children can reserve a place. This leads to the almost comical sight of young parents presenting their cards for stamping attendance to the church official at the church door, just as they might at Starbucks to qualify, in time, for a free treat.

Jenkins wrote that during his two-year research project on cathedrals, he concluded that a cathedral is both a museum and a place for music. That may be, if the Boomers I interviewed are indicative of that trend, a significant factor because, as he noted, it is the 'sung Evensong that they attend, not the Sunday or midweek service'.

In another research project, Simon Coleman and Marion Bowman (2018, 3) also noted the 'supposedly "traditional" religious space that seems, counter-intuitively, to have undergone a revival in recent years' despite trends of pluralism and urbanisation, the usual mainstays of secularisation theory. They draw on the work of Martyn Percy (2013, 125) who described the current increase as an example of what he termed 'episodic belief'. By this he meant the phenomenon of people increasingly attending specific religious services, while overall church membership does not increase: 'Indeed, what seems to flourish in modern European mainline denominational Christianity is pilgrimage, memorialisation and celebration, all of which are episodic in character, rather than intrinsically dispositional.' Coleman and Bowman (2019, 3) suggest that it may be important to ground the idea of 'episodic belief' in a wider understanding of what may be habitual:

For instance, the crowds who come to cathedrals at Christmas may only come once a year, and many do not see themselves as Christian, but their visits still draw on an annually kindled habitus of participation tied to the season, and indeed to familial, regional or work-related obligations.

Their thoughts resonate with what Boomers told me about visiting cathedrals.

Boomers often referred to 'church music' as something they loved and may still listen to or even sing in cathedrals or churches. The experience, however, was not for them 'liturgical', meaning it was not a religious experience, tied to acts of church-based worship. Below, I will discuss what their experience may signify, and why it so resonates with that generation.

Church Music: 'Not to the Glory of God; It's to the Glory of Brahms'

Baby Boomers retained a love for what they called 'church music', by which they meant the pre-classical music created before 1750 primarily of the medieval, Renaissance, and early Baroque eras. What they were describing coincides with what musicologists call 'early music revival', referring to the nineteenth- and twentieth-century activities to rediscover principally choral music from earlier centuries. This process gathered pace in the early twentieth century and became more widespread in the 1960s with several independent, specialist orchestras performing and recording works that became popular.

When she was studying in Cambridge, for example, anti-religious Jennifer 'went all the time' to sung Evensong. She was a member of school, university, and community choirs and described as one of her high points singing with her choir in the Sistine Chapel. Annabel was one of the only Baby Boomers I interviewed who fondly remembered hymns, particularly those 'rousing, evangelical hymns' she recalled from her childhood. I note that these were precisely the sort that put Sally off when she listened to what she described as the 'manipulative' hymns of the Pentecostal choir she encountered in her teens, as I described in Chapter 6. Annabel said she later became familiar with other forms of music often sung in cathedrals and is now a member of a (non-religious) Baroque choir.

Carol Lieberman (1997, 92) argues that this musical turn may be at least partly explained by the growing desire in the mid-twentieth century for 'authenticity':

> Through the use of 'authentic' or 'period' instruments, performers strive to recreate music of the past as it was originally performed, collaborating with musicologists to reinterpret seventeenth- and eighteenth-century aesthetic and stylistic treatises.

This 'authenticity' extended beyond the voice, to the 'authenticity' of the instruments, such as the lute and harpsichord: 'In addition to the coherence and "objectivity" of Baroque and Classical forms, the instruments themselves, especially the harpsichord, were appealing. The purity and clarity of their sound provided a welcome antidote to the lush, overblown scoring of the German Romantics' (Lieberman 1997, 92).

As Carine Hartman (2019, 3) wrote, this revival showed how 'performers searched for an "authentic" way of performing early music' with orchestras and ensembles adopting a concept termed by musicologists as 'Historically Informed Performance'. Quoting musicologist John Butt, Hartman (2019, 4) explains that 'the aim of HIP was to perform early music works in a reconstructed way, that is to associate early music with its original performance practice, as John Butt puts it'.

Part of the commitment to authenticity further extended beyond the voice and instruments to the place for the music to be performed. As early music was composed principally for churches, it would be inauthentic, argued Peter Kivy (1995, 244), to perform it elsewhere, such as a concert hall. That was not just a question of acoustics or history, but of intent. It would not be problematic to have, he suggests, a composition originally composed for a garden performed in a concert hall because the purpose of the composition was musical enjoyment. It would be significantly different, however, 'to remove a Bach cantata from a church setting for which it was designed as a part of liturgical worship'.

It was, for Boomers, a secular experience even if generated originally from music performed for religious liturgies. Carl, for example, drew out that point strongly in describing how he feels when singing church music in the secular choir to which he belongs: 'not to the glory of god; it's to the glory of Brahms'.

This rupture, of secular and sacred music, reflects a distinction Rowan Clare Williams (2019, 11) described as follows:

The enduring popularity of sacred music performed out of its liturgical context, for example by groups such as The Sixteen or the Tallis Scholars (or indeed by King's choir itself), suggests that even if a piece was written for a specific context, the relationship between style, form and purpose is not necessarily fixed.

While, she noted, scholars disagree about definitions of church or sacred music, she quotes (2019, 21) musicologist Wilfrid Mellers (2002, xii) describing that 'sacred music . . . can include music which speaks to anyone who has ever wondered about the "big questions" of human life: purpose, meaning or beauty'. She further refers to Mellers (2002) 'defining "religious" music as that which is "good because it embraces the heights and depths of human consciousness"'. Williams also quotes a Jewish composer Robert Saxton in 'suggesting that liturgical music does not have a monopoly on the sacred'.

Baby Boomers I interviewed did not explicitly refer to 'the sacred' in discussing such music, but it is still appropriate, I would argue, to point out here that 'sacred' has been discussed widely in terms of its non-religious meanings. It can mean religiously holy, special, set apart, or non-negotiable (see, for example, the edited volume Day et al. 2013).

Another music revival, although not often related to church, may further strengthen the association I am making between music and a Boomer desire for authenticity—the mid-twentieth century revival of 'folk music', Although evading a single definition, folk music usually refers to songs that have been passed through generations via oral tradition and is often related to ethnic groups or nationalities. The folk music revival describes a post-war movement where new songs were written and recorded by artists frequently mentioned in my interviews, primarily Joan Baez and Bob Dylan. Although many Boomers may have followed and enjoyed such artists, few were members of the counterculture, drug-infused 'folkniks' who were: 'a very esoteric minority, while the majority of popular music concerned itself over ninety percent of the time with themes of courtship and everlasting love' (Lund and Denisoff 1971, 396).

Christmas Church—A Secular Sacred Ritual

Even in countries where Christianity and church attendance has significantly declined, attendance for Christmas services, particularly midnight mass, has increased. It seems that such events 'possesses the capacity to capture the attention of an otherwise largely apathetic', at least in religious terms, population (Coleman, Bowman, and Sepp 2019, 242).

Although churches do not have age-related statistics for those events, I suggest they are likely to be over-represented by the people attending with their families, including children. It is unlikely that those who have never attended church would suddenly appear at a Christmas mass or church-based carol service and, indeed, surveys show only one in 10 people fit that profile (Francis et al. 2021).

The theme of music in Baby Boomers' non-religious, occasionally church-associated lives, also arose in relation to their attendance at Christmas midnight mass services. Sometimes, this was remembered nostalgically as a time when Boomers recounted the Christmases of their youth: 'My mom and I only attend church once a year,' said Fran, 'to hear the Christmas Carols at Christchurch cathedral.' Philip said he 'probably' attends services on most Christmas Days, through habit, drawing on childhood experiences of attending church before the festivities started: 'probably feels like you have to before getting on with enjoying the rest of the day,' he said.

The act of annually attending a Christmas service may be described as a ritual, following Catherine Bell's (2000, 383) definition of ritual as how:

> people can visibly, formally and explicitly attest to a whole cosmos of implicit assumptions about the nature of reality. Ritual activities, from the elaborate *jiao* to the modest bow, promote particular attitudes toward reality in a notably uncoercive and experiential way.

Clifford Geertz drew attention to how through ritual 'the world as lived and the world as imagined, fused under the agency of a single set of symbolic forms, turn out to be the same world' (1973, 112).

What I therefore suggest the Boomers may be doing, in their Christmas service rituals, is marking a 'sacred', social, non-religious time. Emile Durkheim (1915) argued that all time is social time because people always think of objects as spatially and temporally located. Edmund Leach wrote that 'We talk of measuring time, as if time were a concrete thing waiting to be measured; but in fact we create time by creating intervals in social life. Until we have done this there is no time to be measured' (1971, 135).

Just as 'sacred time' may be that which characterises rituals, the performance and repetition of rituals such as feasts and festivals have dual effects:

not only do participants remember those earlier times, but they are also in an emotional and psychological sense returned there. Gordon Lynch observed that those experiences are effective even if those hours, or even moments, of 'returns' are brief because but they provide an important focus 'on fleeting moments of ecstasy, transgression, creativity, and communitas, which give life by temporarily releasing people from cultural structures' (2012, 20).

The effect of 'communitas' may be particularly applicable to Baby Boomers who have spoken deeply about the importance of family and other relationships. Maurice Bloch (1977) argues that rituals are structured according to a special time sequence experienced by participants as sacred. They therefore help to reinforce wider society's shared sense of time. In this way, I suggest, Boomers are experiencing the Christmas service as a time when people in most countries in this study are inundated with Christmas messages that far exceed religious elements. On Christmas Day it is hard to ignore the comparative silence in city centres as families gather for their annual Christmas gift exchange and feast. Such ritual activities or actions can also be understood temporally through recognising the three-step sequence described originally by Arnold van Gannep (1960) and elaborated by Victor Turner (1977). I suggest we can partly apply Turner's definition of ritual as a 'stereotyped sequence of activities involving gestures, words, and objects, performed in a sequestered place, and designed to influence preter-natural entities or forces on behalf of the actors' goals and interests' (Turner 1977, 183). It is unnecessary to include a requirement for the 'actor' to hope to influence other-than-human forces. It is sufficient that the 'actor' experiences some kind of journey through the ritual, beginning with when a person leaves his or her old life, such as home or the workplace, passes through an interim liminal time, such as the carol service, before emerging a new, refreshed state. As Durkheim (1915) considered festivals as ritual, so, I suggest, can I in so configuring the Christmas carol service and later parties and feasts as an annual ritual for many Baby Boomers.

Bell (1992) showed that rituals had different purposes, depending on the people and the event. The Boomers I interviewed created most of these common rituals at some time in their lives in order to celebrate and dramatise major events such as birth, coming of age, marriage, and death.

The non-religious Baby Boomer persistence of church weddings and christenings to please older parents is an example of the ritual's strength in their imaginations and practice. Celebrating Christmas through church attendance and family festivals are typical 'calendrical rites' that impose a secular, sacred construction on time's passing. Lesley expressed this by saying, several times in our interview, that she retained a deep 'fondness' for the way the Anglican church structures the year. For example, she said, there is Good Friday, Easter, Ascension, Advent, and Christmas. These observed occasions, as discussed above, impose a sacred construction on the passage of time.

Another of Bell's typology is a rite of exchange and communion, of gifts and sacrifices. She adds that these are important in order to please gods and to reinforce earthly order and authority; the same can be said for the way secular families usually visit or otherwise involve senior members of the family at Christmas, at least temporarily re-establishing their familial lines of authority. Rituals of feasting, fasting, and festivals allow people, religious or otherwise, to demonstrate publicly their collective sense of belonging and cultural sentiments, whether at school fairs, village fetes, or music festivals.

Whatever type of ritual that Baby Boomers experience, they are demonstrating the common theme all ritual genres share: social construction of time and activity. Such rituals all create a sense of 'sacred time', marking out that which is removed from daily everyday activities. The result is that rituals, always being group events, serve to bind a group. For people in the countries studied here, particularly the UK and Canada, the power of cultural, secular Christianity is evidenced by these annual gatherings of social, rather than religious, significance. For the Boomers I studied, the effect they were seeking and which they created was a celebration and reinforcement of a social, collective memory of sacred time. The embodied nature of ritual requires participants to perform certain specific actions such as decorating a Christmas tree, wrapping presents, buying and cooking a large turkey, and sometimes attending carol services, that embed memory of the ritual's character and meanings in collective knowledge. Through music, such as carols, words, such as 'Happy Christmas' and movements, such as dressing in new, special clothes with a touch of humour (the 'Christmas jumper', the Santa hat) or a touch of sparkle, the knowledge of what the ritual means, how it is performed, and when it is performed, is passed down through families. Sacred, secular time is thus learned, remembered, and performed (Connerton 1989; Halbwachs 1992 [1925]).

Francis et al. (2021, 3) note that researchers have identified carol services within cathedrals and churches as important for bringing together groups of people who would not usually 'sign up for the kind of membership that entailed a weekly activity'. They also found (Francis et al. 2021, 10) through looking at two types of Christmas services at Liverpool cathedral, that most people attending were not regular church goers. Further they found that the vast majority surveyed (93 per cent) said they attended because of the music, following by motivations to keep to a Christmas tradition and to be with friends. The least common reason, at 59 per cent, was 'to worship the Son of God'. The study found (2021, 13) 'that the religious profile of the participants reveals that the Christmas services brings into the Cathedral a significant number of people who would generally regard themselves as unconnected with church and with the Christian tradition'. And yet, of those who indicated a religious identity, most were Anglican. These may, I suggest, fall into an ex-churched Anglican category, such as that represented by the Baby Boomers in my study. Francis et al. also incorporate studies by David Walker who profiled the motivations and psychological types of people who attend harvest festivals and carol services, finding that most were not regular church goers and fit the psychological profile of people defined as pursuing a 'quest'. Although this is described by Francis et al. as a religious orientation, many people, I suggest, may find the existential questions on the survey a feature of secular orientation as well: sometimes considering issues about the meaning of life and expressing religious doubt are what many of the more humanist Baby Boomers I interviewed would experience.

Rowan Clare Williams suggested, an appeal of Christmas carols is that they are not fixed to a particular 'worshipping community' and thus are not seen as 'church music' in 'the narrow sense, because they do not belong to a particular worshipping community: their appeal and application is wider than the particular context for which they were written' (2019, 26).

David Hebert, Alexis Anja Kallio, and Albi Odendaal (2012) conducted in-depth ethnography in Finland to explore the cultural significance attached to the Finns' attachment to Christmas church music. Although set in a different country from those studied as part of this Baby Boomer research, the non-religious attraction to such events presented a similar puzzle and the researchers' analysis provides helpful insights. As with the UK and Canada, Finnish Christmas carol events are more popular and much better attended than regular church services. About one-fifth of the Finnish population attends *joulumusiikki*—church-based carol services in the Sundays before Christmas. The research aim was to explore such events as 'taken-for-granted, annual occurrences in which contemporary Finnish culture is explored, affirmed and celebrated' (Hebert et al. 2012, 404). Drawing on the work of Hobsbawm (1983, 4), they argued that such cultural patterns represent 'a process of formalisation and ritualisation, characterised by reference to the past'. Further, they relate Hobsbawm (1983, 2) insights about the effect of modernity on people who may respond to conditions on constant change through attempts 'to structure at least some parts of social life within it as unchanging and invariant'.

The research drew on the work of musicologist Christopher Small (1998, 80) who developed the term 'musicking' to reflect 'the ideal relationships of the participants, relationships that are celebrated through taking part in musical events'. They also discussed at length Catherine Bell's (1992, 81) work that showed ritual as a way to reconfigure or reproduce the order of power in the world.

Attending carol services is not, therefore, an individualised expression of personal religiosity but, as one priest they interviewed described it, deeply relational (Hebert et al. 2012, 412):

> You come to the church, and the church is full, when it was Saturday here there were 1200 people! You feel the belongingness together, with the past generations and this one. You don't normally get to go to events where there are that many people singing songs, and you can sing with your own voice, and if you don't have such a good voice, no one hears it, that's the main thing. I think Christmas is somewhat important for Finnish people because they remember the older generations, and that comes through these songs and traditions. something like this with our family, and we go to the grave sites to light candles*these are the things that don't change, when everything else is changing around the world. It is comforting and it's not bad melancholy; it feels good.

As one participant said: 'I think it is more that the music is connected to childhood memories and the time of year is kind of special, so not really religious actually, it's more of the feeling.' Like Fran, quoted earlier in this chapter, many of their research participants identified family connections linked to their attendance, either because a family member was performing or because they were attending with family (Hebert et al. 2012, 418).

The study concluded with the observation that: 'Our descriptions and interpretations have highlighted Helsinki *joulukonsertti* and *joululaulu* events as rituals that both maintain traditions and mediate cultural and societal change through transforming understandings, practices, beliefs and behaviours' (Hebert et al. 2012, 420). As such, they suggest, with reference to Ivo Supicic (1987, 295) music should be studied as something that can relate to ceremony, ritual, magic, or spirituality. 'music itself can become more or less "ceremonial" or "ritual," "magic" or "spiritual," and should be studied as such'.

It may be that the combination of music, lights, and family singing together is a 'magic' that requires little explanation. Christmas celebrations have changed throughout history, as have pre-Christian winter festivals. As Bruce Forbes writes, Christmas is partly a winter festival as well as a religious one, which is one reason it remains popular. Particularly for people who live in the Global north, long months of dark, cold weather 'can be a real challenge, a midwinter break featuring lights, evergreen decorations, feasts, and good times with friends is just what is needed for the sake of sanity . . . expecting Christmas to be a purely spiritual celebration is a desire for something that never was' (2007, 406).

Reclaiming the 'Magic' of Christmas: 'We Totally Invented Greed'

I have discussed thus far how Christmas may be a time of nostalgia for many of the Baby Boomers I interviewed. I will explore now a particular aspect of that nostalgia, one related more to family and a life they recall as being perhaps less materialistic than contemporary society.

As even the casual reader of mainstream media in an average December would see, much is written and lamented about the apparent commercial-isation of Christmas. Perhaps, as I have written elsewhere, the focus on non-religious aspects may be offensive to some, but it is by far the most common way Christmas is publicised in North America and the UK:

> I'm always struck when I visit the United States in December by the lack of religious imagery surrounding Christmas. It's all about family, friends and presents. The angry Conservative Right will claim this is political correct-ness gone wrong in a time of aggressive multiculturalism but they are badly mistaken. If there's anything Americans sanctify more than their flag and their guns, it's their families.
>
> (https://www.huffingtonpost.co.uk/abby-day/meaning-of-christmas_b_4459215.html)

Drawing on the sociologist Marcel Mauss (1990, I argued that gift exchange amongst family members is a social, sometimes sacred act, that connects people through processes of reciprocity, debt, and obligation. It is steeped in meaning, tradition, and expectation. That observation connects, I suggest, to the sometimes-wistful note amongst the Baby Boomers I interviewed when they approached the topic of materialism.

Sherry said she thought societies, from the 1960s onwards, have become more consumerist. People, she said, are 'a lot more materialistic—they want something with branding on it. A lot of people have got to have the new car, "that will make me happy" they think.'

Roger concurred. Although post-1960s was certainly an era of opportunity, and 'the country was becoming more settled' it was also, he said 'maybe more materialistic'.

Bruce also agreed. Following the 1960s, he said he became more 'antagonistic to the neoliberal capitalist agenda, particularly the materialism and selfishness from the late 70s, 80s'. Part of the problem, Terry thought, was the sheer size of the Baby Boomer generation. 'Baby Boomers are a big generation, there are lots of people, so they marketed to us.' As a consequence, he said, 'we totally invented greed, turned it into "greed is good" and got away from some good values about looking after the world'.

In those discussions, about materialism and greed, the topic of family sometimes arose. Martin, for example, said there were good things in society post-1960s. It was a time of change, permissiveness, music, and social life, when it seemed 'money is no object'. Things then 'were better, cheap, but people can't save now. We were the very lucky generation and enjoyed the best of times.'

Then, he said, post-1960s 'shops began to open on a Sunday, people would rather look at furniture stores. I think that's a bit much, a little over the top, people should have some special day for meeting family.' I suggest that it is a mark of Baby Boomer relationality that he was missing family, not church, as a way to spend time on Sundays.

Pam described her family Bibles as relics of history, relationships, and literature, not religion. 'For a humanist household we have a surprising number of Bibles,' she told me. As we were chatting with our cameras on, she said she wanted to show me something, and held up the family Bible dating back to the early nineteenth century. This was from her great, great grandfather she said, turning the pages to reveal handwritten entries. 'I don't think one should dismiss such things,' she said. She likes dipping into it for the memories and also for the language, beautifully written, she said, in the time of Shakespeare. 'Some people might want to burn it, but I say absolutely not. I've read it a lot.'

In summary, in this chapter I have reviewed a number of ways that may appear to contradict Baby Boomer non-religious orientation such as enjoying 'church music', cathedral attendance, and Christmas celebrations. I have tried to reveal what may connect those predilections to their ex-churched identities and have found that the 'lingering trails' of their former exposure to church were steeped mainly in non-religious, family experiences. I have also argued that their desire for 'authenticity' that marked their generation also may explain their continuing, at times avowedly atheistic, participation in the period of early music and folk music.

One possibility, that Boomers returning to church for carol services could lead to their eventual more permanent return, did not arise in my interviews. This is probably not surprising, given that most research confirms that religious identity is stable throughout adulthood and that transmission through families, of both religion and non-religion, is key to generational change. I explore this in more depth in Chapter 11. The record in the UK to date shows regular church attendance is in decline even while Christmas carol services remain popular.

I touched briefly on the idea that many Boomers may experience nostalgia for what they recall as an earlier, less materialistic time. This may resonate with Max Weber's work on 'disenchantment' whereby it was argued that rationalisation and bureaucratisation within modernity led to people being imprisoned with an 'iron cage' of their own and society's making. His pessimistic view included his prediction that, with modernity, people would become more individualised and their pleasures less communal. That was not a tendency I discerned from my interviews. Other than occasional asides about materialism, almost all the Boomers I interviewed were remarkably upbeat and often cheered by society's turn away from 'enchantment'. Simon, for example, said the world was better off being more attuned to science than religion—'there are a million other things going on, like evidence-based science, without mumbo jumbo'. Jay, a retired British journalist born in 1943, said it was part of western culture now, perhaps because of science, that people were 'able to make sense of things'.

I will discuss in the next chapter another apparent contradiction: the common reports from non-religious Baby Boomers about experiencing first-hand, or though others, the possibility of communication with deceased loved ones. Whether this is classified in academe as 'secular', 'religious', or 're-enchantment' may depend on, I will argue, the orientation of the scholar. For the Boomers I have studied it is largely interpreted as a secular, sacred, supernatural phenomenon.

PART III

SHAPING BELIEF AND BELONGING

9

Belief in Spirits

Extraordinary Relationality

Introduction: 'I More Easily Dismiss the Idea of a God than the Idea of the Paranormal'

Rejecting gods is one thing; rejecting ghosts of loved ones is quite another. As Harry said: 'I more easily dismiss the idea of a god than the idea of the paranormal.' If the ex-religious Boomers left God behind, the same cannot be said for their continuing relationships with their beloved deceased grandparents, parents, or partners. As discussed throughout this book, and in more detail in Chapters 11 and 12, Boomers have a strong sense of community, family ties, and commitment. For many, an alteration of that relationship through death brings another dimension to that relationship, rather than its termination.

In this chapter I turn to the ex-religious Boomers' continued relationships with deceased relatives, even amongst the most atheistic. These experiences of a god-less afterlife are, for many, a felt, embodied reality of an 'other' world elsewhere that is accepted unquestionably. Others, while accepting its possibility, believe that science will one day explain such experiences. Either way, their responses fit within their own systems of values and aspirations, the most important of which is the ethos of non-judgemental acceptance of others' authentic experiences.

As discussed in this book, the boundaries between meaning, purpose, and belonging seem remarkably blurred and porous for this generation. Their tendency to simply accept some experiences without requiring greater explanation seems consistent with several aspects of their pasts: their general ethos of 'being real', rejecting the social conventions of, amongst other things, church attendance; the quiet ambivalence of some of their parents who, as discussed earlier, nudged them to self-authority; and their teenage years, spent in an era where old certainties were shattered. One of the few things the Boomers were sure about was their conviction that other people's experiences should be respected and accepted, echoing 1960s' mantras,

Why Baby Boomers Turned from Religion: Shaping Belief and Belonging, 1945–2021. Abby Day, Oxford University Press. © Abby Day 2022. DOI: 10.1093/oso/9780192866684.003.0009

inspired by cultural heroes like Fritz Perls, Baba Ram Dass, Timothy Leary, and the Beatles of 'doing your own thing' and respecting those whose 'thing' may be different from one's own.

Privileging experience over abstract theorising is part of the Boomer 'being real' ethos. This was the generation who, as discussed in Chapter 2, had been forced as children to do 'the social thing' of attending church and performing what they intuited was a pretence of commitment and spirituality. Many spoke strongly about the hypocrisy they had witnessed: parents who paid, literally, 'lip service' to the creed and prayers by speaking them once a week, but not integrating Christian or, at least, 'golden rule' (Ammerman 1997) beliefs or practices into their weekday lives; neighbours and family friends those children knew to be harsh or otherwise unpleasant who would on Sundays in church present a forced false face of kindness. As discussed then, few Boomers felt any sense of spiritual connections during those church-based hours. But what were those mirages of spirituality against the sense of being visited and comforted by the spirit of a deceased loved one?

Understanding those experiences poses a challenge for me and other scholars steeped in an epistemological tradition that privileges a binary between sacred and secular and theories that presume 'modernity' leads inevitably to increased rationality and disenchantment (see, for the roots of such ideas, for example, Tylor 1958 [1871] and Weber 1922). Charles Taylor is one who seems convinced that the so-called 'buffered self' is not open to 'a world of spirits' (2007, 300). Such an assumption, I suggest, shows an ignorance both of popular culture, where stories about vampires, ghosts, reincarnation, and such are popular, but also of contemporary beliefs where revitalisation of animism and spiritualism show continued and perhaps growing significance amongst otherwise non-religious people.

Taylor further claims (2007, 302) that there is a malaise in a 'disenchanted' world, which explains why some people may be turning more towards spirituality. He does not give evidence to substantiate that claim, and further misses the point that, as I have argued earlier, people may be turning away from religion because they have become disillusioned with that institution as a site of illegitimate authority.

In a disapproving tone, Taylor (2007, 419) states that 'The modern ideal has triumphed. We are all partisans of human rights.' While I think the Baby Boomers I interviewed would agree and approve, many would disagree with his view that 'secular humanists' share an 'illusion of a good beyond life and the illusion of the beyond' (Taylor 2007, 637). As I have shown in earlier chapters, not only do Boomers share values and morals of what is 'good' but, as I will discuss here, many also share a belief in something 'beyond'.

Admitting to a secular belief in 'something beyond' may, however pose challenges to some people who consider themselves to be atheists but are reluctant, due to societal pressures, to openly self-identify as such. Such beliefs in a god-less afterlife are not always welcome by others. Research in the USA shows that antipathy towards atheists is high, with some studies finding that people regard atheists as untrustworthy as rapists. Psychological experiment-based research designed to test the sources of that mistrust looked at two prominent theories (Cook et al. 2015). The widely accepted cultural evolutionary theory argues that, in societies that look to religion to keep morals and values stable, an atheist who does not believe in God is thought to be without morals and is therefore untrustworthy. A separate theory is that most people live in terror of death and seek ways to manage that fear. Religion is one source of such terror diminishment, and an atheist who does not affirm religious teachings on the afterlife may be seen as an existential threat.

Understanding the 'Secular Supernatural'

I wondered to what extent the ex-religious Baby Boomers might have experienced something that I, for lack of better vocabulary, may describe as supernatural. Further, if they had, I was curious about how they might rationalise, explain, or absorb such experiences. In obtaining answers to these questions, I hoped to gain not only a better understanding of their beliefs and practices but also insights into what they might have absorbed from their parental generation and passed on to their own children.

In practice, during my interviews it sometimes happened that they raised discussion of those experiences before I had a chance to ask about them. If they had not, then towards the end of the interview I asked them if they had ever experienced something that might be described as supernatural, or paranormal. While some immediately answered in the negative, I was surprised to find several who seemed to belie their earlier statements about rejecting religion in the name of reason by revealing complex and, for them, significant experiences of other worldliness.

I discuss here three main types of belief that seem to be held by those who had, either directly or indirectly, some experience of the 'supernatural'.

1. *A belief in the authenticity of others.* Many Boomers did not seek to explain reports of such experiences, even if it is something they have never experienced themselves. This attitude aligns with their general moral framework, as discussed earlier here and particularly in Chapter 6, to accept other people's experiences as unique and authentic without trying to convert them into their own worldview or having to fit apparent anomalies into a wider, stable fabric of 'meaning'.

2. *A belief in the ultimate truth of science and human agency.* Their faith in science allows them to put aside the need for an immediate explanation because they believe one day science will explain it. Some are content to muse about how such phenomena could be explained, before shrugging to say that while they did not know how, they did not 'dismiss it'. One day, they believe, people will be able to construct an understanding of scientific laws that will explain it.

3. *A belief in the continuity of the soul.* Because those experiences align closely with their deeper personal and cultural values about human and more-than-human relationships, they do not strike them as controversial. The sense of a continuing presence of their deceased loved ones provides the qualities of comfort and continuity described by other scholars as 'ancestor worship'.

I elaborate on that typology below, but first I would like to attend to the word I have chosen to use above: belief. Unusually within disciplines that study religion, throughout this book I have distinguished between what some philosophers and anthropologists (see, for example, Needham 1972; Ruel 1982) have recognised as a 'propositional' belief, that is, an intellectual engagement with the likely plausibility or not of a given statement, such as, for example, 'I believe a God exists because the universe is too perfect to have been merely created through a chance occurrence' and a faith-like, or, I would argue, emotional statement of fealty, loyalty, or love as in, for example, 'I believe in your love and commitment to our marriage'.

When scholars do not differentiate between those types of belief, they can, I suggest, be misled by questionnaires that ask such undifferentiated questions as 'Do you believe in God'? or, as I will discuss below, 'Do you believe in heaven or hell?' The extent to which and how that belief matters[1] also needs to be understood.

When I interviewed, in 2003 and 2004, nearly 70 people (Day 2011) to probe why they might self-identify as Christian, it was important to keep questions as open-ended as possible to avoid imposing religious ideas and vocabulary. I therefore did not ask people if they believed in God, or 'heaven' or 'hell'. Such matters often arose in discussion when they answered my wider, more existential questions. When I was talking to one teenager (Day 2011, 159), about how she thought the universe came into being, she said, almost grudgingly, that it might have been brought about by God. It seemed, by her tone, that she was providing what she assumed I might be expecting as a correct answer. Before I had an opportunity to add another question she hastily added, that 'I don't, like worship him or anything!' She was the daughter of Baby Boomer parents. I suggest now that her emphatic qualification that she does not 'worship him' may be partly a result of being raised by a generation of people who, as I have argued in earlier chapters, dispensed with automatic deference to, in their eyes, dubious sites or persons of authority in favour of more 'authentic' and emotional relationships. Those Baby Boomers raised a generation of young people who felt more liberated to explore alternative forms of other-worldly belief and spirituality as, perhaps, evidenced by the growth in benign forms of teenage witchcraft and paganism (see, for example, Berger and Ezzy 2007; Cush 2010; and Luhrmann 1989 for a discussion of Baby Boomer involvement in witchcraft). Further, while earlier generations may have protected grief as a private matter, researchers have also noted the trend for young people to engage publicly in conversations with their deceased relatives on Facebook (Brubaker, Hayes, and Dourish 2013; Kasket 2012). I will return to the topic of non-religious belief transmission in the final chapter.

What might appear as too equivocal and fluid to those adhering to stricter belief systems, the middle ground of doubt and epistemological generosity is an ethical orientation of many ex-religious Baby Boomers. As Peter Berger (1967) argued, the plausibility statements of religion weakened amongst this generation and allowed both the possibility of other religions but also, I found, possibilities of fluidity and shape-shifting. In the place, I argue, of bounded forms of religiosity or spirituality, arose strong desires for emotional, relational frameworks. When I use the term 'belief' here, I am therefore embedding it in an emotional, relationship framework.[2]

A belief in the authenticity of others

When I asked Harry if he had ever experienced something uncanny, perhaps a sense of something outside himself, he said that he did not believe in the supernatural. And yet, in a manner similar to several other of my interviewees, he suddenly stopped himself for a moment and paused, as if remembering something important he momentarily either forgot or was unsure about sharing. I waited in the silence, and then he continued.

'No, I don't, but my mother was a bit like that.' He then told me his story, beginning when he was in his twenties and left university abruptly, determined not to finish his studies. He returned home, not sure what he wanted to do, apart from being sure that he did not want to be at university. He began to apply for jobs but never mentioned it to family and friends, worried that they might intrude on his decision-making or offer judgements. One morning he joined the family for breakfast as usual, knowing he was going for a job interview later that day, but saying nothing about it. His mother remarked over breakfast that she had had an intense dream the night before in which she saw Harry in a large room surrounded by bits of plastic. It was not a bad dream, she mused, but it was strange, nonetheless. That afternoon, Harry arrived at his job interview and was shown into the company's boardroom where he was asked to sit down and wait for the interview. He looked around and saw that the walls and much of the floor spaces were decorated with displays of the plastic objects they produced. Surrounded by plastic , as his mother had described, he felt himself suddenly relax with the overwhelming and, it transpired, correct realisation that he need not worry, he would get the job. 'She was quite fey,' he commented about his mother.

He then recalled another experience when he was with his then partner, staying at her parents' house while they were away on holiday. She awoke early one morning, distressed. She rushed to a window and cried out that her father, who was supposedly away on holiday, was actually in the driveway in his car. Harry went to the window where she was standing but saw nothing. They learned later that day that her father had died early that morning. Telling me that story, Harry then shook his head as if he were lost for an explanation: 'I don't dismiss that kind of thing,' he said. 'There could be different levels of communication in the world, and some people might be more tapped into those than others.'

Todd, a Canadian doctor born in 1953, said he did not believe in anything that could be described as supernatural or paranormal, but added that his wife 'believes that spirits are around'. While he did not believe in ghosts, he said, he did think that mediumship may one day be explained through, for example, discovering that 'mediums are somehow connected to people's brain waves and can pick up memories from childhood'.

Vikki also told me stories about her relatives believing in spirits: 'My cousins are into spiritualism and Buddhism. I'm not convinced about all that, but I accept their feelings about it. I don't say "you're stupid".'

A belief in the ultimate truth of science and human agency

Ex-religious Boomers who have themselves experienced, even fleetingly, 'supernatural' phenomena, are often able to accept those experiences as things to be explained in time with a greater understanding of science.

Mary, who described herself as an 'existentialist', told me in answer to my question that she does not believe in anything 'supernatural'. She began to describe herself as 'cynical' before pausing, as if catching herself with a memory. It appeared to me that she was hesitating, mulling something over. I waited for a moment or two, and then she picked up the story. There was one incident, she explained, that happened many years earlier when she was just beginning her medical training. She had suddenly woken from a deep sleep at around 1.45 a.m. feeling 'the hairs standing up on the back of my neck'. She could not at the time understand why, but the next day back at work she discovered that one of her patients had died at exactly that time. I asked her what she made of that experience, and she replied: 'I don't know, but I don't dismiss it.'

Two others made similar comments, such as Paul, who said that he knew people who believed in ghosts, but, reflecting on his earlier education in physics and biology, as 'a trained scientist with an aversion to god, I would look to science for an explanation'. Sheila, a retired British biologist born in 1948, said she would consider the neurological context if someone said they had seen a ghost: 'Perhaps people have had some kind of brain spasm,' she said. 'As a scientist I'm a firm believer there is a rational explanation for everything.'

One Boomer I interviewed spoke harshly against people who held beliefs in the continuing presence of deceased relatives. Michele said she was relieved to break away from her church which was 'oriented towards literal truth'. Michele said she did not ever feel that she needed God, even when her father died when she was two years old, and her mother when she was 14. Her sister, she said, 'became very spiritual, but not religious'. Her sister claims she is psychic, Michele said, with a note of scorn: 'Nothing makes me angrier. I get comfort from rationality.' On the other hand, as I mentioned in

Chapter 5, some Boomers were both rational and sometimes something else: Annabel had said that although she considered herself to be a rationalist, there were moments like once when she was standing on a windswept beach watching the waves when she experienced a 'sudden feeling of peace, an indescribable, I would say, spiritual experience'. Charlotte told me of similar experiences which she said might be described as spiritual, for example, 'walking on hill tops, even now, maybe more so with Covid' and while she doesn't 'meditate or do mindfulness or anything like that', she often feels intensely thankful and filled with love. 'It's magical.' She recounted how she and her husband would take their two children out at night sometimes when they were young, 'when it was very clear and they'd get into their sleeping bags outside and look at the stars'.

A belief in the continuity of the soul

To illustrate the complexity of some ex-religious Boomers' relationships to both religion and spirits, I will discuss in detail the case of Rebecca, a retired British doctor born in 1946, and now active in alternative healing groups and practices. Rebecca was raised in a strict religious family who regularly attended church, but she felt alienated at an early age from what she described as the church's rigid, patriarchal structure. Indeed, during our interview and subsequent correspondence she frequently referred to 'the church' rather than 'Christianity', a distinction that resonates with earlier discussions here about the 'structures' of religion and the propensity of ex-religious Boomers to signal a deliberate move away from 'institutions'. For Rebecca, one notable exception to that memory of institutional rigidity was the feeling of awe, bliss, and spiritual connection she experienced when she was baptised as a young child. Nevertheless, as she grew into her teens and early adulthood she drew away from 'the church' and its 'framework', finding an illogical pattern of, she said, 'punishing people when they're bad, but not praising them when they're good'.

At university she drifted even further away from 'the church' and eventually stopped attending. Pursuing a career in medicine, she enjoyed her life and circle of friends and even sometimes visited churches on her travels. There, she explained, she could feel 'spiritual as long as I didn't listen to the words'. She and her husband felt the same way about 'church' but often longed to belong to some kind of group; they eventually satisfied that need through forming a Quaker community.

And yet, nothing had prepared her for an intense spiritual experience she felt when visiting the Australian outback. Walking in the bush, she saw a glade ahead of her and felt drawn towards it. At the end of the glade was a single, tall, white tree. As she approached and drew nearer, she was overwhelmed with a deep feeling of awe and love.[3] It made her realise, she explained, that she could only experience spirituality outdoors. That realisation was so strong that she decided to work part-time to enable her to connect more to art and nature, and eventually to train as an art therapist.

The outback experience was her first but not last encounter with nature spirituality. During our interview and subsequent correspondence, she recounted several more such events, all of which combined to convince her to spend more time communing with nature. A pivotal moment was when, alone on a beach sitting in front of a small fire she had built, she felt her deceased father's spirit join her. He encouraged her to keep up with her photography and her exploration of nature spirituality, so much so that she became involved in shamanism and believes this helps her to heal herself and others. Her own healing is necessary, she explained, to rid her of the traumas caused by a childhood spent in a religion that forced a separation between mind and body and neglected what she described as 'the feminist sacred'. Those experiences helped her to gradually rebuild her spiritual orientation and her relationship with her father.

A sense of paternal protection was also felt by Simon, who began to tell me about it when I asked him if he had ever felt something paranormal or supernatural. The problem with that question, he said, was that his experience involving his deceased father felt completely natural and was not 'super' or 'para' anything. I had fallen into the trap of imposing a preconceived category and apologised. He continued with his account, describing the first such occasion as one of several when his son had been critically ill. Simon was sitting, distressed, at his son's hospital bedside, and suddenly had an overwhelming sensation that his deceased father was standing behind him, his hand on Simon's shoulder and was telling him not to worry, that everything would be fine. And, Simon added, he was right, his son recovered. Since that time, in similar situations with his son and in other very difficult moments, he has felt a similar presence he described as 'his hand on my shoulder' and a feeling that his father was reassuring him that all would be well and, importantly, that he was not on his own. 'I've never tried to explain it,' he said. 'It felt quite natural. Obviously, it's not natural, but that's how it felt.'

Alice, a retired British teacher born in 1947, described a similar experience involving her father. The day he died, she had been at her office and then had returned home, feeling 'totally unsettled, thinking of my dad, when I felt an arm around my shoulder and his smell, feeling him say "I'm at peace"'. She later learned that this had occurred at exactly the same time he had died. Two days later she went to see his body at the funeral parlour and 'he wasn't there—whatever the energy is inside me that makes me, with him, it was gone'.

Joan also told me that she and other family members often feel their father, who had died 15 years earlier, was with them 'in a good way'. They frequently talked about him, re-telling family stories and jokes: 'We kind of keep him alive,' she said. When I asked her how she would explain that, she answered: 'Maybe it's through a deep love for someone, you want to remember the details about someone, to remember details, to hold them in a different place in your head, not in a shrine.' Her reference to a 'shrine' evoked images of a Buddhist temple or special place in a family home set aside for the ancestors, perhaps with candles, and small items of food and drink for their sustenance. While Joan was marking her own practices as different from those, perhaps in places she imagined as Africa or China, I would suggest that in terms of function it may not be so different. What all those activities have in common is the desire to keep the deceased ancestors close, and in some senses, alive.

Memory, as discussed by, for example, Maurice Halbwachs (1992), Elizabeth Tonkin (1992), and Janet Carsten (2007) is a social experience that supports social relations such as a family as it functions to bind individuals within groups. Memories are embedded through storytelling, just as Joan described, and also sometimes with events designed to commemorate—or 'memorialise'—significant social moments and important related characters.

When anthropologist Meyer Fortes studied ancestor-related practices amongst the Tallensi and Ashanti people in west Africa he concluded that the purpose of ancestor worship was to ensure continuity of social boundaries and norms (Fortes 1987, 67). Raymond Firth, who studied indigenous people in New Zealand and islands of the southern Pacific Ocean (1955) saw ancestor veneration practices as a way to reinforce the social structure, not just individual memory. American anthropologist James Spickard (1993, 6) suggested from his research that such experiences are 'social products' learned, or at least presupposed in some way through familial or friendship associations. Those anthropologists' conclusions focused on the societal, cohesive aspects rather than those of individual experience.

Whether or not those practices are folded into an institution or community may vary, although it is interesting to note that Spiritualism, a comparatively young religion founded in the 1800s, has apparently seen growth recently in the numbers of young people joining. The way such beliefs are practised may not be the same as, say, the popular practice of seances in the late nineteenth and early twentieth centuries.

The essence of Spiritualism is the belief that contact with the dead is possible, and believers actively encourage such experiences. Census evidence in the UK, for example, shows that the number of people who define themselves as 'Spiritualist' grew by 22 per cent between 2001 and 2011. While some may attend Spiritualist churches, others will share their extraordinary experiences with close friends and families. What Tony Walter (2019, 394) has described as a discourse of the 'pervasive dead' seems to have been emerging since the late 1990s, 'picturing the dead as no longer separate from everyday life but pervading it' but continuing the bonds between the dead and the living (see also Klass, Silverman, and Nickman 1996).

The stories of continuing relationality remind me of an interview I had many years earlier which helped me begin to explore the idea of a secular supernatural (Day 2011). Patrick, a successful lawyer, and Baby Boomer born in the 1950s, established early in our interview that he identified as an atheist. The idea that there was some external power that organised events on earth was, he exclaimed, 'utterly ridiculous'. As someone who had dedicated his life to enforcing rules and laws, arguing his way in and out of situations on behalf of his clients, his scorn and dismissal of such ideas fit the stereotype of the modern, rational atheist. And yet, he continued, he did believe in something he said he could only describe as 'the human spirit'. To illustrate that, he described how several years earlier he had been overwhelmed and devastated by his mother's death, so much so that he had not even felt able to even attend her funeral. At home that morning, with the funeral planned for early afternoon, he sat weeping, alone and distraught when suddenly, seemingly out of nowhere, a strong sense of warmth and peace surrounded him. It was as if he were, he recounted, being physically cloaked with her warmth, love, and comfort, so much so that he garnered the strength to attend her funeral feeling peaceful and calm. The continuity of 'the human spirit' was, he said, the only logical explanation for that and so many other seemingly inexplicable feelings and events.

The relevance of that interview in the context of this current Baby Boomer project is to emphasise that difference between reason and emotion, and presence and power. It seems evident that the Baby Boomers did not follow a Weberian adherence to rationality and a conception of modernity as a sterile, secular space. Their tendency to valorise emotion led them to accepting phenomena that may be inexplicable, but no less real for that.

For ramifications of this emotional-relational turn in scholarship, I will turn now to a discussion of how early definitions of religion may have misled scholars.

A Belief in Spirits: 'Whatever It Is that Makes Me, Me'

The scholarly discussion about non-religious people who believe in the spirits of their deceased relatives is blurred by definitional problems. Most studies that cue contemporary beliefs in what is variously called the super-natural or paranormal cite aliens, reincarnation, or 'ghosts' but, less so, the presence of deceased relatives. Further, in much of the sociology of religion, religious studies, and theology research, these 'other-worldly' accounts tend to be described as 'religious experiences' even when reported by people who were not religious. The studies are further complicated, perhaps, by institu-tionalised religions' condemnation of such ideas and practices as commu-nicating with the dead.

The language used by the researchers may further obscure the non-religious character of such experiences because scholars generally ask ques-tions about supernatural beliefs that are already embedded in religious language (see Day 2011 and Rice 2003). A Pew Research survey, for example, asked questions about whether Baby Boomers believed in 'heaven'; it was perhaps unsurprising that most of those who answered and identified as non-religious did not (https://www.pewforum.org/religious-landscape-study/ belief-in-heaven/among/generational-cohort/baby-boomer/).

Another example of the imposition of religious language that is particu-larly revealing is drawn from work conducted by the Alister Hardy Trust, based at the University of Wales, Trinity St. David. They were established in 1969 (see Hardy 1979) to conduct research into what they describe as the phenomena of sensing a presence outside of oneself. People are invited to write in describing such experiences, and in 1982 a report was published to summarise the record thus far (Hay 1982). It concluded that although most reports did not name God and 'premonitions, encounters with the dead and encounters with an evil presence were often ruled out of the category religious' (Hay 1982, 152), the Trust would continue to use the term 'religious experience' as a kind of shorthand. Indeed, more recently the Trust has been conducting research in China through its 'religious experience research centre' and found that while only 8.7 per cent of the Chinese people surveyed described themselves as 'religious', 56.7 per cent report that they have experienced the sense of 'a kind of power that people cannot control or explain clearly'.

This move, while ill-serving those who deliberately declined that term, is steeped in an earlier definition of religion which scholars still find hard to shake off. These early views of religion clearly demarcated the 'everyday' from the 'other', with Edward Burnet Tylor's (1958 [1871]) formulation of religion as 'belief in spirits' maintaining prominence more than two centuries later. As anthropologist Michael Lambeck (2002, 21) noted: Tylor's theories 'remain congenial to many contemporary thinkers and [are] indeed almost a part of western "common sense" on the subject'. The reliance on nineteenth-century anthropologists is, however, diminishing within both anthropology and sociology, as scholars challenge the dominance of colonial-era empirical and theoretical work and its continued legacies (see, for a longer discussion and examples of practical steps being taken in universities worldwide, Day et al. 2022). The legacy of Tylor's limited view of 'spirits' is a good example of such 'coloniality' where coloniality, as distinct from 'colonialisation' refers to the ongoing processes and assumptions that predominate and are still promulgated within academia (for a concise overview see Bhambra 2014).

One of the most damaging assumptions of nineteenth-century scholars was the view that the so-called 'primitive' cultures they were studying were examples of 'survivals'. Tylor argued that in studying such people scholars could see what apparently earlier and supposedly less advanced, forms of social organisation looked like. Contemporary scholars do not tend to align themselves to such views (and for a comprehensive overview and critique of Tylor, see Tremlett et al. 2017). Tylor applied that thinking to develop his theories of animism, the belief that everything has a soul, which was rooted in the phenomenon of people reporting that they had seen their deceased relatives. These experiences were, Tylor argued, but the stuff of dreams and their related practices of what he termed as 'ancestor worship' would, he argued, dissipate as cultures became more 'advanced', by which he meant, become like the northern European societies with which he was familiar and monotheistic religions of Christianity, Judaism, and Islam. In keeping with that tradition of 'primitive' vs. 'advanced' societies, early anthropologists studied 'ancestor worship' in, largely, 'other', more religious, and what they envisaged as more 'exotic' (Said 1979) societies in Africa and Asia rather than Euro-American contexts.[4]

While Tylor argued that those beliefs were child-like symptoms of societies that have not yet fully evolved to Western standards, evidence today tells a strikingly different story with many people reporting that they are sensing, and sometimes communicating with, deceased loved ones. Indeed, a little-known unpublished research project of Tylor's was his own fieldwork investigating spiritualism in London (Stocking 1971; Kalvig 2017). He attended several seances and, although he dispensed with much of what he witnessed at those events as trickery and manipulation, he reflected on how he could not completely discount those spirits may exist. In a troubling sleight of hand, Tylor forced his data into one of his pre-existing frameworks that relegated such beliefs into the domain of the 'primitive' and uneducated, hiding the inconvenient fact that those who attended the seances were mainly middle class and educated. Tylor was determined to retain his theories despite the evidence, as Stocking notes (1971, 90)

> He suggested that the development of religion was a series of stages reflecting 'the long-waged contest between the theory of animation' and 'a slowly-growing natural science which in one department after another substitutes for independent voluntary action the working out of systematic law'—although new errors occasionally arose and old ones were sometimes revived, as in the case of 'modern spiritualism, [which] as every ethnographer may know, is pure and simple savagery both in its theory and the tricks by which it is supported.' (Tylor 1866, 83–5)

I have discussed in this chapter that 'belief in spirits' remains strong in contemporary societies and therefore Tylor's generally accepted definition of religion may require etymological corrections. As Tremlett et al. (2017) discuss, some religions such as Theravada Buddhism do not incorporate a belief in spirits, and new forms of animism (Harvey 2017) revere other-than-human entities besides ancestors. I have argued here that while some religious belief-systems may not include spirits, spirits may be included in a range of non-religious belief systems. Such an 'anthropocentric' orientation to spirits (Day 2011) tends to be neglected within the sociology of religion, religious studies, and secular studies. Joseph O. Baker writes that such topics as a secular belief in the paranormal tend to be either dismissed or condemned by scholars:

That is to say, secular studies is in no way alone in ignoring—or in the case of organized skeptic groups, condemning—the paranormal. Indeed, the paranormal is, by definition, the doubly damned castoff of both organized religions and secular scientism. et damnation doesn't make the paranormal go away. It always returns.

(https://nonreligionandsecularity.wordpress.com/2017/11/24/whither-the-paranormal-in-secular-studies/amp/)

As Baker points out, beliefs in the paranormal have been steady over time, even as the number of people who self-identify as religious has declined. He cites the General Social Survey which shows that in 1973, 77 per cent of Americans believed in life after death; in 1991, and again in 2016, that percentage was 81 per cent.

A survey by the Pew Research Center revealed that nearly a third of those surveyed said they have felt in touch with someone who is deceased (http://www.pewresearch.org/fact-tank/2015/10/30/18-of-americans-saytheyveseen-a-ghost/).

Analysing data from the General Social Survey of 58,000 people, Twenge et al. (2016) found that, during the preceding 40 years, beliefs in life after death had increased as had levels of atheism. The numbers of atheists in the USA increased between 1984 and 2014 to 22 per cent while between 1972 and 2014 belief in the afterlife rose from 73 to 80 per cent.

The researchers, however, brushed aside any in-depth analysis of what that might mean, deriding instead those who held such beliefs: (Twenge et al. 2016, 11). 'One plausible, though speculative, explanation is that this is another example of the rise in entitlement—expecting special privileges without effort.' They presumably do not recognise the effort required to sustain loving relationships during and after life.

An analysis of the European Values Survey (Haraldsson 2006) found that a majority of those surveyed from Nordic countries believe in life after death and 43 per cent in reincarnation. Lambert (2003) also examined that European Values Survey data to show how Christian adherence declined but a belief in an afterlife increased. Those accounts, combined with others, led me to conclude that many otherwise non-religious people believed in the continuing presence of their deceased, loved ones and, further, while I and colleagues within my discipline wrestled with what we saw as a contradiction, they were unencumbered by such doubts or intellectual machinations.

That so many of the Baby Boomers interviewed for this current study reported 'supernatural', non-religious experiences may help explain why the generations that followed them, Generation X, Millennials, and currently Generation Z, are more likely than previous generations to be both non-religious *and* open to such other-worldly, numinous experiences. The monopoly traditional religion held over other-worldly experiences is neither upheld nor respected amongst the Boomers and their progeny. This life, next life, and multiple lives beyond do not, for them, need a sacred canopy of deities and doctrines. Apparent contradictions between findings on badly worded questionnaires do not need the Boomers' intellectual effort to unravel. For many, even amongst the self-identified campaigning Humanists I interviewed, a reconciliation between their beliefs and those of organised religion is unnecessary. As discussed in Chapters 1 and 2, they (like many of their ambivalent parents) never had strong religious beliefs as children, even though they attended church and were confirmed. Indeed, as discussed in Chapter 4, it was often the experience of their confirmation that turned them finally away. The 'confirmation' for them was their identity as grownups who could make their own decisions and were respected by their parents for doing so.

The dominance of certain theories during the last century or so may obscure forms of relationality which, to many people, trump forms of rationality. Max Weber's gender-blind view of religion and 'meaning' will be discussed further in the next chapter. For here, the point I suggest is that were scholars to dispense with a Max Weberian, masculinist theoretical dependency on theories of modernity and rationality, the consistent pre- and post-death relational experiences of non-religious people would not seem contradictory. Indeed, recent work (Solms 2021) in neurology positions emotion, not rational cognition, as the source of consciousness; perhaps a revision of the Cartesian formula is required: 'I feel, therefore I am'. The work of Ole Riis and Linda Woodhead (2010) on religion and emotion also contributes to this ongoing conversation.

More research is necessary on these phenomena, especially as experienced by non-religious and ex-religious people. Progress within the discipline of anthropology of religion shows promising results, built around the concept of 'elsewhere' and the affective relationships people have with the people, places, and objects so located. In their introduction to a special section of the annual journal *Religion and Society: Advances in Research*, the editors (Kasmani et al. 2020, 94) note that while such complex relationships with 'differently corporeal, nonhuman, or more-than-living figures across other/ worldly realms (angels, djinns, saints, spirits, mythical creatures, ghosts, etc.)' have been known to academics, a sustained intellectual engagement has been lacking:

> The fact is that ideas of corresponding with the godly and the unknown, spiritual relations, or mystical becomings have long captured the imagination of those who have studied religion and society. Despite a vibrant intellectual history, it is startling that a critical and sustained engagement with informed ideas of affect, which so often are embedded in people's relations with and perceptions of divine, other-worldly or more-than-human figures, has not taken place.

Several of the themes explored here, particularly concerning affective relationships and belonging, are taken up in the next chapter when I focus on how ex-religious Baby Boomers respond to ideas of meaning and purpose. While theologians and other scholars within the study of religion often criticise those who are non-religious and do not express sentiments about 'meaning' or higher purposes, often ensuring that whatever the topic, meaning is something that, as Joel Robbins (2006, 211) remarked, gets 'lobbed in', I explore here how ex-religious Boomers frequently challenge the idea that 'meaning' is important, at least when it is bound up in religious or philosophical frameworks. They tend to speak more about their relationships, their work, their communities, and, in many cases, their causes. Meaning and 'belonging' often overlap. As one Boomer commented: 'It's not what you think but what you do.'

In summary, in this chapter I have tried to disconnect experiences of an other-than-human entity from discourses of religion. Reviewing Baby Boomers' personal experiences of such phenomena, and the way in which they described similar accounts of those close to them, convinced me that imposing a religious or spiritual vocabulary distorts what they meant and what scholars can learn in order to revise theory.

For theoretical reflection, I suggest the following three interventions:

1. Reduce a theoretical dependency on outdated theories of modernity that presume and dictate a modern/enchanted binary. Both are simultaneously compatible.
2. Revise theories of secularisation that assume that a decline of Christianity, at least in the Global North, is due to modernising influences of rationality and individualisation. Research into

non-religious, other-worldly experience demonstrates the high degree of relationality and preparedness to permit wonder and doubt. Christianity's decline, I have argued throughout this book, is more likely to be due to a decline of deference to patriarchal and other forms of authority deemed to be illegitimate.

3. Reject the Tylorean mandate defining religion as a 'belief in spirits' as this implicitly assumes that belief in spirits is religious while, as shown here and through references to other work, belief in spirits is also strong amongst non-religious people. Beliefs are not always consistent, at least to the outside observer, but can reflect complex ideas and experiences.

I will review in more depth in Chapter 11 the implications for understanding how Baby Boomers have transmitted their non-religious belief in spirits to Millennials and younger generations.

Notes

1. Or even, as Charles Kadushin (2007) argued, whether it is 'theologically correct' when within some religions, such as Judaism, the experience rather than the belief in God, is most significant.
2. This is not to say that religious people are unemotional: see Ole Riis and Linda Woodhead 2010 for a unique sociological discussion of religious emotion.
3. The way she described this in our interview reminded me of her description of her baptismal experience, and may be an example of vestiges, or trails of religion.
4. For further discussion of anthropologists' tendency to avoid studying the Christian societies in which they live, see Joel Robbins 2007.

10

Belonging and Behaving

Troubling 'Meaning': 'It's Not Religious, But Humanistic'

While religious scholars claim, and criticise, an apparent lack of purpose or 'meaning' amongst younger, secular, generations they are sometimes echoing wider theories prevalent in more general social science relating to conditions of modernity and postmodernity (see, for example, Taylor 2007; Mason et al. 2007; Smith and Denton 2005). Boomers, on the other hand, frequently challenge the idea that 'meaning' is important, at least when it is bound up in religious or philosophical frameworks.

Beginning with the religion-specific literature, it struck me when I was conducting, between 2001 and 2011, multi-generational longitudinal research in northern England on 'belief' and 'belonging' (Day, 2011, 2013, 2014) that a tension pervaded between researchers and their research participants. What people often talked about in terms of what was important to them left many researchers disappointed. This may be because some of the academics held strong Christian beliefs and identities of their own, and while they produced interesting and often robust findings, there was an underlying assumption that people 'should' have larger frameworks of meaning—what, perhaps, a sociologist might describe as 'grand narratives'. As much of their research involved young people, I will return to their work in the next chapter as I discuss the generations raised by the Boomers.

Religious studies and the sociology of religion disciplines are influenced by key sociologists of the early twentieth century, including Max Weber, and it is his work on 'meaning' that has arguably had the most impact. Weber assumed a universalist stance on 'meaning', both in an existential sense related to a 'meaning of life'; and to what he described as the problem of meaning, created when adherents' strong beliefs in a good god is threatened by bad events. Both interpretations are relevant to this study of Baby Boomers; I will begin with the existential problem.

Why Baby Boomers Turned from Religion: Shaping Belief and Belonging, 1945–2021. Abby Day, Oxford University Press. © Abby Day 2022. DOI: 10.1093/oso/9780192866684.003.0010

Meaning and/of Life

Weber's assumption (1922, 117) that all people everywhere are searching for meaning is rarely empirically tested or challenged by scholars who tend to accept that:

> the metaphysical needs of the human mind as it is driven to reflect on ethical and religious questions, driven not by material need but by an inner compulsion to understand the world as a meaningful cosmos and to take up a position toward it.

Religious scholars often take such an assumption and apply it, uncritically, throughout their work. Peter Berger, for example, a sociologist and theologian, wrote that there exists 'a human craving for meaning that appears to have the force of instinct. Men [sic] are congenitally compelled to impose a meaningful order upon reality' (1967, 22). The gendered aspect of 'meaning' has only been occasionally discussed within the sociology of religion (see Woodhead 2001 and Day 2020), particularly with regard to Weber's famous 'iron cage' of rationality, based on his assumptions about participation in the waged 'public sphere', a domain from which women were traditionally excluded. The occupational groups he selected for analysis (Weber 1922, 95–117) were male dominated, sometimes exclusively so: the warriors, artisans, missionaries, and tent-makers, leaving invisible the religious predilections of women in work as domestic labourers, queens, nurses, mothers, teachers, or wives.

Fraser, for example, when we discussed whether he believed there may be a 'meaning to life', said that there may be, 'but I believe that is not religious, but humanistic, the things that binds people together are the principles'.

Marianne Weber, a sociologist who was married to Max Weber, took exception to his insistence that everyone everywhere was in search primarily for a rationalised 'meaning' and that that was the main function of religion. She argued (as cited in Lengermann and Niebrugge-Brantley 1998, 204) that patriarchy allowed men's needs to be satisfied at the expense of women's who were forced to sublimate them. Taking a womanist perspective, she listed these as:

> the embodied practical need for material existence; the embodied sensual need foerotic and sexual gratification; the psychic need for agency, or

self- directed action; the emotional need for intimacy; and the ethical needs for moral autonomy and harmony with others.

Those needs were often mentioned by the women Baby Boomers I interviewed. As I discussed in earlier chapters about women's rights, several female Boomers were outspoken about the benefits of being able to enjoy sex without worry, they were damning about men's need to control, both in religion and secular relationships, and talked about being able to follow their own career paths. When it came to 'meaning' women often talked about their careers and relationships. Stephanie had said that she had 'agonised a lot when I was younger, that if I had stayed an Anglican would I be a better person?' As she got older, she stopped worrying about it.

She described her sense of belonging to her career, her volunteering now that she is retired, and to her friends, most of whom are not 'observant' apart from the Muslim ones. 'Do I mourn not having a faith?' she mused. 'No, not at all. You make your choices and then you live with them.' Those choices included, for her, not having children and not having 'organised religion in my life'.

Following Marianne Weber's ideas, I note that my own preference for participant and non-participant observation, impossible in the pandemic, can help to illuminate and elaborate more of those women's perspectives about their everyday and lived non-religion. Nevertheless, the continued narratives I heard from the Boomers all tended to stress other people as embedded in any sense of meaning or belonging they felt. This somewhat contradicts Thomas Luckmann, a sometime collaborator with Berger, who shared with Berger an assumption that there is something essential and universal that leads humans to religion. Reflecting the Weberian assumption that people are engaged in a search for meaning, Luckmann further asserts that the search for meaning is religious. Again, without evidence, Luckmann (1967, 98–9) argued that people create meanings 'in a relatively autonomous fashion'.

Troubling the meaning of meaning has arisen more frequently in anthropology than in sociology, beginning with Talal Asad (1993) pointing out that formulations about belief were Christian. He disrupted the implicitly Weberian approach to meaning by arguing that it was universalistic and created without showing how, and under what conditions, meanings are constructed. Asad's work radically shifted earlier anthropological understandings based on unproven ideas about meaning and order to one that would become more temporally and spatially situated.

The lack of an empirical record therefore makes it intellectually dubious to claim that any apparent search for meaning may have changed over time. There is no evidence to suggest that people today are less or more in search of meaning than people centuries ago. As I have mentioned earlier, anthropologist Joel Robbins observed that there is a tendency to impute or propose 'meaning' or the lack of it, when it is perhaps the researcher, not the informant, who is seeking it: 'meaninglessness is always something untoward, lobbed in unexpectedly' (2006, 218).

It was therefore a conversation I approached cautiously with the Baby Boomers. I suggested in our interviews that some people might feel that having a 'meaning' to life was important and might receive comfort from that idea. Perhaps, I prompted, a life without religion may be less meaningful? As I found in my longitudinal research (Day 2011, 2103) with three generations, including Baby Boomers, most people disagreed.

I asked Virginia what she thought about meaning, and if she thought it was possible to have meaning without religion. She paused for a moment and then mused, 'Meaning? Not church. Meaning, my life? No. can't say I've spent much time thinking of that, we all go through times, thinking of my purpose, I guess.'

Although Virginia described herself as not religious, and had, like so many Boomers, given up church attendance decades earlier, she continued the conversation by making a distinction between what she believed as a higher power and the idea of meaning; 'I certainly have faith, knowing, I may not be able to articulate it, knowing some things to be true—a higher power, he, she.' On the subject of meaning, however, she added 'No. I never stopped to think about it. I may not think about it, but I can say I do have meaning in my life in relationships and community and a sense of always trying to do better.'

Belonging to like-minded groups, or somehow contributing to a 'community' was a mode of behaving and belonging that many Boomers mentioned, as discussed below. For now, I will note that the kinds of meaning that Virginia mentioned, reluctant as she was to fully apply that term to her life, were relationally embedded, not theological or philosophical.

I therefore have no evidence to support Luckmann's (1967) idea that meaning, such that it may be, is created relatively autonomously. As I have discussed earlier, while most people may say that they are responsible for their own decisions (it would, perhaps, be cavalier to suggest otherwise), they also nest those decisions in practice in relationality.

In his study of Spring Harvest, for example, the largest annual charismatic-evangelical conference in Britain, Rob Warner (2008) showed that the event's format allows individuals to choose how they will experience the festival, but within a strong connection to the wider religious group. He described that process as 'bricolage within boundaries'. As discussed in Chapter 4, Bellah et al.'s (1985) report about one of their research partici-pants, 'Sheila Larson' and her 'own little voice', it would, I suggest, be an unwarranted leap to claim that people who believe in their inner voices or their ideas about meaning are completely self-oriented or individualistic, when they are probably reflexive in a highly socialised way.

Some Boomers gave the idea of 'meaning' rather short shrift. Sam, a retired British architect born in 1948, wanted to know if by 'meaning' I meant the meaning of life. I said not necessarily, and I was interested in what he thought meaning was or could be. He laughed: 'What about the meaning of life...when anyone says they wonder why they are here, I tell them it's because their parents had sex.' Religion was not necessary to provide meaning, he said: 'you have to find your own purpose or meaning'.

The 'Problem' of Meaning

Another relevant interpretation of 'meaning' is Max Weber's analysis of the 'problem' of evil, or the problem of meaning. As discussed in Chapter 6, the problem proposes that it is inconsistent to believe that an all-good, all-powerful god would allow bad things to happen to good people.

I return to this topic now, elaborating on one of the points of discussion raised in Chapter 7 concerning events of the 1960s: the threat of immediate annihilation. Although, as I noted, several Boomers mentioned this, I do not think scholars of religion take as seriously as we should that life-altering psychological impact on childhood. Writing in *Jewish Currents* (https://jewishcurrents.org/baby-boomers-and-the-bomb), Lawrence Bush reflects on this time and expresses surprise that the impact of that event on 'the American psyche' has not been featured within the other waves of nostalgia Boomers display towards their childhoods. He remarked that he found that odd, 'given the enormous nostalgia baby boomers express for the culture of our childhoods':

> Do we not remember those bomb shelter drills, in which we made exodus to the school basement and stood nose-to-scalp, listening to each other's

breathing and envisioning Armageddon for a few minutes only to return to our classrooms and resume our lessons without so much as a discussion of the Bomb's radically disruptive meaning?

Have we forgotten the sense of existential absurdity engendered by the notion that each of us, our families and best friends, might be annihilated due to a political argument, a failed communication, a stupid computer glitch?

As he notes, Baby Boomers were regularly watching the supernatural series, *The Twilight Zone*, which frequently featured episodes about nuclear war. Even as teenagers, Boomers were all familiar with facts about atomic bombs and most would have covered in school the details about how a bomb devastated Hiroshima and would also be up to date with figures showing that the Americans and Soviet had thousands of much bigger bombs available at the touch of a fingertip. He recalled that, as children, Boomers experienced together the same day in 1962 when the Cuban Missile Crisis brought the world to the brink of nuclear war.

He cites Robert J. Lifton (1982) as one of the few scholars who has taken this event and associated traumas seriously. Lifton proposed that a condition he named as 'nuclearism' may describe the effects of such trauma: a sense of increased 'ephemeralism', characterised by doubting permanence and authenticity leading, possibly, to the 'drop-out' attitudes of the 1960s' hippies; a growing desire for fundamentalism exhibited by hardline doctrines about life and community; a move towards transcendence, assisted by psychedelic drugs.

I further suggest that Lifton's discussion of 'nuclear numbing' (1982, 100–10) may also be instructive. He argued that the horror of probable instant annihilation of all that people know and love was simply unimaginable and therefore buried in their psyches. Being, at the time, children and adolescents the effect on their psyches may, arguably, have been formative.

Gertrude S. Goldberg (1984) suggests the effects of such trauma may engender a sense of helplessness because the problem seems too immense to remedy. What is required, she argues, is a sense of urgency that might propel social action. Her hypothesis can explain both of the movements amongst Baby Boomers to either 'drop out' or to actively protest with songs and marches. Indeed, as mentioned in Chapter 7, many Boomers did become involved in organisations such as the Campaign for Nuclear Disarmament (CND). Florence Braithwaite described CND as one of the 'first of the 'new social movements' built around issues like peace, gender, race, sexuality and environmentalism, which exploded from the late-1960s onwards' (2016, 134).

In comparing the horrors of nuclear war to the trauma people experienced in the plague-ridden fourteenth century, Goldberg notes that the current threat is known to be caused by humans, whereas the earlier events were thought to be God-driven: 'Our twentieth-century plague, we may argue, is man-made. Yet, we treat it as if it were inexorable' (1984, 482).[1]

It also became evident that even in those most challenging, life-threatening times, the Boomers I interviewed did not reach to religion for solace or meaning but to their friends and family—dead, as I discussed in the last chapter, or alive.

Pippa Norris and Ronald Inglehart (2004) suggested that pockets of religiosity in different societies can be partly explained by conditions that promote and maintain 'existential insecurity'. While, indeed, it may be common sense to assume that during times of crisis people turn to religion, spirituality, or other grand narratives, my empirical research with Baby Boomers was conducted in 2020 and 2021, during the first phases of the global Covid-19 pandemic. I did not find a shift towards increased religiosity and nor, in comparison, did such a trend appear in wider polling. The UK think tank *Theos* commissioned UK polling company *YouGov* to ask questions probing meaning, religion, and spirituality in May and June 2020 (https://www.theosthinktank.co.uk/comment/2020/08/06/religious-trends-in-a-time-of-international-crisis). In response to the statement, 'I'm searching for a sense of meaning in my life', 32 per cent agreed while a larger proportion, 37 per cent, did not. The largest age group amongst that 37 per cent was the older cohort, aged over 65—the Baby Boomers. They were also most likely to say that the pandemic did not prompt more of a search for meaning than before.[2]

That research reminded me of something one of my interviewees said on the subject of finitude: Stephanie said that since she was about 25, 'I stopped worrying about the hereafter'. Further, she added, 'Meaning has to be discovered, it can't be laid on from above. I don't like people prescribing things for me.'

Wade Clark Roof (2000) conducted research on Baby Boomers as he contended that they are the 'lead generation' who have been responsible for creating the nation's cultural, religious, and political moods. He also argued that the Boomers have been behind the cultural shift away from religion towards other values, some spiritual and others more diffuse, tied to their beliefs and post-materialist values. Those were centred on, for example, the environment, the role of women, holistic orientations, and quality of life. He argued that this trend was found throughout the West, not only the USA, and showed that while people's beliefs were no longer rooted in Christianity, they showed an openness to a range of insights drawn from other religions and metaphysics.

Roof's original research in 1988 (see Carroll, Roof and Roozen, 1995; Roof 1993) included a telephone survey of 1400 randomly selected people born between 1946 and 1962, intensive telephone interviews with 536 (and later follow-up interviews in 1995–96 with 411 of the 536), and face-to-face interviews with about 100 of them. One of his several significant findings relevant here addressed the point being made in this and earlier chapters: 'Approaching the end of the twentieth-century, people are aware that it has been one of the bloodiest of centuries, remembered for wars, global environmental destruction, AIDS, and the Holocaust,[3] and that increasingly, humanity holds within its own hands its destiny' (Roof 2000, 4–5).

Roof argues that the concept of modernity is important as it presumes greater control over life, while also making people more aware of their responsibility for making the right decisions. While Roof detected a growth of 'spiritual quests' amongst his research participants, my own findings stress an awareness of existential questions. His knowledge of the kinds of responsibilities people may feel in an era of 'modernity' may also help to illuminate why it is that Baby Boomers seemed not to have joined traditional organisations such as trade unions. As noted in Chapter 6, Grace Davie argued that church attendance declined at a time when participation in other organisations, such as political parties and trade unions was also diminishing (2002, 18). Taking the idea of 'modernity' further to consider, for example, Shmuel N Eisenstadt's idea of 'multiple modernities' (and see also Danièle Hervieu-Léger 2003) the Baby Boomer experience makes sense as:

the best way to understand the contemporary world—indeed to explain the history of modernity—is to see it as a story of continual constitution and reconstitution of a multiplicity of cultural programs. These ongoing reconstructions of multiple institutional and ideological patterns are carried forward by specific social actors in close connection with social, political, and intellectual activists, and also by social movements pursuing different programs of modernity, holding very different views of what makes societies modern.

Social movements, characterised as fluid, often leaderless, issue-based, orga-nisations fit that generational preference perhaps more than the highly structured, hierarchical, and patriarchal organisations populated by their parents. As Christopher Einolf pointed out in his study, discussed in more detail later here, 'Boomers are less likely to volunteer in traditional associ-ations such as churches and neighborhood groups' (2009, 196).

Perhaps, in conclusion, the Weberian 'problem of meaning' is no longer relevant to increasingly non-religious populations. As non-religious Baby Boomers, and their progeny, do not believe in an all-powerful, all-loving God, there is no reconciliation to make. I will return now to the kinds of non-religious belonging that matter to Boomers.

Duty, Care, and Belonging with Family

Many Boomers told me about their significant family relationships and the acts of care they often performed in wide networks of belonging. As would be expected in an era where divorce was more common than in their parents' generation, the idea of 'family' extended beyond a tightly bound, and static, nuclear family of two parents and 2.5 children. Before attributing an increased divorce rate solely to Baby Boomer behaviour, it is important to note, as described in Chapter 3, that the most significant increase in divorces occurred during the 1940s amongst the Baby Boomer parents' generation. An increasingly acceptable precedent was set (https://www.ons.gov.uk/people populationandcommunity/birthsdeathsandmarriages/divorce/bulletins/divorce sinenglandandwales/2011-12-08).

Baby Boomers often spoke of their family including their parents and sometimes stepparents/partner, grown-up biological children, step-children, and grandchildren. This would be consistent with anthropological under-standings of what constitutes 'family'. As David Schneider (1980) showed, people do not necessarily view their 'kin' in strictly biological terms. Who and what is a family is often more than simply the people one is raised with, but those with whom one has developed strong bonds.

Those bonds included commitments that Boomers make with time, money, and care. The oft-quoted 'bank of Mum and Dad' is real for many Boomers, who often expressed keen awareness that their children's gener-ations, born in the 1970s, '80s, and early '90s, did not enjoy levels of employment and prosperity that Boomers did. I will discuss that in more detail in Chapter 11.

Honouring their father and mothers

While Boomers did not quote the fifth commandment to 'honour thy father and mother', this is what many did, often on a daily basis. Parents of the Boomers are living longer than previous generations, often in poor health. Merril Silverstein and Roseann Giarrusso (2010, 1039) note in an extensive review of the literature on care:

> Improvements in life expectancy have changed the structure of multigenerational families; joint survivorship within and across generations has resulted in extended periods of support exchanges (including caregiving) and affective connections over the life span.

In other words, Baby Boomers shoulder more caring responsibilities for their parents than their parents did for theirs, mainly because older, and sometimes increasingly frail, people are living longer. Baby Boomers also, as Silverstein and Giarrusso note (2010), often simultaneously occupy several different roles within wider family networks, as spouse, sibling, as a child themselves of an older parent, as a parent to an adult child, and as a grandparent. This multiple locatedness demands considerable emotion, physical, and intellectual agility.

An example of that agility is the experience of Charlotte who visited her dying aunt's bedside frequently. Her aunt's Bible lay on a table beside her— 'As an evangelical woman she was never without her bible,' Charlotte said— and she felt moved to read some of her aunt's favourite passages to her. Her rational mind said she shouldn't bother, Charlotte told me, as those words 'meant nothing', but her 'emotional brain said that the words would mean something to my aunt, and my emotional brain won', and so Charlotte sat beside her aunt during her last hours and read to her the Lord's Prayer and Psalm 23 ('The Lord is my shepherd') because she knew it would comfort her.

The Boomers' duties to parents included physically looking after those unable to care for themselves, sometimes in their parents' homes and sometimes by visiting them in care facilities, for which the Boomers often need to pay.

Another means of care was the extent to which the Boomers performed religious actions to please their parents, perhaps helping to explain the sometimes-anomalous facts that even non-religious Boomers got married in churches and had their own children baptised, despite their lack of religiosity, commitment, or religious behaviour. Jay, for example, married a woman whose father was a Church of England vicar and felt strongly that they should be married in a church. Jay said they even had to attend several pre-marital sessions with the officiating minister. To please the parents, he explained, they went along with this, but never attended church thereafter. Terry supplied a similar story, saying that he had been married twice in his life, and the first time was in a church. This wasn't because his wife was religious, he explained, but because his mother 'wanted a traditional wedding'. Some non-religious boomers also had their children christened for much the same reason: I will return to this in more detail in Chapter 11.

Duties of care for grandchildren

Fran, for example, told me that she looks after her granddaughter three days per week. It is 'an economic necessity,' she said, as well as a pleasure. Her labour not only helps her children in their roles as working parents but also fuels the economy, she explained. Indeed, the unpaid, informal labour of Baby Boomer child carers is rarely acknowledged as an essential part of the market economy.

The high cost of childcare has meant that parents who are employed outside the home increasingly rely on their Baby Boomer parents for childcare help. Surveys show that on average 85 per cent of UK families rely on grandparents to look after children. Baby Boomers spend on average 10 hours per week on childcare, and more in school holidays, ranging from looking after children at home, to picking them up from school and taking them to and from extra-curricular activities. The saving in childcare costs may be up to £2.2 billion per year (see, for example, https://www.themoneypages. com/household-bills/grandparents-save-working-families-22-5b-childcare-costs/ https://www.earlyyearscareers.com/eyc/latest-news/grandparents-help-look-children-reduce-childcare-costs/https://www.independent.co.uk/life-style/health-and-families/grandparents-childcare-costs-save-money-families-a963 7926.html).

Belonging to Communities: 'All Shapes and Sizes'

I asked Boomers in interviews to reflect on the idea that some people suggest religion is necessary to create and sustain 'community', and I wanted to know the extent to which they would agree with that notion, and what, if any, activities in groups or associations they might have. This was intended to probe associational and relational kinds of belonging, particularly given alternative theories (see, for example, Beck and Beck-Gersheim 2002) that argue people today are increasingly individualistic. The term 'community' is highly contested in disciplines such as anthropology and human geography, perhaps because of their place-based methodological and epistemological histories. Its potential for diverse interpretations remains relatively untouched in the area of religious studies or sociology of religion.

The Boomers I interviewed took exception to the idea that religion was necessary for 'community', whatever that might mean. Virginia, for example, said 'community can come in all shapes and sizes, with various levels of connection and empathy'. She would be supported here by those scholars, primarily from geography and anthropology, who have grappled with that term. As discussed in my earlier work with geographer Ben Rogaly (Day and Rogaly 2014), ideas of community have shifted from place-based 'community studies' common in the mid-twentieth century to an understanding of social relationships and symbolic identities. We noted (Day and Rogaly 2014, 76–7) that 94 different definitions of community were identified by George Hillery who observed that it largely 'consists of persons in social interaction within a geographic area and having one or more additional common ties' (1955, 111). Marilyn Stacey (1969) critiqued 'community studies' as myth, perpetuating the idea that cultures and places were cohesive and bounded when, she argued, people's associations would be better studied as processes or movements.

In relation specifically to religion we further noted (Day and Rogaly 2014, 77–8) that the dominant discourse of 'faith community' may, as Adam Dinham (2011) pointed out, be used to mean something that is either cohesive or fragmentary tool, depending on who is defining it and for what purpose.

The word community often serves to mask conflict and diversity. 'The discourse of faith community can therefore be used to further the interests of people for religious and non-religious purposes. Sometimes, "community" can work to obscure structural inequalities' (Day and Rogaly 2014, 77). We drew on Gerd Baumann's (1996) study of Southall in London where he analysed how communities becoming defined as being composed of an apparently stable 'ethnic' culture entrenches ethnic identities and in so doing reduces all other social complexities. Following Baumann, I suggest that 'community' also serves to 'other' people who one group decides do not, and should not, belong. As Baumann pointed out, we may hear people being described as members of a Muslim 'community'; but why are people never described as members of a Jehovah's Witnesses community? Baumann argued that of the many possibilities available to it, any dominant discourse will choose to ascribe to a 'community' whatever socio-demographic characteristic seems most important in a particular social context. While this may, and often does, draw on a dominant discourse of cultures being, as Paul Gilroy argued, 'supposedly sealed from one another by ethnic lines' (1987, 55), there may also be, I suggest, imposed categories of religion, of non-religion, or of gender, age, sexuality, skin colour, or social class.

Returning to my conversation with Virginia, I note that the several 'communities' to which she belonged included diverse contexts, from work associations to a journaling group she had joined to help with her grief following the death of her husband. She, like the non-religious middle-class man quoted in research on non-religious identities (Cheruvallil-Contractor et al. 2021, 340) would not accept being non-religious had to mean being non-involved in communities: 'I think, somehow, a big, big assumption is made that you don't contribute to the local community unless you are religious. It is more annoying than necessarily discrimination.'

Indeed, the lines between religious and non-religious communities may be blurred for some. I was surprised, for example, to hear from one of my interviewees, Roger, that he is an active member of his church's handbell group despite being an atheist and never attending church. As well as helping to instigate the revival of early music, as discussed in Chapter 8, Boomers were key proponents of the largely secular, handbell music revival of the 1960s. Even before then, handbell ringing was periodically seen as a non-religious activity. According to a history of handbell ringing written by a Lincolnshire handbell ringing guild (https://www.ldgcb.org.uk/history/), bellringing has been a secular pursuit since the time of Queen Elizabeth I: 'From this time on bellringing became a secular sport, with very little connection with the building in which bells were hung. Probably the survival of bellringing was actually because it was regarded as a secular sport.' There was an attempt by churches in the 1800s to incorporate handbells with the services, but that practice had diminished by the beginning of the twentieth century. A revival occurred in the 1960s, accompanied by residential courses. Although there is no literature on the reasons for the handbell ringing revival, the repeated words of 'traditional' and 'authentic' on their web pages suggest that the revival's timing coincided with a cultural turn in the 1960s to both new and apparently authentic historic musical forms: previous discussions of early music and folk music revivals may resonate here.

Humanist and Atheist 'Community': 'Like-Minded People'

As I discussed in Chapter 5, Paul had described his way of thinking as 'humanist'. Many Baby Boomers did not adopt any specific terminology to define themselves, whereas others said clearly that they would use words like humanist, atheist, or secular to describe their way of believing and also of belonging and behaving. Paul, for example, said he had joined the UK national society, Humanists UK when he first heard about them and felt an impulse to belong to an association with, as he described it, fellow 'like-minded people' where others felt like he did about himself and the wider world. He did not get involved in their activities, he told me, but contributed to them financially through his member subscription, and read their regular newsletter. Like many Boomers I interviewed, he was concerned, for example, about the role of religion in public life, and wanted to support campaigns to reduce that:

> [T]o say the UK is a Christian country is wrong—it's old-fashioned, a harking back to some earlier times. That we have Bishops in the House of Lords is ridiculous, particularly as they are all from the Church of England. What about Methodists? Catholics?

Anthropologist Matthew Engelke joined the Humanists UK (then known as the British Humanist Association) and trained to be a celebrant in order to learn more about them. He regularly observed one gathering of members in particular, which he called the Thames Path Humanists, composed mainly of the same age group represented in most of the organisation: people in their 50s, 60s, and 70s; in other words, although he did not used the term to describe them, 'Baby Boomers'. The people who join are not always the hardened, intellectual atheists epitomised by, for example, Richard Dawkins. Engelke (2015, 298) observed that 'Humanism is embodied; humanism is incorporated' aspects that are often ignored in wider public discourse. The humanists he studied enjoyed their coffee morning, helping out at a local soup kitchen, and even their Christmas party. They also sometimes participated in ritual activities with a trained specialist, for example marking marriages, births, and deaths. He suggested that 'the humanists do not want belief, but they do want belonging; they do want the sense of community'. While I agree with Engelke that the humanists I interviewed did not want religious beliefs, they sometime hold non-religious beliefs; as Ben said: 'Atheist means without God which is a negative linguistic statement whereas Humanist is an ethical approach to life, it's active, positive identification with a belief system or value system.'

Engelke found that local humanist groups 'are doing the kinds of things that religious groups have traditionally done' such as paying social visits to elderly members in their homes, volunteering for local charities and participating in 'community fairs and civic life' (2015, 80). As the members explained to him, they involve themselves in such activities because it 'fosters happiness and well-being. God has nothing to do with it' (and see also Greg Epstein 2009 about how secular humanists support each other and other groups).

Some of the Baby Boomers in my study joined such organisations because they wanted to campaign against the intrusion of religion in public life, while others joined because they wanted to read the newsletter and feel like they were engaging with like-minded people. Annabel, for example, explained that she and her husband both joined a humanist group because they 'thought people of no religion should have political clout' and they did not like the way government seemed to 'fall over themselves to appease religion'. Plus, she added, 'it was also quite nice to say what I was rather than what I wasn't'.

Several who identified themselves as humanists spoke strongly about the place of religion, rather than its content. Philip, for example, said he often enjoyed talking to 'vicars' he might encounter on his walks or in the park with his dog. He told me this because he was trying to make the point, he said, that he does not 'mind people being religious, but I don't think they should have special privileges' any more than someone who, for example, supports a football team, attending matches, and wearing their t-shirts, or he himself who plays bridge.

Several Boomers mentioned that they were shocked when Donald Trump got elected, especially when they realised that so much of his support came from Evangelical Christians. Most were mystified that people with apparently high moral standards would support someone as outwardly immoral, at least when it came to sexual impropriety and, arguably, other issues such as equal rights. One Boomer remarked that 'Trumpism is a new religion, with the evangelicals' and, he said, 'Evangelical Christians were not well educated but were predisposed to believe anything they're told. They are mentally vulnerable, religion has something to do with that.'

As I have discussed in earlier work (Day 2020, 26–8), Trump benefited in his campaigns for presidency by the way in which he engaged evangelical, fundamentalist Christians. Surveys show that he has been supported by nearly 90 per cent of those who self-identify as Evangelical Christians. It was not, I argued, 'his character as a moral, god- fearing Christian that was important in this case, but his ability to wield power in the right direction' (Day 2020, 27). Trump promised, and largely delivered, a tough stance on abortion and greater backing of Israel, for example.

The place of religion is particularly complicated in the UK. As discussed in more detail, (Day 2020, 57–74), the UK is one of only two countries in the world with the practice of reserving places for religious leaders in government (the other is Iran). The Lords Spiritual, as the 26 bishops in the House of Lords are known, represent only 3 per cent of the Lords' total composition, but their influence has been felt on a wide range of issues, such as opposing same-sex marriage. This influence appears to be part of a larger pattern to which many humanists object because the Church of England enjoys 'more institutional opportunities than other religious bodies to shape the cultural landscape of the nation' (Guest et al. 2012, 68).

Philip said he had been involved in related campaigns conducted by Humanists UK to remove Bishops from the House of Lords: 'They shouldn't be there. The majority of people in the country are not religious.' Others spoke up against Bishops being in the House of Lords, saying this was an example of a larger, misplaced example of influence with the church being so close to the state.

Another place of contention is religion's role in education. There is a long history of religion being interwoven with education in the UK, and to some extent in Canada, but some Baby Boomer humanists object strongly to that. Roger said he did not get involved in humanist activities, but he did sometimes contribute financially to their campaigns, 'like religion in schools—I'm not keen on that'.

The UK's 1944 Education Act allowed for the provision of state funding to Christian schools. This was extended in the 1990s to a wider selection, including Jewish, Muslim, and Sikh schools (Flint 2009, 164). At the time of writing there were 7000 (including independent Church of England and Church of Wales) religious schools, providing education to a quarter of primary school pupils and 6 per cent of secondary schools.

Communities of Care: 'Working for the Benefit of Society'

Boomers discussed various ways in which they devoted voluntary labour to non-religious organisations they believed in. An everyday visible form of such participation can be seen on high streets throughout Britain and widely on main streets and shopping centres in other countries, such as Canada. Charity shops are those retail outlets run by a charity where people donate and purchase secondhand goods. These are often known, in Canada and the USA, as 'thrift shops'. Familiar names in the UK and Canada will be, for example, The British Red Cross, Oxfam, Goodwill Industries, and Value Village. Any visitor to such shops will likely notice what appears to be the disproportionate numbers of volunteers who are women and well over 60. That is not a skewed observation: research shows that women of this age, equivalent to the 'Baby Boomer' cohort, form the largest single largest group (see, for example, Harrison-Evans 2016).

Further, the number of people volunteering is growing, contra to predictions by, for example, Robert Putnam (2000) that as religious participation declines, so will wider forms of voluntary labour. For example, Christopher Einolf (2009) sought to test the Putnam thesis that religion is linked to social capital and therefore when religion declines, so will the associated social capital activities, such as volunteering. He analysed data from 1995 and 2005 waves of the *Midlife in the United States* panel study to assess the level of Baby Boomer volunteering compared to earlier cohorts and found no support for Putnam's theory. On the contrary, he found that Baby Boomers volunteered more than previous generations and that, given past volunteering behaviour is a good predictor of future volunteering behaviour, there is no reason to think this will diminish in future. He concluded that 'the future increase in elderly volunteers may be so large that non-profits might not have to devote special efforts to recruiting them. In fact, the large size of the baby boom cohort and the increasing proportion of elderly who volunteer may create a situation in which organizations have more volunteers than they are able to manage' (Einolf 2009, 197).[4]

Research conducted by the UK think tank *Demos*, written up by Peter Harrison-Evans (2016), found that in 2017 there were an estimated 220,000 volunteers working in the sector. They used both quantitative and qualitative techniques, including quantitative surveys of the public, charity shop managers and volunteers. These included commissioning a nationally representative survey of 2000 British citizens, a survey of more than 650 people working in charity shops and interviews with staff, managers, and volunteers. They examined several demographics related to age, gender, religion, and ethnicity with reference to those who donated, shopped, or volunteered in the charity shops. The effect of religion was notable only when examining data about the donors: people of non-Christian religions, particularly Muslims, are more likely to donate than Christians. Of those who volunteered in 2015, 39 per cent were over 65, and 79 per cent were women. The researchers did not find that religion was a statistically significant variable. When it came to reasons people volunteered in charity shops, researchers pointed out that the motivations were polarised according to age: younger people were hoping to acquire skills and experience, often in period of unemployment or transition from full-time education, whereas older people, who were often retired or working part-time, wanted to feel a sense of belonging, social contact, and a sense they were contributing to their chosen charity. This finding mirrored what Rosie Jones and Frances Reynolds (2019) discovered in their research into ageing: volunteering in charity shops gave older people, particularly those in periods of transition related to, for example, bereavement or retirement, benefits of structure, belonging, and agency.

Penny, a retired Canadian teacher born in 1957, told me said she felt she was 'working for benefit of society' through her volunteering: 'Working in the community is driven by my commitment to society and humanity in general, not to do with church,' she said. Pam also emphasised the non-religious nature of her voluntary labour, in her case with the Girl Guides. She said her activity as an adult began when she moved house to a new location and wanted to make friends as well as contribute to a worthwhile organisation. As I discussed in Chapter 3, she was strongly opposed to the then religious-based 'promise' in the Girl Guides.

As Roof noted above, sites of volunteer labour include social welfare and environmentalism. Following two chance encounters in two separate countries with people engaged in practices of sea turtle conservation, religious studies scholar Lori Beaman decided to look in depth at that activity in order to explore forms of non-religious practice. She focused on sea turtle rescue efforts in Cape Cod, where young turtles are often washed ashore and need help (Beaman 2017, 10). She set out to explore people's motivations to rescue sea turtles, the ways in which the 'sea turtle rescuers understand their place in the world and in the environment in which they live', the location of their activities in, perhaps, ideas of transcendence and immanence, and the language they might use.

Beaman (2017, 20) focuses on one person she interviewed, Ann, a Baby Boomer who seemed to be emblematic for others in her study:

> During the process of our conversation Ann revealed herself as 'not a church goer . . . I broke with the church that I was raised in,' that 'I do believe I have a soul,' and 'I do believe in spiritual elements, and I definitely feel it with these animals—with the turtles I definitely feel it.' She located all living beings on a similar plane.

Beaman emphasises that Ann, like others she interviewed, was involved in 'world repairing work' (2017, 21). They were not 'seekers', or 'individualistic'. Of the 21 people she interviewed, only four practised religion, although most of the others, like my sample in this volume, had experienced religion somewhere in their early lives. Many had lived through the 1960s, a significant period, she notes, for environmental consciousness. It was an era when human relationships with nature and animals became highlighted and, to a large extent, reconfigured. It was not, she wrote, only a decade of student upheaval and political protests (and see Chapter 7 in this volume) but it was also a period marked by environmental disasters such as a massive oil spill off the coast of England, intensive logging in India, and the emerging realisation, mainly through Rachel Carson's work (1961, 1962) of the dangers of pollutants and insecticides.

In summary, as I have discussed in this chapter, non-religious Baby Boomers seek belonging in non-religious ways and behave accordingly. While religious scholars may argue that 'meaning' is an essential driver of humanity, the Baby Boomers studied here located meaning in deeply embedded relationships and as noted earlier, because they do not believe in an all-loving, powerful god, the Weberian 'problem of meaning' is of no consequence. Even when faced with, arguably, the century's most chilling worldwide threat of nuclear war, Boomers turned to each other rather than to a god. Their actions of duty occurred in a variety of contexts, notably family, charitable organisations, and environmental work.

It may be analytically helpful to summarise the difference between those who seek meaning from religion and those who do not as a distinction between those who orient themselves—their identities, beliefs, and practices—towards other people and those who orient themselves towards a god. As proposed in my earlier longitudinal work on belief and belonging (Day 2011, 2013), the former group can be termed as 'anthropocentric' and the second as 'theocentric'. Most people involved in my earlier longitudinal

and the Baby Boomers here 'believe in'—meaning have faith in—the relationships in which they belong, specifically those who were important to
them and with whom they have adherent, affective reciprocal relationship:
partners, family, and friends.

Further, many Boomers resist the more vocal growth of religion in the
public sphere, and some joined campaigning humanist organisations as a
result. Indeed, as Cimino and Smith suggested, '*Something* [italics theirs]
happened in American society in the last three decades that mobilized
nonbelievers into action, and we believe that something is the increasing
public—often political—presence of religion' (2014, 3).

These orientations and modes of belief, behaviour, and belonging had a
formative impact on the next generation, as I will turn to now in Chapter 11.

Notes

1. See also Sibylle K. Escalona 1982 and Barbara Tuchman 1978.
2. 7 De Graaf and Grotenhuis (2008, 595) noted a similar, perhaps counter-intuitive,
   finding. As the welfare state in the Netherlands shrunk and people became less
   protected by social security: 'Interestingly, and in contrast to Norris and
   Inglehart's prediction, secularization is still going on.'
3. Studies of Judaism indicate that many Jews turned from God after the Holocaust
   because they could no longer tolerate the idea of an all-powerful god who allowed
   that genocide. I use the term 'Holocaust' to cover the period from 1935, when the
   Nuremburg laws stripped German Jews of all their rights until 1945, when the war
   ended and concentration camps were liberated.
4. That general trend may be at least temporarily disrupted due to restrictions and
   health concerns imposed during the global Covid-19 pandemic when older people
   were encouraged to remain indoors (https://www.theconversation.com/older-
   volunteers-are-being-pushed-out-of-charity-shops-thanks-to-the-pandemic-152347).

11

The Next Generations

Raising the 'Nones'

Introduction

The category of 'no religion' has displaced Christianity as the largest religious category in the UK and other countries are not far behind. The surge is powered primarily by the generations following the Baby Boomers: Generation X, Millennials, and Generation Z. Baby Boomers are the parents and grandparents of these younger, less religious generations, and therefore are at least partly responsible for their upbringing and turn away from religion. The trend is, as I have argued throughout this book, generational and therefore possible to predict. In the Netherlands, for example, De Graaf and Grotenhuis (2008, 595–6) concluded that religious belief will continue to decline, mainly due to generational factors.

The impact of the Baby Boomer effect can be discerned partly by its timing. As corroborated by surveys both in the UK and elsewhere, the decline was dramatic. In Canada, for example, the decline in mainstream Christianity is occurring because members of the mainstream denominations are ageing and not being replaced by younger generations. In the USA, one-quarter of the population now identifies as not religious. Between the 2001 and 2011 UK censuses, the number of people who said they had no religion nearly doubled, mostly accounted for by younger people.

The reasons for the decline, I have argued here and elsewhere (Day 2020, 2011) cannot be attributed to personal loss of faith amongst young people. Like their parents, these younger generations never had faith to lose (and see also Callum Brown's 2015 detailed oral history of ex-Anglicans). As Linda Woodhead notes from her analysis of the British Social Attitudes survey: 'children brought up Christian have a 45 per cent chance of ending up as "nones", whereas those brought up "no religion" have a 95 per cent probability of retaining that identification' (2016, 249).

This chapter explores the kinds of values the Boomers say they transmitted to their children. I move away from the subtraction story of 'nones' to an

Why Baby Boomers Turned from Religion: Shaping Belief and Belonging, 1945–2021. Abby Day,
Oxford University Press. © Abby Day 2022. DOI: 10.1093/oso/9780192866684.003.0011

addition narrative, exploring the stories of the Baby Boomers I interviewed, and stories found in other research to understand more about how Baby Boomers transformed belief and belonging for, arguably, generations to come.

Breaking the Chain of Memory

As Boomers rejected practices of church attendance and religious beliefs, they were, I suggest, following Danièle Hervieu-Léger (2000) in actively breaking the 'chain of memory' that perpetuates religion. Hervieu-Léger argued that a function of religion is to preserve associated memories and traditions that help bind people to the religion and then, by transmitting the memories, ensures its continuation. As I have detailed in this book, the Baby Boomers I interviewed were quick to cease attending church post-confirmation, in common with many other young Anglicans of their generation. They never returned and did not, in common with their childhood experience, practise anything religious at home. It was into that religious vacuum that their children were born.

Some of the non-religious Generation X and Millennial young people participated in a global, but short-lived, movement known as the Sunday Assembly which, as Josh Bullock (2018) showed, partly replicated the format of a Sunday morning Christian church service. He suggests that Hervieu-Léger's concept of a chain of memory is useful here to interpret the Sunday Assembly movement as part of the transition to a post-Christian society.

One Baby Boomer I interviewed talked explicitly about how children need to be raised in religion in order to be religious. Philip said he thinks Christianity, at least in the Global North, has been declining because parents stopped taking young people to church, and they in turn have not been taking their children. Religion, he said, 'has to be impressed on someone very early'. He has two sons and although they were both christened, he said they were not raised to be religious. Nevertheless, there seems to be a fondness in the family for their local church: both sons were married there and Philip, who describes himself as non-religious, said he usually attends church on Christmas Day.

As an example of how difficult it would be to repair the chain of memory once broken, Nicola told me about the negative effect of sudden exposure to church. She said her children were never baptised: 'we had a celebration at home'. She did not attend church with her children, which was probably one reason her daughter became frightened at a church on a school trip when she was six. A year later her daughter went to a Christingle service (a church event when people carry oranges, representing the world, with a candle at its centre) and 'didn't make the whole thing—she was so unnerved'.

Sally mentioned a similar event with her daughter. She had never been to church and yet one day expressed interest in attending. Sally respected her decision and took her to a church service. After the first time, her daughter said she did not want to go back. I suggest this demonstrates the necessity of being to some extent indoctrinated early into religious habits and sentiments; otherwise, such events may seem strange and even, to a child, spooky.

Viv said her children were christened, but not because of any 'religious feeling': 'it was just a big party with their godparents'. Despite not attending church, Viv said she 'went to great lengths' to have her children enrolled in church activities, such as Brownies and Guides. As a requirement, she had to attest that she believed in God: 'I went along with it', she said, explaining that as she did not believe it, and he did not exist, then it did not matter. Other than for those activities, the children did not attend church, she explained, and her grown-up children are still not religious.

Those experiences are understandable in the context of definitions of religion that stress the importance of socialisation. While the Boomers' parents at least ensured that their offspring attended Sunday school and confirmation, the Boomers were in no position to act in a similar way. There was, for them, no familiar church to attend and bring their children. As they had ceased church attendance in their own teens, by the time they were adults and parents, church attendance was a distant, usually insignificant, and often unpleasant memory.

However, they shared accounts of performing a religious practice that demonstrated in my view one of their most important values—care for their family. George, for example, described getting married in a registry office but then having a church 'blessing; to please the parents'. He went along with it because, he said with a shrug: 'all I had to do was say yes'. Later, when his sons were born, they were baptised due to 'peer pressure from family'. He did not believe in the ritual as a religiously important moment for him 'but we had a good party'. Acknowledging the needs of his Catholic partner's parents was what prompted Peter to allow his daughter to be christened in the Catholic church and to go to a Catholic school, even though he was an atheist. Jay, discussed in Chapter 10, said he was fairly sure his children had been baptised but could not recall the detail. Jay had married a woman whose father was a Church of England vicar and yet his own children did not attend church because they 'hadn't shown the slightest bit of interest'. Their grandmother, he said, 'thought that was terrible'.

Sherry described having her children christened because of pressure from her husband's family. Her Millennial children now have children themselves, 'and didn't get them Christened,' she said.

Terry also described choosing a religious wedding although he was not religious. He had been married twice in his life, and the first time was in a church because his mother 'wanted a traditional wedding'. However, his children were not baptised and were not religious. He explained that he and his wife felt if their children wanted to embrace religion they would do so as they are adults, but they did not.

Family pressure sometimes had negative consequences. Annabel said that she had her child baptised because her mother and sister were exerting 'silent disapproval' when she said that she did not want this to happen. Annabel succumbed to the pressure but later resented it so much she became angry and never attended any kind of church service again. When we were discussing her adult son being non-religious, I asked her if his children had been christened: 'No! absolutely not!' she exclaimed, hinting at an antipathy that may have been carried across the generations. Lesley also reported a sense of conflict through giving into parental pressure. She 'compromised' by getting married in a church and having her children baptised. An exception amongst the Baby Boomers I interviewed, her son, but not her daughter, began attending church in his twenties.

Ben was one who specifically raised the difficult, but to him non-negotiable, experience of refusing to have his daughter baptised, much to his mother's chagrin. 'My mother got really annoyed about that,' he said, but he did not give in: 'I'm very much the pussycat on most things, but on that I stood my ground.'

Bruce reported more familial strife than compromise with family relations. His daughter was baptised 'against my will' but it was something his wife had wanted as she was starting to attend a church. His 'wife won', he said and took their daughter to church as a child. He and his wife divorced when the daughter was still young and his daughter stopped attending church by the time she entered high school, and never resumed.

Alice recounted a disturbing story of succumbing to familial pressure out of fear. The church, she said, 'just want people in the church to marry and produce more little church attenders'. She had three sons and they were all christened because their father was religious. She attended church with the children and their father because she thought 'that wouldn't do them any harm, but I also thought I couldn't stop'. Her then husband 'was an unpleasant man. He might have beaten me up.' Her sons did not feel religious but sang in the choir 'for the pocket money for weddings. They got paid! They couldn't actually sing, but just stood there opening their mouths, looking angelic.'

A lingering sense of wider social pressure, beyond family, convinced some Boomers to have their children christened, although this concession did not last long enough to lead to church attendance. Roger said his children were born in Liverpool during the 1970s at a time when it was 'the norm even then to have the children baptised'. He and his wife took the children to church for a short time possibly, he said, because they thought they should be exposed to some 'religious indoctrination', but they never insisted the children go to church. They left Liverpool in 1980 and the family never returned to church. His adult daughters have children, who have neither been baptised nor attended church.

Charlotte said both her children were christened for much the same reason: 'We didn't even think about it, it's just what you did.' Apart from the christening, however, she did not involve her children in religion and never attended church herself. Her children have remained non-religious.

Helen reported a similar experience. She and her husband did not raise their children to be religious, although they were christened because 'that's what you did then'. Her children did not become religious as they got older and have not christened their own children. Later in her life, she was divorced and remarried. Her stepchildren were not raised to be religious, she said, and are not religious now and did not christen their children.

Eleanor said when she remarried, her stepchildren were christened because 'that's what you did then' but were otherwise raised as non-religious. Their children have not been raised with religion either, she added.

Sometimes, Boomers had their children christened for more pragmatic reasons. Joan, for example, had her two girls christened because she wanted them to attend the local church school, and proof of baptism was a condition of entry.[1] When the children grew older and no longer attended the church school, they stopped going to church entirely and have not taken their own children.

Wendy told me that she 'married young', at 18, in a registry office not in a church. When she had children, despite parental pressure she 'refused to have them baptised'. Although they never attended church, this was not a problem at the local Church of England primary school. The school head-master said to her at the time: 'We don't mind if your children aren't religious, as long as you don't mind if we are.' Wendy laughed, recalling how her child was confused about some religious ideas: at the age of four her daughter asked her 'if god made the world what was he standing on at the time?' Her daughter went on to take religious education at A-level and did well, said Wendy, but she added, as if to confirm that this was not a religious experience, 'that was when RE was more about philosophy and ethics'.

Not all the Baby Boomer parents I interviewed were supportive of church schools. Charles said that when his son was born in 1980, he was not christened. Charles was an atheist and his wife an agnostic:

[I]t never occurred to us to have him christened and we were absolutely clear we didn't want him to go to religious primary school. The one close by was CofE, but we didn't send him. It's one of the things I feel most strongly about. I don't think religious organisations should have any involvement in the upbringing of children.[2]

Laura said she never took her children to church, 'wanting them to make up their own minds'. She said she was pleased that, in her daughter's case, she 'dodged going to the CofE school' because there was another, local alternative.

The above examples give texture to the theoretical work of Hervieu-Leger, adding weight to her argument that reinforcement of religious tradition and memory is critical to its continuation. They also corroborate the data introduced here by Woodhead: if children are raised by non-religious parents, they are likely to remain non-religious. Further, the examples echo the evidence and argument provided earlier in this book, particularly in Chapters 2 and 3, that in most cases the Boomers did not have a religion to lose, let alone to transmit.

The discussion so far has centred on the importance of practice, particularly regular church attendance; I will next explore the kinds of non-religious beliefs and values Boomer parents transmitted to their children.

Non-Religious Belief Transmission: 'Treat People as You Would Wish To Be Treated Yourself, with Respect'

As I discussed in my earlier, longitudinal qualitative research (Day 2011, 2013), having 'no religion' is not the same thing as being an atheist, and being an atheist includes more than just disbelief in God. As I mentioned at the beginning of this chapter, there is a richness to non-religious beliefs, values, and morals that is often under-estimated by scholars bemoaning the decline of Christianity. Charles Taylor (2007, 488) correctly, I suggest, observed that churches and the Christian Right moral majority movement align to reconnect America with theism: 'For all these groups, the idea remains strong that there is a link between Christian faith and civilizational order.' The Baby Boomers I interviewed would likely agree that such an alliance exists, while disagreeing that Christianity is an ordering force for 'civilization'. Most of them refuse Christianity on the grounds that it is, in their view, deeply immoral, patriarchal, and intolerant of other faiths and beliefs.

Their beliefs and morals tend to cluster around faith in equality, human rights, and authenticity. As I discussed in Chapter 10, the Boomers I interviewed also expressed strong beliefs in maintaining bonds, particularly for their children. Those bonds included commitments that Boomers make with time, money, and care. The oft-quoted 'bank of Mum and Dad' is real for many Boomers, who often expressed keen awareness that their children's generations, born in the 1970s, '80s, and early '90s, did not enjoy levels of employment and prosperity that Boomers did.

Taylor (2007, 299) was partly correct in his description that the latter half of the twentieth century has been characterised by 'a generalised culture of "authenticity" or expressive individualism, in which people are encouraged to find their own way, discover their own fulfilment, "do their own thing"'. As I have argued throughout this book, Baby Boomers are relational and committed to their family and friends, and while they told me about their values that would, indeed, mirror such terms as 'authentic', they did not convey a commitment to leading insular, self-centred lives.

As I suggested in earlier chapters, particularly Chapter 3 when I discussed parental ambivalence, this invocation to 'make up their own minds' seems to apply only to discussions about church attendance after confirmation. By all accounts from my own research, and in comparison to others, I do not see a general turn to anarchy where households descended into a constant chaos of everyone individually 'doing their own thing' (see also Wilson 2001). As I discussed primarily in Chapter 3, the parents of the Baby Boomers may have been ambivalent towards church and therefore found it difficult to coerce their children into regular attendance.

There was, nevertheless, arguably a wider societal turn towards postmodernity where taken-for-granted certainties and a strong adherence to 'tradition' were diminishing. It is, however, essential to point out that 'tradition' is not a neutral concept. As Martha Nussbaum (1999, 29) importantly discussed, the idea of 'tradition' often masks a universalised masculine authority:

> Depressingly, many traditions portray women as less important than men, less deserving of basic life support or of fundamental rights that are strongly correlated with quality of life, such as the right to work and the right to political participation. Sometimes, ... the women themselves resist these traditions. Sometimes, on the other hand, the traditions have become so deeply internalized that they seem to record what is 'right' and 'natural,' and women themselves endorse their own second-class status.

An apparent aversion to 'tradition' and 'authority' therefore needs to be appreciated as complex. I reported (Day 2011, 83) on the conversation with a Millennial (aged 15 when I interviewed him), who:

> often cited people whom he respected as authorities in the field and credited his school for his knowledge about history and his father as political inspiration. Like many young people, he would not respect authority for its own sake, particularly if perceived as authoritarian.

He also thought it was a mistake to look back to past decades or centuries as more moral or preferable than those today. He told me that (Day 2011, 133):

> in this country I think it's less than one per cent of people go to church every week, but we've got less crime, we don't have 12-year-old prostitutes like we did a couple of hundred years ago, we don't have the same sort of immorality as then and yet religion has declined.

Researching Millennials when they were teenagers and young adults, I found (Day 2011, 83) that they were articulate about what kind of authority and tradition was worth their respect. They honoured important relationships in which they believe and have faith:

> They are characterized by feelings of love, affection, trust, and protection gained from and given to certain people. Those are the people in whom they believe, and to whom they belong, often in a post-nuclear family, where the structures are flexible and the boundaries shift, defined and

maintained by the members' conceptions of who legitimately belongs, or not.

Those relationships, I found, included siblings, stepsiblings, grandparents, teachers at school, and friends. I also found that those Millennials expressed belief in the same sorts of moral codes as their Baby Boomer parents treating people with respect, not killing or stealing, doing well at school, and getting a job afterwards or continuing to university. What religion scholars such as Charles Taylor and Bryan Wilson seem to conflate is morality, gender, and sexuality. In discussing how secularity increased post-World War II, Taylor said that the US Supreme Court and Canadian Prime Minister Pierre Trudeau revoked criminality of homosexuality saying, 'the state has no business in the bedrooms of the nation' (2007, 485). He then cites legalisation of 'abortion, divorce reform, authorization of pornographic films, and so on' suggesting that 'the heart of this revolution lies in sexual mores' which mainly happened in 'the 60s for general classes though earlier for elites' and had an impact on churches which had always, he said, emphasised a strict moral code. As I have discussed in earlier chapters, the Baby Boomers I interviewed do not conflate sexuality with morality and were highly critical of the church's values and ethics, particularly those assuming a masculine authority and an inward gazing 'community'.

While some scholars have expressed concern that a less religious world would be a less moral world, non-religious Baby Boomers are satisfied that they have transmitted the right core values to their children. In discussing the kinds of values embraced by the Baby Boomers who came of age in the 1960s, Varon et al. (2008, 6) wrote:

> Richard Flacks, a co-founder of Students for a Democratic Society and later a scholar of social movements, wrote in the 1980s that, 'the great personal hope of the Sixties was that one would be able to live a life of ongoing self-examination, a life of scrutinizing the social content of one's actions, a life grounded in principle and social responsibility, a life of service, care, and commitment to justice and social betterment'.

The Baby Boomers I interviewed tended to reflect those values in raising their children. Charles for example, said he 'brought up my son to treat people as you would wish to be treated yourself, with respect'.[3] He described the Ten Commandments as a set of moral values that is common to all religions, 'the only way we can effectively behave as a society. You shouldn't steal from a sweet shop, not because God said so but because you shouldn't take something that doesn't belong to you.'

In an interesting story of three-generational belief transmission, Vikki told me that her Millennial daughter describes herself as a 'Desideratist'. The descriptor refers to a long prose poem, Desiderata, written in 1927 by Max Ehrmann, who advised readers to 'Go placidly amid the noise and the haste', listen to others, be honest, and remember that you are a child of the universe. The poem made such an impact on Vikki's father that he learned calligraphy just so that he could copy it out beautifully. When her daughter read it she agreed with her grandfather that is perfectly encapsulated the best way to live. Vikki and I began to recite the poem together, and then faltered by the second verse. 'My daughter can say it word for word, but I have to look it up,' she laughed. One line was perhaps particularly pertinent to our conversation, Vikki said: 'be at peace with god whatever you conceive him to be'. It reminded her, she told me, of the British comedian Dave Allen, an irreverent, political commentator who hosted a one-man television show in the 1970s and 1980s. He often poked fun at religions, she recalled, and yet ended each programme with his catch-phrase:

Goodnight, thank you, and may your God go with you.

Other surveys and research show that those young people who describe themselves as having no religion are also likely to respect the rights of others to hold different beliefs. For example, when considering contemporary issues, Linda Woodhead found that the UK 'nones' were more cosmopolitan and internationalist than those who self-identified as Anglican. She also found that the nones' views about abortion, divorce, and assisted dying were more liberal than conservative religious adherents and the wider general population. Woodhead summarised the characteristics of the typical 'none' as 'younger, white, British- born, liberal about personal life and morals, varied in political commitment but cosmopolitan in outlook, suspicious of organised religion but not necessarily atheist, and unwilling to be labelled as religious or to identify with a religious group' (2016, 252). She observed that in choosing to self-identify as having no religion, the nones appeared to be making a negative rather than a positive choice. They were refusing to align with existing religious categories and were actively disaffiliating from orga- nised religion. I suggest that, given the constant theme running through this book that Baby Boomers found organised religion unethical, it is indeed likely that such an attitude was transmitted to the younger generations.

Sacred Pluralism: 'Not the Only Thing To Believe'

The issue of pluralism has been discussed earlier in this book, partly in terms of its effect on secularisation. The Boomers' parents, Generation A, were the first generation to see significant waves of new immigration in the UK and North America. Peter Berger (1967) highlighted this in identifying 'pluralism' as one of the defining characteristics of the more secular age. But there is, I suggest, an ethical dimension to pluralism that has been accented by Baby Boomers and their descendants. Acknowledging that there are significant global variations, and therefore advising against hasty generalizations, Linda Woodhead (2016) notes that in some regions, particularly the UK and Scandinavia, there seems to be a general trend towards greater liberalism, supporting the argument that pluralism makes it increasingly difficult for any one religion to claim and sustain absolute truth, particularly when freedom of religion and belief is becoming increasingly enshrined in legislation. She argues that this, in the UK at least, reflects an increasing trend towards ethical liberalism, where individuals want the right to choose their beliefs and practices while embracing the rights and practices of others.

In their research into American Millennials. Pew found that Millennials' attitudes towards other countries are generally favourable and appear to be stable through their life course (https://www.pewresearch.org/fact-tank/2020/07/08/u-s-millennials-tend-to-have-favorable-views-of-foreign-countries-and-institutions-even-as-they-age/). This suggests that they may be influenced by their Baby Boomer parents who, as discussed earlier in this book, expressed similar attitudes mainly brought about by meeting and living with different groups of people, at university and through foreign travel. Pew also found that Millennials and Generation Xers are almost twice as likely as their grandparents (the parents of the Baby Boomers) to believe that immigrants have a beneficial impact on society (https://www.pewtrusts.org/en/trend/archive/winter-2018/the-millennials-arent-kids-anymore).

Evidence of decreasing racism amongst young people has been attributed to a number of factors, including improved education, increased social diversity, and general societal discouragement of racist discourse (Ford 2008). Those changes may reflect a desire for more acceptance of pluralism and socially diverse modes of meaning and authority. Younger people are also less likely to express national pride than previous generations, argue Tilley and Heath (2007) because they grew up in more diverse areas and are more familiar with mixed, nuanced identities. I would also add that the Millennials are likely to have absorbed the more pluralistic beliefs of their

Baby Boomers parents with their insistence that only legitimate forms of authority should be respected. Adherent social relationships were, for both generations, the most commonly sited locations for legitimacy and authority.

Joan, mentioned above, had her children christened as a condition of entry to the local Church of England school. The family did not attend church, although the school held a monthly service for the children. When Joan's children asked questions about some of what they were hearing at the services, she 'told them it was not the only thing to believe', thus emphasising not so much the importance of their choices, but the importance of assessing a number of different options and not simply believing one because it was upheld by the school, or church. Samantha expressed a similar value when she said to me that 'If children can believe in themselves, that would be a good thing'.

For some scholars, self-belief can be taken too far. Jean Twenge (2016a, 2016b, 2014) has written various books that all indicate a trend towards unhealthy narcissism amongst Millennials. The evidence is partly drawn from a widely used psychological instrument, the narcissistic personality inventory, and from General Social Survey data. Much of his argument centres on the experiences and focus of Millennials on digital media, which Twenge finds harmful and leading to self-absorption. However, according to Roberta R. Katz, Sarah Ogilvie, Jane Shaw, and Linda Woodhead (2021, 26), he may be overstating the case and reflecting his own anxiety, a form of 'moral panic', common in periods of rapid technological change.

Ensuring young people were aware of a range of belief systems was a value not only shared by the Baby Boomers who were parents. Jennifer, although she did not have biological children, was a godparent. She told me that 'I'm a godmother, I took it seriously, so I introduced him to more religions'. She gave her godchild a Bible, the Qur'an, and a book about Daoism.

In a study of the Baby Boomers, Wade Clark Roof (2000) found that, for Baby Boomers, pluralism was not just a fact relating to diversity, although their generation was the first to be so immersed in such a widely felt reality. It was also, he argued, important to them for relating to other values they held in high esteem: tolerance and respect for other people. Given their role as the 'lead generation' of their time, the Baby Boomers were influencing wider society beyond religion and, I suggest, influencing generations to come. A similar study (Hoge et al. 1994) found the same strong faith in pluralism shared by the Boomers who disaffiliated from (American

Presbyterianism) religion after becoming confirmed; the majority agreed that all religions shared similar aspects that could help people in their own search for truth.

As I have discussed throughout this book, Baby Boomers were born into the era of human rights. Although he is obviously dismissive of this orientation, Charles Taylor (2007, 419) is, I suggest, correct in observing that 'The modern ideal has triumphed. We are all partisans of human rights.'

A Secular Sacred Turn

As religion fades amongst younger generations, some claim that religion is being replaced by spirituality. A research team at Lancaster University in the UK led by Paul Heelas and Linda Woodhead (2005) set out to investigate that, and the theories they developed were pathbreaking. For two years the team conducted surveys, interviews, observations, and archival research to explore what they described as the 'contemporary patterns of the sacred', searching for the less obvious, nuanced examples in people's religious and spiritual lives. They divided the population into two broad areas: the 'congregational domain', composed of churches, chapels, and other Christian institutions, and the 'holistic milieu', a diverse and often hard to identify population whose activities had, in their own terms, a spiritual dimension, such as discussion groups meeting in private homes, circle dancers, yoga practitioners, Tai Chi groups, and complementary therapy practitioners. One of the main differences they found related to where people located authority. Those in the 'congregational domain' positioned their beliefs in the realm of a higher, external power, such as God, while those in the holistic milieu focused internally on their own bodies and emotions or, in the researchers' words, 'subjective lives'. The research team found that 7.9 per cent of the Kendal population belonged to the 'congregational domain', while 1.6 per cent were in the 'holistic milieu'. While the authors did not conclude that religion would diminish entirely and be replaced by spirituality, they argued that certain forms of religion would continue to lose their appeal and plausibility as some forms of spirituality increase in popularity and credibility. They concluded that, if the current rates of respective decline and growth continued in Kendal, within 40 years the 'holistic milieu' would grow proportionately and the congregational domain would decline, reversing positions.

As discussed in Chapter 9, a belief in an afterlife seems to be growing amongst younger people. The Baby Boomers I interviewed were often open to experiences of post-death continuity and it is therefore reasonable to assume that those beliefs have been transmitted. Helen, for example, said that her non-religious stepdaughter was very close to her father, and had reported seeing his ghost. One problem in researching such phenomena is the language researchers use, particularly when trying to form short questions for surveys. Reflecting on the difficulty of knowing what people may mean by heaven or afterlife, a report in the Canadian news magazine *Macleans* reported on a survey of Generation Xers (https://www.macleans. ca/society/life/the-heaven-boom/_):

> 1970 British Cohort group—9,000 people, currently 42 years old—found half believed in an afterlife, while only 31 per cent believed in God. No one has yet delved deeply into beliefs about the new afterlife—the cohort surveyors didn't ask for details—but reincarnation, in a newly multicultural West, is one suggested factor. So too is belief in what one academic called 'an unreligious afterlife,' the natural continuation of human consciousness after physical death.

Future Generations: 'You Could Be a Christian, a Muslim, or a Vegetarian'

At the time of writing, the Baby Boomers are in their 60s, 70s, and 80s. The next generation of Generation X and Millennials are adults in their 30s, 40s, and early 50s. Many are now raising their own children, and in ways more familiar to their Baby Boomer parents than would be to their grandparents and great-grandparents. An acceptance, even an embrace, of inter-connectivity and the benefits of pluralism seem to inflect the current young adults known as Generation Z. These young 20-somethings are also sometimes described as digital natives, post-millennials, and zoomers. In their interdisciplinary, international research project into the lives and beliefs of Generation Z, carried out between 2016 and 2020, Roberta R. Katz, Sarah Ogilvie, Jane Shaw, and Linda Woodhead argued that the temporal location of that generation is unique and significant as they are the first generation ever to have always known the Internet: born and raised 'only knowing the world with the possibility of endless information and infinite connectivity of the digital age' (Katz et al. 2021, 1). The researchers were struck by the way their research participants discussed their lives and values bound together by a strong sense of connections and collaboration. The researchers argue (Katz et al. 2021, 5) that the values of Generation Z are ones all generations can adopt to their benefit, and to that of the wider world:

Be real, know who you are, be responsible for your own well-being, support your friends, open up institutions to the talents of the many not the few, embrace diversity, make the world kinder, live by your values.

Sally's remark in my own Baby Boomer research resonates here. We were discussing the beliefs of the younger generations and she said that she thought ideas about fairness, and how to be a good citizen prevailed. She recounted a time when her granddaughter, a member of Generation Z, said she had learned in her religious education class that day that 'you could be a Christian, a Muslim, or a vegetarian'. Indeed, as detailed elsewhere (Harding and Day 2020) beliefs such as veganism have been recognised by the UK as a 'protected characteristic', like religious beliefs, according to the Equality Act 2010.

It is also interesting to note the focus on connectivity and collaboration that Katz et al. (2021) found. This may help to explain and point to an important shift that speaks directly to the way future religion, and other beliefs, may be transmitted amongst those who engage every minute of their lives with friends, acquaintances, and media influencers. A three-year, multi-country project, directed by Peter Nynäs at Åbo Akademi University, explored the religious and non-religious life views of young people, namely, members of Generation Z and the Millennial generation. The 'Young Adults and Religion in a Global Perspective' project examined global media influence, consumerism, social movements, and increasing polarisation between pluralism and radicalisation. An important early paper developing the area of religious socialisation was authored by Ben-Willie Kwaku Golo and his colleagues (Golo et al. 2019). They show that while most existing theories in the sociology of religion identify the family as a key area for religious socialisation, the current millennial generation also ascribes secondary sources of socialisation, such as friends, media, and secular education.

Whatever the values that are being formed by Generation Z, they are unlikely to be religious. As I have argued throughout this book, the Baby

Boomer ex-Anglican parents I interviewed experienced little of what previous generations would have understood as 'religion' in both belief and practice and, accordingly, transmitted few if any of those beliefs and practices to their offspring. This helps explain another finding of Katz et al. (2021, 67): 'For postmillennials in the UK and US, more than for any previous generation, it is common to have had no exposure to religion in their upbringing.' They point to the rising numbers of people who say they have 'no religion': just over half of British postmillennials and a quarter of US postmillennials. They show that the parents of those postmillennials (late Boomers and early Generation X and Millennials) were raised without religion and also identify as having no religion:[4]

> Thus, it was no surprise to find that, for many, religious identity was simply not on their radar, though that did not necessarily make them closed to the idea of exploring it. Whether this was out of politeness, respectfulness, or genuine interest was not always clear.

In summary, I conclude here that clarity will come as members of Generation Z mature and have families of their own. It does not appear that the evidence so far, and the theories we sociologists of religion understand, indicate a religious revival. Modes of practice, belief, habit, and the turn to legitimate authority all suggest less religious, but profoundly connected and ethical futures.

My study here has been limited by its dependence on interview data, a consequence of the Covid-19 circumstances in which it was undertaken (see Chapter 1 for more reflection on this). Participant observations had been intended originally and could provide rich, ethnographic data, particularly concerning the inter-generational dynamics. My primary empirical data was also intentionally focused on a sample of 'ex-Anglicans' located in the UK and Canada as a follow-up from my previous (Day 2017) study. It is therefore primarily mono-classed and ethnicised, reflecting a predominance of middle-class white Anglicans of the Global North. There are, of course, other stories to be told within the Baby Boomer and subsequent generations about people who remained or became religious or have held more fluid beliefs (see, for example, Day and Lynch 2013; Collins-Mayo and Dandelion 2010; Savage et al. 2006; Ward 1996).

Further research is necessary.

Notes

1. The UK Equality Act 2010 allows sex and religious discrimination in the cases of single-sex schools and schools of a religious nature.
2. As noted in Chapter 10, state-funded religion-based schools provide education to a quarter of primary school pupils and 6 per cent of secondary school pupils. Supporters of state-funded faith schools argue that they provide high-quality education, and promote justice and fairness for religious communities, while promoting social cohesion and the integration of minority communities into the life of the state; on the other hand, opponents claim that faith schools use state money to proselytise and to disadvantage other schools through selection procedures, and do not promote social cohesion because they separate pupils of different religious and non-religious backgrounds (Jackson 2003, 89). For a more recent detailed analysis of the legal frameworks and implications, see Suhraiya Jivraj 2013.
3. While this idea may echo a Christian teaching that one should 'do unto others as you would have them do unto you' or Jewish instruction to 'love thy neighbour', for discussion of it as an ethic of reciprocity spanning most religions and cultures see, for example, the edited volume by Bruce Chilton and Jacob Neusner 2008.
4. Indeed, the provocative title of Gordon Lynch's (2002) book about Generation X-ers frequenting clubs, *After Religion*, positions this generation as one that may be post-religion but not, according to his findings, post-meaning or authenticity.

Bibliography

Ackerman RA, Witt EA, Donnellan MB, Trzesniewski KH, Robins RW, Kashy DA. 2011. 'What Does the Narcissistic Personality Inventory Really Measure?' *Assessment* 18(1): 67–87. doi: 10.1177/1073191110382845.

Alexander, Alison, Louise M. Benjamin, Keisha Hoerrner and Darrell Roe. 1998. ' "We'll Be Back in a Moment": A Content Analysis of Advertisements in Children's Television in the 1950s'. *Journal of Advertising* 27(3): 1–9.

Alexander, Jeffrey C. 2004. 'Toward a Theory of Cultural Trauma'. In Jeffrey. C. Alexander, Ron Eyermar Bernard Gieson, Wail J. Smelser and Piotr Sztompka (eds), *Cultural Trauma and Collective Identity*, 1–30. Berkeley, Los Angeles and London: University of California Press.

Alderson, Priscilla 2016. *The Politics of Childhoods Real and Imagined: Practical Application of Critical Realism and Childhood Studies*. Volume 2. London: Routledge.

Amit, Vered 2000. 'Introduction: Constructing the Field. In Vered Amit, *Constructing the Field: Ethnographic Fieldwork in the Contemporary World*. London: Routledge.

Amira, MZ. 2008. 'Experience Beyond Belief: The "Strangeness Curve" and Integral Transformative Practice'. *Social Analysis* 52(1): 127–43.

Ammerman, Nancy. 1997. 'Golden Rule Christianity: Lived Religion in the American Mainstream'. In David Hall (ed), *Lived Religion in America*, 196–216. Princeton: Princeton University Press.

Ammerman, Nancy T. 2007. *Everyday Religion: Observing Modern Religious Lives*. Oxford and New York: Oxford University Press.

Anderson, Benedict. 1991. *Imagined Communities: Reflections on the Origins and Spread of Nationalism*. London and New York: Verso.

Arat, Alp. 2016. 'Practice Makes Perfect: Meditation and the Exchange of Spiritual Capital'. *Journal of Contemporary Religion* 31(2): 269–80.

Ariès, Phillipe. 1962. *Centuries of Childhood*. New York: Alfred A. Knopf.

Arnold, John. 2005. *Belief and Unbelief in the Middle Ages*. London: Bloomsbury.

Asad, Talal. 1993. *Genealogies of Religion: Discipline and Reasons of Power in Christianity and Islam*. Baltimore: Johns Hopkins University Press.

Ashworth, Jacinta and Ian Farthing. 2007. *Churchgoing in the UK*. Teddington: Tearfund.

Baker, Christopher. 2013. 'Moral Freighting, Civic Engagement: A UK Perspective on Putnam and Campbell's Theory of Religious-based Social Action'. *Sociology of Religion*. 74(3): 343–69.

Baker, Christopher and Jonathan Miles-Watson. 2008. 'Exploring Secular Spiritual Capital; An Engagement in Religious and Secular Dialogue for a Common Future'. *International Journal of Public Theology* 2(4): 442–64.

Bandura, Albert. 1986. *Social Foundations Of Thought And Action: A Social Cognitive Theory*. Englewood Cliffs: Prentice- Hall, Inc.

Bardi, Anat, Julie Anne Lee, Nadi Hofmann-Towfigh and Geoffrey Soutar. 2009. 'The Structure of Intraindividual Value Change'. *Journal of Personality and Social Psychology* 97(5): 913.

Barker, Eileen. 2012. 'Aging in New Religions: The Varieties of Later Experiences'. *Diskus: The Journal of the British Association for the Study of Religions* 12.

Barthes, Roland. 1967. *The Elements of Semiology*. London: Cape.

Baumann, Gerd. 1996. *Contesting Culture: Discourses of Identity in Multi-Ethnic London*. New York: Cambridge University Press.

Beaman, Lori. 2017. 'Living Well Together in a (Non) Religious Future: Contributions From The Sociology of Religion'. *Sociology of Religion* 78(1): 9–32.

Beaudoin, Tom. 1998. Virtual Faith: The Irreverent Spiritual Quest of Generation X. San Francisco: Jossey-Bass.

Beck, Ulrich and Elisabeth Beck-Gernsheim. 2002. *Individualization: Institutionalized Individualism and its Social And Political Consequences*. London: Sage.

Bell, Catherine. 1992. *Ritual Theory, Ritual Practice*. Oxford: Oxford UP.

Bell, Catherine. 1997. *Ritual, Perspectives, and Dimensions*. New York and Oxford: Oxford University Press.

Bell, Catherine. 2000. 'Acting Ritually'. In R Fenn (ed), *The Blackwell Companion of Sociology of Religion*, 371–87. Oxford: Blackwell.

Bellah, Robert, Madsen, W.M. Sullivan, A. Swidler, and S.M. Tipton. 1985. *Habits of the Heart: Individualism and Commitment in American Life*. Berkeley: University of California Press.

Bengston, Vern and Merril Silverstein (eds). 2019. *New Dimensions in Spirituality, Religion and Aging*. New York: Routledge.

Bengtson, Vern, Hayward, R.D., Zuckerman, P. and Silverstein, M. 2018. 'Bringing up Nones: Intergenerational Influences and Cohort Trends'. *Journal for the Scientific Study of Religion* 57(2): 258–75.

Bengtson, Vern, Kang, S.L.C., Endacott, C.G., Gonzales, G.G. and Silverstein, M. 2019. 'Emerging Developments in Spirituality, Religion, and Aging'. In Vern Bengtson and Merril Silverstein (eds), *New Dimensions in Spirituality, Religion and Aging*, 1–26. New York: Routledge.

Berger, Helen A and Douglas Ezzy. 2007. *Teenage Witches: Magical Youth and The Search for the Self*. New Brunswick: Rutgers.

Berger, Peter L. 1967. *The Sacred Canopy: Elements of a Sociological Theory of Religion*. New York: Doubleday, and Luckmann, Thomas 1966. *The Social Construction of Reality: A Treatise in the Sociology of Knowledge*. Garden City, N.Y.: Anchor Books.

Bergin, Allen E. 1980. 'Psychotherapy and Religious Values'. *Journal of Consulting and Clinical Psychology* 48(1): 95.

Bhambra, Gurminder K. 2014. 'Postcolonial and Decolonial Dialogues'. *Postcolonial Studies* 17(2): 115–21.

Bielo, James S. 2015. *Anthropology of Religion: The Basics*. Abingdon: Routledge.

Blackwelder, Julia Kirk. 1979. 'Southern White Fundamentalists and the Civil Rights Movement'. *Phylon (1960–)* 40(4): 334–41.

Bloch, Maurice. 1997. "The Past and the Present in the Present". Man 12 (2): 282.

Bourdieu, Pierre. 1977. *Outline of a Theory of Practice*. Cambridge: Cambridge University Press.

Brewer, John D. 2000. *Ethnography*. Buckingham: Open University Press.

Brierley, Peter. 2000. *The Tide is Running Out*. London: Christian Research.

Brierley, Peter. 2006. *Pulling out of the Nose Dive: A Contemporary Picture of Churchgoing; What the 2005 English Church Census Reveals*. London: Christian Research.

British Social Attitudes. 2019. 'Religion: Identity, Behaviour and Belief over Two Decades'. http://www.bsa.natcen.ac.uk/media/39293/1bsa36religion.pdf.

Brooke, John Hedley. 1991. *Science and Religion: Some Historical Perspectives*. New York, Port Chester, Melbourne, and Sydney: Cambridge University Press.

Brown, Callum G. 2015. 'How Anglicans Lose Religion: An Oral History of Becoming Secular'. In Abby Day (ed), *Contemporary Issues in the Worldwide Anglican Communion, Powers and Pieties*, 245–66. Aldershot: Ashgate.

Brown, Andrew and Linda Woodhead. 2017. *That Was The Church That Was: How The Church Of England Lost The English People*. London. Bloomsbury.

Brown, C Mackenzie. 2003. 'The Conflict Between Religion and Science in Light of the Patterns of Religious Belief Among Scientists'. *Zygon: Journal of Religion and Science* 38(3): 603–32.

Brown, Callum. 2001. *The Death of Christian Britain*. London: Routledge.

Brown, Callum G. 2010. 'What was the Religious Crisis of the 1960s?' *Journal of Religious History* 34(4): 468–79.

Brown, Callum G. 2017. *Becoming Atheist: Humanism and the Secular West*. London and New York. Bloomsbury.

Brown, Callum and Gordon Lynch. 2012. 'Cultural Perspectives'. In Linda Woodhead and Rebecca Catto (eds), *Religion and Change in Modern Britain*, 329–35. Routledge: London.

Brubaker, JR, GR Hayes, and P Dourish. 2013. 'Beyond the Grave: Facebook as a Site for the Expansion of Death and Mourning'. *The Information Society* 29: 152–63.

Bruce, Steve. 2002. *God is Dead: Secularization in the West*. Oxford: Blackwell.

Bruce, Steve. 2011. *Secularization: In Defence of an Unfashionable Theory*. Oxford: Oxford University Press.

Buch, Elana D and Karen M Staller. 2014. 'The Feminist Practice of Ethnography'. In Sharlene Nagy Hesse-Biber (ed), *Feminist Research Practice: A Primer*, 107–44. 2nd edn, Thousand Oaks, London, and New Delhi: Sage Publications.

Buchanan, Constance H. 1992. 'The Anthropology of Vitality and Decline: The Episcopal Church in a Changing Society'. In Catherine M. Prelinger (ed),

Episcopal Women: Gender, Spirituality, and Commitment in an American Mainline Denomination, 310–29. New York: Oxford University Press.

Bullock, Josh. 2018. *The Sociology of The Sunday Assembly: 'Belonging Without Believing' in a Post-Christian Context*. (PhD thesis), Kingston University.

Buss, Allan R. 1974. 'Generational Analysis: Description, Explanation and Theory'. *Journal of Social Issues* 30(2): 55–72.

Butler, Judith. 1990. *Gender Trouble: Feminism and the Subversion Of Identity*. New York: Routledge.

Caliandro, Alessandro. 2018. 'Digital Methods for Ethnography: Analytical Concepts for Ethnographers Exploring Social Media Environments'. *Journal of Contemporary Ethnography* 47(5): 551–78.

Caliandro, Alessandro and Alessandro Gandini. 2017. *Qualitative Research in Digital Environments: A Research Toolkit*. New York: Routledge.

Cameron, Jane. 2013. 'Sartorially Sacred or Fashion Faux Pas? Visual Interpretations of Modesty Online'. In Abby Day, Giselle Vincett, and Christopher R. Cotter (eds), *Social Identities Between the Sacred and the Secular*, 23–39. Aldershot: Ashgate.

Campbell, Colin. 1993 [1971]. *Toward a Sociology of Irreligion*. London and Basingstoke: MacMillan.

Carroll, Jackson W, Wade Clark Roof, and David A Roozen (eds). 1995. *The Post-War Generation and Establishment Religion: Cross-Cultural Perspectives*. Boulder: Westview Press.

Carson, Rachel. 1961. *The Sea Around Us*. New York: Oxford University Press.

Carson, Rachel. 1962. *Silent Spring*. Boston: Houghton Mifflin.

Carsten, Janet (ed). 2007. *Ghosts of Memory: Essays on Remembrance and Relatedness*. Oxford: Blackwell.

Chae, Ryan. 2019. *Overprotective Parents and a New Generation of American Children Berkeley Political Review*, 16 April. https://bpr.berkeley.edu/2019/04/16/overprotective-parents-and-a-new-generation-of-american-children/.

Cheruvallil-Contractor, Sariya, Kingsley Purdam, and Paul Weller. 2021. 'Much More Than a Negation of Religion: A Qualitative Exploration of the Diversity of Non-Religious Identities in England and Wales'. *Journal of Contemporary Religion* 36(2): 329–48. doi: 10.1080/13537903.2021.1936966.

Chilton, Bruce and Jacob Neusner. 2008. *The Golden Rule: The Ethics of Reciprocity in World Religions*. London and New York: Continuum.

Cimino, Richard and Christopher Smith. 2014. *Atheist Awakening: Secular Activism and Community in America*. Oxford and New York: Oxford University Press.

Clark, David. 1982. *Between Pulpit and Pew: Folk Religion in a North Yorkshire Fishing Village*. Cambridge: Cambridge University Press.

Coleman, Simon and Peter Collins. 2006. 'Introduction'. In *Locating the Field Space, Place and Context In Anthropology'*, 42. ASA Monographs. London: Routledge.

Coleman Simon and Marion Bowman. 2019. 'Religion in Cathedrals: Pilgrimage, Heritage, Adjacency, and the Politics of Replication in Northern Europe'. *Religion* 49(1): 1–23.

Coleman, Simon, Marion Bowman, and Tiina Sepp. 2019. 'A Cathedral Is Not Just for Christmas: Civic Christianity in the Multi-Cultural City'. In Pamela E. Klassen and Monique Scheer (eds), *The Public Work of Christmas: Belonging and Difference in Multicultural Societies*, 240–61. Montreal: McGill-Queen's University Press.

Cornman, John M and Eric R Kingston. 1996. 'Trends, Issues, Perspectives, and Values for the Aging of the Baby Boom Cohorts'. *The Gerontologist* 36(1): 15–26.

Coleman, Simon. 2019. 'On Praying in an Old Country: Ritual, Replication, Heritage, and Powers of Adjacency in English Cathedrals'. *Religion* 49(1): 120–41.

Connerton, Paul. 1989. *How Societies Remember*. Cambridge: Cambridge University Press.

Connerton, Paul. 2009. *How Modernity Forgets*. Cambridge and New York: Cambridge University Press.

Cook, Corey L, Florette Cohen, and Sheldon Solomon. 2015. 'What If They're Right About the Afterlife? Evidence of the Role of Existential Threat on Anti-Atheist Prejudice'. *Social Psychological and Personality Science* 6(7): 840–6.

Cook, Hera. 2004. *The Long Sexual Revolution: English Women, Sex and Contraception 1800–1975*. Oxford: Oxford University Press.

Copson, Andrew. 2017. *Secularism: Politics, Religion, and Freedom*. Oxford and New York: Oxford University Press.

Copson, Andrew and AC Grayling. 2015. *The Wiley Blackwell Handbook of Humanism*. Chichester: Wiley Blackwell.

Cornwall, Marie. 1987. 'The Social Bases of Religion: A Study of Factors Influencing Religious Belief and Commitment'. *Review of Religious Research* 29: 44–56.

Cornwall, Marie. 1988. 'The Influence of Three Agents of Religious Socialization: Family, Church, and Peers'. In Darwin L Thomas (ed), *The Religion and Family Connection: Social Science Perspectives*, 207–23. Povo Utah: Religious Studies Center, Brigham Young University.

Cornwall, Marie. 1989. 'The Determinants of Religious Behavior: A Theoretical Model and Empirical Test'. *Social Forces* 68(2): 572–92.

Coupland, Douglas. 1991. *Generation X: Tales for an Accelerated Culture*. New York: St. Martin's Press.

Cush, Denise. 2010. 'Teenage Witchcraft in Britain'. In *Religion and Youth*, edited by Sylvia Collins-Mayo and Pink Dandelion. (eds) 2010. *Religion and Youth*. Ashgate: Aldershot. 74–81.

Campbell, C. 2007. *Easternization of the West: A Thematic Account of Cultural Change in the Modern Era*. Colorado: Paradigm Publishers.

Davidov, Eldad, Peter Schmidt, and Shalom H Schwartz. 2008. 'Bringing Values Back in: The Adequacy of the European Social Survey to Measure Values in 20 Countries'. *Public Opinion Quarterly* 72(3): 420–45.

Davie, Grace. 1994. *Religion in Britain since 1945: Believing without Belonging*. Oxford: Blackwell.

Davie, Grace. 2002. *Europe: The Exceptional Case: Parameters of Faith in the Modern World*. London: Darton, Longman & Todd.

Davie, Grace. 2007. 'Vicarious Religion: A Methodological Challenge'. In NT Ammerman (ed), *Everyday Religion: Observing Modern Religious Lives*, 21–36. Oxford and New York: Oxford University Press.

Davie, Grace. 2012. 'A Short Afterword: Thinking Spatially About Religion'. *Culture and Religion* 13(4): 485–9.

Davies, Christie. 2017. *Strange Death of Moral Britain*. London: Routledge.

Dawkins, Richard. 2006. *The God Delusion*. New York: Houghton Mifflin.

Day, Abby. 2005. 'Doing Theodicy: an Empirical Study of a Women's Prayer Group'. *Journal of Contemporary Religion* 20(3): 343–56.

Day, Abby. 2011. *Believing in Belonging: Belief and Social Identity in the Modern World*. Oxford: Oxford University Press.

Day, Abby. 2012. 'Extraordinary Relationality: Ancestor Veneration in late Euro-American Society'. *Nordic Journal of Religion and Society* 25(2): 57–69.

Day, Abby. 2013. 'Varieties of Belief Over Time: Reflections From a Longitudinal Study of Youth and Belief'. *Journal of Contemporary Religion* 28(2): 277–93.

Day, Abby. 2014. Invited essay: 'The Problem of Generalizing Generation', *Religion and Society: Advances in Research* 4: 109–24.

Day, Abby. (ed). 2015. *Contemporary Issues in the Worldwide Anglican Communion: Powers and Pieties*. Abingdon and Burlington: Routledge.

Day, Abby. 2016. 'Believing in Belief: Towards the Secularization of Faith in Global Economies'. In P. Zuckerman (ed), *Beyond Religion*, 53–69. Farmingham Hills: Macmillan.

Day, Abby. 2017. *The Religious Lives of Older Laywomen: the Last Active Anglican Generation*. Oxford: Oxford University Press.

Day, Abby. 2018. 'Rationality and Belief'. In Hilary Callan (ed), *The International Encyclopaedia of Anthropology*. New York: Wiley-Blackwell.

Day, Abby. 2018. 'Sacred Time'. In Hilary Callan (ed), *The International Encyclopaedia of Anthropology*. New York: Wiley-Blackwell.

Day, Abby. 2019. 'Lived Belief in Cross-Cultural Comparison'. In James Walters (ed), *Religious Imaginations and Global Transitions*, 143–8. Ginko: London.

Day, Abby. 2020. *Sociology of Religion: Overview and Analysis of Contemporary Religion*. Abingdon: Routledge.

Day, Abby and Ben Rogaly. 2014. 'Sacred Communities: Contestations and Connections'. *Journal of Contemporary Religion* 29(1): 75–88.

Day, Abby, Giselle Vincett, and Christopher R Cotter (eds). 2013. *Social Identities between the Sacred and the Secular*. Ashgate: Abingdon and Burlington.

Day, Abby et al. (eds). 2022. *Diversity, Inclusion, and Decolonisation: Practical Tools for Improving Teaching, Research and Scholarship*. Bristol: Bristol University Press.

De Certeau, Michel. 1984. *The Practice of Everyday Life*. Berkeley, Los Angeles, and London: University of California Press.

De Graaf, NanDirk and Manfred te Grotenhuis, 2008. 'Traditional Christian Belief and Belief in the Supernatural: Diverging Trends in the Netherlands Between 1979 and 2005'. *Journal for the Scientific Study of Religion* 47: 585–98.

Demerath III, NJ. 1965. *Social Class in American Protestantism*. Chicago: Rand McNally & Co.

Devine, Paula. 2013. 'Men, Women, and Religiosity in Northern Ireland: Testing the Theories'. *Journal of Contemporary Religion* 28(3): 473–88.

Dinham, Adam. 2011. 'What is a "Faith Community"?' *Community Development Journal* 46: 526–41.

Dumont, Louis. 1980. *Homo hierarchicus: The Caste System and Its Implications.* Trans Mark Sainsbury, Louis Dumont, and Basia Gulati. Chicago: University of Chicago Press.

Durkheim, Émile and Marcel Mauss. 1963 [1902]. *Primitive Classification.* Trans from the French and edited with an introduction by Rodney Needham. London: Cohen.

Durkheim, Émile. 1915. *The Elementary Forms of the Religious Life.* London: George Allen and Unwin.

Dudley, Roger L., and Margaret G. Dudley. 1986. 'Transmission of Religious Values from Parents to Adolescents'. *Review of Religious Research,* 3–15.

Eccles, Janet. 2014. 'Older English Churchgoing Women as Voluntary Providers of Welfare'. *Journal of Beliefs & Values: Studies in Religion & Education* 35(3): 315–26.

Engelke, Matthew. 2015. 'Good Without God: Happiness and Pleasure Amongst the Humanists'. HAU, *Journal of Ethnographic Theory* 5(3): 69–91.

Engelke, Matthew. 2014. 'Christianity and the Anthropology of Secular Humanism'. *Current Anthropology* 55(10): 292–01.

Engelke, Matthew. 2015. 'The Coffin Question: Death and Materiality in Humanist Funerals'. *Material Religion* 11(1): 26–48.

Epstein, Greg M. 2009. *Good Without God: What a Billion Nonreligious People Do Believe.* New York: Harper.

Erikson, Erik. 1950. *Childhood and Society.* New York: Norton.

Evans-Pritchard, EE. 1976 [1937]. *Witchcraft, Oracles, and Magic among the Azande.* Oxford: Clarendon Press.

Eyerman, Ruth and Bryan S Turner. 1998. 'Outline of a Theory of Generations'. *European Journal of Social Theory* 1(1): 91–106.

Ecklund, ElaineH and Jerry Z. Park, 2009. 'Conflict Between Religion and Science Among Academic Scientists?' *Journal for the Scientific Study of Religion* 48: 276–92.

Edmunds, June and Bryan S Turner. 2002. *Generations, Culture and Society.* Buckingham: Open University Press.

ECOTEC Research and Consulting Limited. 2004. The Economic and Social Impacts of Cathedrals in England. http://www.ecotec.com.

Einolf Christopher J. 2009. 'Will the Boomers Volunteer During Retirement? Comparing the Baby Boom, Silent, and Long Civic Cohorts'. *Nonprofit and Voluntary Sector Quarterly* 38(2): 181–99.

Eisenstadt, Shmuel N. 2000. 'Multiple Modernities'. *Daedalus* 129(1): 1–29.

Ellwood, Robert S. 1997. *The Fifties Spiritual Marketplace: American Religion in a Decade of Conflict.* New Brunswick: Rutgers University Press.

Escalona, Sibylle K. 1982. 'Growing Up with the Threat of Nuclear War: Some Indirect Effects on Personality Development'. *American Journal of Orthopsychiatry* 52: 605–6.

Field, Clive. 2015. 'Religion-in-Great-Britain-1939-99-A-Compendium-of-Gallup-Poll-Data': http://www.brin.ac.uk/wp-content/uploads/2011/12/Religion-in-Great-Britain-1939-99-A-Compendium-of-Gallup-Poll-Data.pdf.

Findlay, James F. 1990. 'Religion and Politics in the Sixties: The Churches and the Civil Rights Act of 1964'. *The Journal of American History* 77(1): 66–92.

Finke, Roger and Rodney Stark. 2006. *The Churching of America, 1776-1990: Winners and Losers in our Religious Economy.* New Brunswick, NJ: Rutgers Univ. Press.

Firth, Raymond. 1955. *The Fate of the Soul.* Cambridge: Cambridge University Press.

Flint, John. 2009. 'Faith- Based Schools: Institutionalising Parallel Lives?' In Adam Dinham, Robert Furbey, and Vivien Lowndes (eds), *Faith in the Public Realm: Controversies, Policies and Practices*, 163–82. Bristol: Policy Press.

Flory, Richard W and Donald E Miller (eds). 2000. *GenX Religion.* London and New York: Routledge.

Forbes, Bruce David. 2007. 'Christmas Was Not Always Like This: A Brief History'. *Word and World* 27(4): 399–406.

Ford, Robert. 2008. 'Is Racial Prejudice Declining in Britain?' *British Journal of Sociology* 59(4): 609–36.

Fortes, Meyer. 1987. 'Ancestor Worship in Africa'. In Jack Goody (ed), *Religion, Morality and the Person: Essays on Tallensi Religion*, 65–6. Cambridge: University of Cambridge Press.

Fortier, Anne-Marie. 2000. *Migrant Belongings, Memory, Space, Identity.* Oxford: Berg.

Foster, JD, LK Shiverdecker, and IN Turner. 2016. 'What Does the Narcissistic Personality Inventory Measure Across the Total Score Continuum?' *Current Psychology* 35: 207–19.

Foucault, Michel. 1977. *Discipline and Punish.* New York: Pantheon.

Francis, Leslie J, Susan H. Jones, Ursula McKenna, Nelson Pike, and Emma Williams. 2021. 'Belonging through Events? Exploring the Demographic Profile, Motivations, and Experiences of Those Attending the Afternoon Carol Services on Christmas Eve at Liverpool Cathedral'. *Religions* 12(90): 2–16.

Francis, Leslie J, and Susan H Jones. 2020. 'Cathedrals as Agents of Psychological Health and Well-Being Within Secular Societies: Assessing The Impact of The Holly Bough Service in Liverpool Cathedral'. *HTS Teologiese Studies/Theological Studies* [Online] 76(3).

Friedan, Betty. 1963. *The Feminine Mystique.* New York: W.W. Norton & Company, Inc.

Furseth, Inger and Pål Repstad. 2006. *An Introduction to the Sociology of Religion: Classical and Contemporary Perspectives.* Surrey: Ashgate Publishing Ltd.

Geertz, Clifford. 1973. *The Interpretation of Cultures: Selected Essays.* New York: Basic Books, 1973.

Giddens, Anthony. 1991. *Modernity and Self-identity: Self and Society in the Late Modern Age.* Cambridge: Polity.

Giddens, Anthony. 1998. *The Third Way: The Renewal of Social Democracy.* Cambridge: Polity Press.

Gilroy, Paul. 1987. *There Ain't No Black in the Union Jack*. London: Hutchinson.

Goffman, Erving. 1959. *The Presentation of Self in Everyday Life*. New York: Doubleday.

Goldberg, Gertrude S. 1984. 'Adding the Arms Race to the Psychosocial Equation'. *Social Work* 29(5): 481–3.

Golo, Ben-Willie Kwaku, Måns Broo, Sławomir Sztajer, Francis Benyah, Sohini Ray and Mallarika Sarkar. 2019. 'Primary Religious Socialization Agents and Young Adults' Understanding of Religion: Connections and Disconnections'. *Religion* 49(2): 179–200.

Goodhew, David. (ed). 2012. *Church Growth in Britain: 1980 to the Present*. Farnham and Burlington: Ashgate.

Gorsuch, Richard L and Sam G McFarland. 1972. 'Single vs. Multiple-item Scales for Measuring Religious Values'. *Journal for the Scientific Study of Religion* 11(1): 53–64.

Graebner, William. 1980. 'The Unstable World of Benjamin Spock: Social Engineering in a Democratic Culture, 1917–1950'. *The Journal of American History* 67(3): 612–29.

Greenwood, Jeremy and Nezih Guner. 2004. 'Marriage and Divorce since World War II: Analyzing the Role of Technological Progress on the Formation of Households'. NBER Working Paper No. 10772.

Griffiths, Mark. 2009. *One Generation from Extinction: How the Church Connects with the Unchurched Child*. Oxford: Monarch Books.

Guest, Mathew, Elizabeth Olson, and John Wolffe. 2012. 'Christianity: Loss of Monopoly'. In Linda Woodhead and Rebecca Catto (eds), *Religion and Change in Modern Britain*, 57–78. London: Routledge.

Gunderman, Richard. 2019. 'Dr. Spock's Timeless Lessons in Parenting'. *The Conversation*. https://theconversation.com/dr-spocks-timeless-lessons-in-parenting-122377 last accessed 17.08.2021.

Hadaway CKirk and PennyL Marler. 2005. 'How Many Americans Attend Worship Each Week? An Alternative Approach to Measurement'. *Journal for the Scientific Study of Religion* 44(3): 307–22.

Hadaway CKirk, PennyL Marler, and M Chaves. 1993. 'What The Polls Don't Show: A Closer Look at U.S. Church Attendance'. *American Sociological Review* 58(6): 741–52.

Halbwachs, Maurice. 1992. *On Collective Memory*. Chicago: University of Chicago.

Hallin, Daniel C. 1986. *The Uncensored War: The Media and Vietnam*. Berkeley and Los Angeles: University of California Press.

Hamilton, HA. 1964. *The Family Church in Principle and Practice*. Surrey: The Religious Education Press.

Hall, Stuart. 1978. *Policing the Crisis: Mugging, the State, and Law and Order*. London: Macmillan.

Hall, Stuart (ed). 1997. *Representation: Cultural Representations and Signifying Practices*. Maidenhead: Sage Publications, Inc; Open University Press.

Haraldsson, Erlender. 2006. 'Popular Psychology, Belief in Life After Death and Reincarnation in the Nordic Countries, Western and Eastern Europe'. *Nordic Psychology* 58(2): 171–80.

Harding, Kim and Abby Day. 2021. 'Vegan YouTubers Performing Ethical Beliefs'. *Religions* 12(7). https://dx.doi.org/10.3390/rel12010007.

Hardy, Alister C. 1979. *The Spiritual Nature of Man: A Study of Religious Experience.* Oxford: Blackwell.

Hay, David. 1982. *Exploring Inner Space: Scientists and Experience.* Harmondsworth: Penguin.

Harrison-Evans, Peter. 2016. 'Shopping for Good: The Social Benefits of Charity Retail'. London: DEMOS. https://www.demos.co.uk/wp-content/uploads/2017/09/Shopping-for-Good-the-social-benefits-of-charity-retail-.pdf.

Hartman, Carine. 2019, *"Early music is dead, long live early music!" The Holland Baroque ensemble and the Dutch early music revival.* Unpublished Master's dissertation, Utrecht: Utrecht University.

Harvey, Graham. 2017. *Animism: Respecting the Living World.* London: Hurst and Company.

Hebert, David, Alexis Anja Kallio, and Albi Odendaal. 2012. 'Not So Silent Night: Tradition, Transformation and Cultural Understandings of Christmas Music Events in Helsinki, Finland'. *Ethnomusicology Forum* 21(3): 402–23.

Heelas, Paul, Linda Woodhead, Benjamin Seel, Bronislaw Szersynski, and Karin Tusting. 2005. *The Spiritual Revolution: Why Religion is Giving Way to Spirituality.* Oxford: Blackwell.

Hervieu-Léger, Danièle. 2000. *Religion as a Chain of Memory.* Cambridge: Polity Press.

Hervieu-Léger, Danièle. 2003. *Catholicisme, la fin d'un monde.* Paris: Bayard.

Hjorth, Larissa, Heather Horst, Anne Galloway, and Genevieve Bell. 2017. *The Routledge Companion to Digital Ethnography.* New York: Routledge.

Hillery, George. 1955. 'Definitions of Community: Areas of Agreement'. *Rural Sociology* 20: 111–22.

Hine, Christine. 2000. *Virtual Ethnography.* London: Sage.

Hitlin, Steven and Jane Allyn Piliavin. 2004. 'Values: Reviving a Dormant Concept'. *Annu. Rev. Sociol* 30: 359–93.

Ho, Christina. 2011. 'Respecting the Presence of Others: School Micropublics and Everyday Multiculturalism'. *Journal of Intercultural Studies* 32(6): 603–19.

Hobsbawm, EricJ. 1983. 'Introduction: Inventing Traditions'. In Eric J. Hobsbawm and Terence Ranger (eds), *The Invention of Tradition,* 1–14. Cambridge: Cambridge University Press.

Hochschild, Arlie Russell. 2003 [1983]. *The Managed Heart: Commercialization of Human Feeling.* Berkeley, Los Angeles, and London: University of California Press.

Hoge, Dean R, Benton Johnson, and Donald A Luidens. 1994. *Vanishing Boundaries: The Religion of Mainline Protestant Baby Boomers.* Louisville: Westminster/John Knox Press.

Hjarvard, Stig. 2008. 'The Mediatization of Religion: A Theory of the Media as Agents of Religious Change'. *Northern Lights: Film and Media Studies Yearbook* 29(2): 9–26.

Horowitz, Helen Lefkowitz. 1986. 'The 1960s and the Transformation of Campus Cultures'. *History of Education Quarterly* 26(1): 1–38.

Iltis, Ana S. 2012. 'Ritual as the Creation of Social Reality'. In David Solomon, Ruiping Fan, and Ping-cheung Lo (eds), *Ritual and the Moral Life. Philosophical Studies in Contemporary Culture*, vol 21, 17–28. Springer.

Inglehart, Rodney. 1977. *The Silent Revolution: Changing Values and Political Styles Amongst Western Publics*. Princeton: Princeton University Press.

James, Nalita and Hugh Busher. 2009. *Online Interviewing*. London: SAGE Publications.

Jackson, Robert. 2003. 'Should the State Fund Faith Based Schools? A Review of the Arguments'. *British Journal of Religious Education* 25(2): 89–102.

James, Allison and Alan Prout. 1997. *Constructing and Reconstructing Childhood: New Directions in The Sociological Study of Childhood*. Oxford: Routledge.

Jenkins, Philip. 2018. 'The Religious World Changed in 1968, but Not in the Ways We Think'. https://www.abc.net.au/religion/the-religious-world-changed-in-1968-but-not-in-the-ways-we-think/10214328.

Jenkins, Simon. 2016. 'Why Cathedrals Are Soaring: The Church of England's Unexpected Success Story'. https://www.spectator.co.uk/article/why-cathedrals-are-soaring.

Jivraj, Suhraiya. 2013. *The Religion of Law: Race, Citizenship and Children's Belonging*. Basingstoke: Palgrave Macmillan.

Jones, Rosie and Frances Reynolds. 2019. 'The Contribution of Charity Shop Volunteering to a Positive Experience of Ageing'. *Journal of Occupational Science* 26(4): 1–13.

Jones, Michelle and Lori Record. 2014. 'Magdalene Laundries: The First Prisons for Women in the United States'. *Journal of the Indiana Academy of the Social Sciences* 17(1): 1–26.

Jones, Stephen H, Tom Kaden, and Rebecca Catto. 2019. *Science, Belief and Society: International Perspectives on Religion, Modernity and the Public Understanding of Science*. Bristol: Bristol University Press.

Kadushin, Charles. 2004. 'Too Much Investment in Social Capital?' *Social Networks* 26(1): 75–90.

Kadushin, Charles. 2007. 'Theologically Correct Survey Questions'. Paper delivered to 2007 conference of the Society for the Scientific Study of Religion, Tampa, Florida, 4 November 2007.

Kalvig, Anne. 2017. 'Necromancy Is a Religion: Tylor's Discussion of Spiritualism in *Primitive Culture* and in his Diary'. In Paul-François Tremlett, Graham Harvey, and Liam T Sutherland (eds), *Edward Burnett Tylor, Religion and Culture*, 123–40. London: Bloomsbury.

Kasket, Elaine. 2012. 'Continuing Bonds in the Age of Social Networking: Facebook as a Modern-Day Medium'. *Bereavement Care* 31: 62–9.

Kasmani, Omar, Nasima Selim, Hansjörg Dilger, and Dominik Mattes. 2020. 'Introduction: Elsewhere Affects and the Politics of Engagement across Religious Life-Worlds'. *Religion and Society: Advances in Research* 11: 92–104.

Katz, Roberta R, Sarah Ogilvie, Jane Shaw and Linda Woodhead. 2021. *Gen Z, Explained:the Art of Living in a Digital Age*.Chicago and London: University of Chicago Press.

Klass, Dennis, Phyllis R, Silverman, and Steven L Nickman. 1996. *Continuing Bonds: New Understandings of Grief*. Bristol: Taylor and Francis.

Keane, Webb. 2007. *Christian Moderns*. Berkeley and Los Angeles: University of California Press.

Keller, Kate. 2018. 'What Were the Protests about?' https://www.smith sonianmag.com/history/fifty-years-later-france-still-debating-legacy-its-1968-protests-180968963/.

Kelly, Michael. 2020. 'France's Laïcité: Why the Rest of the World Struggles to Understand it'. https://theconversation.com/frances-la-cite-why-the-rest-of-the-world-struggles-to-understand-it-149943.

Kivy, Peter. 1995. *Authenticities: Philosophical Reflections on Musical Performance*. Ithaca: Cornell University Press.

Klatch, Rebecca E. 1999. *A Generation Divided: The New Left, the New Right and the 1960s*. Berkeley, Los Angeles, and London: University of California Press.

Kleinman, Sherryl and Martha A Copp. 1993. *Emotions and Fieldwork*. Newbury Park: Sage.

Kleinman, Sherryl. 1991. 'Field-workers' Feelings: What We feel, Who We Are, How We Analyze'. In WB Shaffir and RA Stebbins (eds), *Experiencing Fieldwork: An Inside View of Qualitative Research*, 184–95. Newbury Park: Sage.

Knott, Kim. 2013. 'The Secular Sacred: In Between or Both/And?' In Abby Day, Giselle Vincett, and Christopher R Cotter (eds), *Social Identities Between the Sacred and the Secular*, 145–60. Aldershot: Ashgate.

Kynaston, David. 2009. *Family Britain 1951-57*. London: Bloomsbury.

Lacquer, Thomas. 1976. *Religion and Respectability: Sunday Schools and Working Class Culture 1780-1850*. London: Yale University Press.

Lanman, J and MD Buhrmester. 2017. 'Religious Actions Speak Louder Than Words: Exposure to Credibility-Enhancing Displays Predicts Theism'. *Religion, Brain & Behavior* 7(1): 3–16.

Lambeck, Michael. (ed). 2002. *A Reader in The Anthropology of Religion*. Malden: Wiley Blackwell.

Lambek, Michael. 1996. 'The Past Imperfect, Remembering a Moral Practice'. In Paul. Antze and Michael. Lambek (eds), *Tense Past: Cultural Essays in Trauma and Memory*, 235–54. New York: Routledge.

Lambert, Yves. 2003. 'New Christianity, Indifference and Diffused Spirituality'. In Hugh McLeod and Werner Ustorf (eds), *The Decline of Christendom in Western Europe, 1750-2000*, 63–78. Cambridge: Cambridge University Press.

Lasch, Christopher. 1979. *Haven in a Heartless World: The Family Besieged*. New York: Basic Books.

Lazerwitz, Bernard. 1961. 'Some Factors Associated with Variations in Church Attendance'. *Social Forces* 39(4): 301–9.

Leach, Edmund. 1971. 'Two Essays Concerning the Symbolic Representation of Time'. In Edmund Leach (ed), *Rethinking Anthropology*, 124–36. London: The Athlone Press, University of London.

Lee, Lois. 2015. *Recognizing the Non-religious: Reimaging the Secular*. Oxford: Oxford University Press.

Lee, Lois. 2019. 'Feeling Rational, Affinity and Affinity Narratives in British Science-Non-Religion Relations'. In H Stephen, Tom Kaden Jones, and Rebecca Catto (eds), *Science, Belief and Society: International Perspectives on Religion, Modernity and the Public Understanding of Science*, 173–96. Bristol: Bristol University Press.

Lefebvre, Henri. 1991. *The Production of Space*. Oxford: Oxford University Press.

Lengermann, Patricia M and Jill Niebrugge- Brantley. 1998. *The Women Founders: Sociology and Social Theory, 1830–1930*. Boston: McGraw-Hill.

Lewis, Reina. (ed). 2013. *Modest Fashion: Styling Bodies, Mediating Faith*. London: IB Tauris.

Lieberman, Carol. 1997. 'Back to the Future: Postmodernism and the Early Music Revival'. *The European Legacy* 2(1): 92–7.

Lifton, Robert J. 1982. 'Imagining the Real'. In Robert Lifton and Richard Falk (eds), *Indefensible Weapons: The Political and Psychological Case Against Nuclear Weapons*, 64–5. Toronto and Ontaio: Canadian Broadcasting Corporation.

Lipsky, David and Alexander Abrahams. 1994. *Late Boomers*. New York: Times Books.

Longenecker, Richard N. 1997. *The Road from Damascus: The Impact of Paul's Conversion on his Life, Thought and Ministry*. Grand Rapids and Cambridge: Eerdmans.

Lövheim Mia. (ed). 2013. *Media, Religion and Gender*. Abingdon: Routledge.

Lövheim, Mia and Evelina Lundmark. 2019. 'Gender, Religion and Authority in Digital Media'. *Essaches* 12(2(24): 23–38.

Luckmann, Thomas. 1967. The Invisible Religion. London: Collier-Macmillan.

Luhrmann, Tanya M. 2007. 'How Do You Learn to Know That it is God Who Speaks?' In D. Berliner, and R. Sarró (eds), *Learning Religion, Anthropological Approaches*, 83–102. New York and Oxford: Berghahn Books.

Luhrmann, Tanya M. 1989. *Persuasions of the Witch's Craft*. Cambridge, MA: Harvard University Press.

Lund, Jens and R Serge Denisoff. 1971. 'The Folk Music Revival and the Counter Culture: Contributions and Contradictions'. *The Journal of American Folklore* 84 (334): 394–405.

Lynch, Gordon, Jolyon P Mitchell, and Anna Strhan. 2012. *Religion, Media and Culture: A Reader*. Abingdon: Routledge.

Lynch, Gordon. 2002. *After Religion: 'Generation X' and the Search for Meaning*. London: Darton, Longman, and Todd Ltd.

Lynch, Gordon. 2007. *The New Spirituality: An Introduction to Progressive Belief in the Twenty-First Century*. London: IB Tauris.

Mannheim, Karl. 1952 [1923]. 'The Problem of Generations'. In Karl Mannheim (ed), *Essays on the Sociology of Knowledge*, 163–95. New York: Routledge & Kegan Paul.

Manning, Christel. 2010. 'Atheism, Secularity, the Family, and Children'. In P Zuckerman (ed), *Atheism and Secularity*. Volume 1, 165–79. Santa Barbara: Praeger.

Manning, Christel. 2015. *Losing Our Religion. How Unaffiliated Parents are Raising their Children*. New York: New York University Press.

Marcus, George. 1995. 'Ethnography in/of the World System: The Emergence of Multi-Sited Ethnography'. *Annual Review of Anthropology* 24: 95–117.

Markham, Ian, S, James Barney Hawkins IV, Justyn Terry, and Leslie Nuñez Steffensen (eds). 2013. *Wiley-Blackwell Companion to the Anglican Communion*. Oxford: Wiley-Blackwell.

Marler, Penny. 2008. 'Watch the Women'. In Kristin Aune, Sonya Sharma, and Giselle Vincett (eds), *Women and Religion in the West: Challenging Secularization*, 23–56. Aldershot and Burlington: Ashgate.

Marler Penny Long, L and CKirk Hadaway. 2014. 'Back to The Future: Why the Sunday School is Key to Denominational Identity and Growth'. *Review & Expositor* 111(1): 17–32.

Mason, Michael, Andrew Singleton, and Ruth Webber. 2007. *The Spirit of Generation Y*. Melbourne: John Garratt.

Massey, Doreen B. 2005. *For Space*. London, Thousand Oaks, and New Delhi: Sage.

Mauss, Marcel. 1935. 'Techniques of the Body'. *Journal de Psychologie Normal et Patholigique* AnnCe XXXII: 271–93.

Mauss, Marcel. 1990. The Gift: The Form and Reason for Exchange in Archaic Societies. London: Routledge.

McCarthy, Rebecca Lea. 2010. *Origins of the Magdalene Laundries: An Analytical History* Jefferson: McFarland & Company, Inc.

McCartney, Caitriona. 2019. 'British Sunday Schools: An Educational Arm of the Churches, 1900–39'. *Studies in Church History* 55: 561–76.

McCloud, Sean. 2007. *Divine Hierarchies*. Chapel Hill: University of North Carolina Press.

McGuire, Meredith B. 1990. 'Religion and the Body: Rematerializing the Human Body in the Social Sciences of Religion'. *Journal for the Scientific Study of Religion* 29: 283–96.

McGuire, Meredith B. 2008. *Lived Religion: Faith and Practice in Everyday Life*. Oxford and New York: Oxford University Press.

McLeod, Hugh. 1993. *Religion and Irreligion in Victorian England*. Bangor: Headstart History.

McLeod, Hugh. 2000. *Secularisation in Western Europe, 1848–1914*. Basingstoke: Macmillan.

McLeod, H. 2007. *The Religious Crisis of the 1960s*. Oxford: Oxford University Press.

Mellers, Wilfrid, 2002. *Celestial Music? Some Masterpieces of European Religious Music* Woodbridge: Boydell Press.

Middlemiss Lé Mon, Martha. 2009. *The In-between Church. A Study of the Church of England's Role in Society through the Prism of Welfare*. Acta Universitatis Upsaliensis, *Studies in Religion and Society* 2. Uppsala: Uppsala University.

Mombo, Esther. 1998. 'Resisting Vumilia Theology: The Church and Violence against Women in Kenya'. In Anglicanism: A Global Communion. ed. Andrew Wingate, Kevin Ward, Carrie Pemberton, and Wilson Sitshebo. London: Mowbray, 219–24.

Mulkeen, Andrea. 2020. Church Commissioners Mission, Pastoral and Church Property Committee Diocesan Rationale for Closures: 2010–2019. https://www. churchofengland.org/sites/default/files/2021-07/MPCP%2820%2925%20-%20Dio cesan%20Rationale%20for%20Closures%202010-2019.pdf.

Nason-Clark, Nancy and Catherine Holtmann. 2015. 'Naming the Abuse, Establishing Networks and Forging Negotiations: Contemporary Christian Women and the Ugly Subject of Domestic Violence'. In Abby Day (ed), *Contemporary Issues in the Worldwide Anglican Communion, Powers and Pieties*, 75–93. Aldershot: Ashgate.

Neal, Sarah and Karim Murji. 2015. 'Editors' Introduction'. 'Sociologies of Everyday Life', a special issue of *Sociology*, 49: 811–19.

Needham, Rodney. 1972. *Belief, Language and Experience*. Chicago: Chicago University Press.

Nelson, Rob and Jon Cowan. 1994. *Revolution X*. New York: Penguin.

Niemelä, Kati. 2008a. *Does Confirmation Training Really Matter?* Tampere: Church Research Institute.

Niemelä, Kati. 2008b. Private email correspondence. 19 May 2008.

Norris, Pippa and Ronald Inglehart 2004. *Sacred and Secular: Religion and Politics Worldwide*. Cambridge: Cambridge University Press.

Nussbaum, Martha. 1999. *Sex and Social Justice*. Oxford: Oxford University Press.

Nynäs, Peter and Andrew Kam-Tuck Yip. (eds). 2012. *Religion, Gender and Sexuality in Everyday Life*. London: Routledge.

Oakley, Ann. 1981. 'Interviewing Women: A Contradiction in Terms'. In Helen Roberts (ed). *Doing Feminist Research*, 30–61. London: Routledge & Kegan Paul.

Oakley, Ann. 2016. 'Interviewing Women Again: Power, Time and the Gift'. *Sociology* 50: 195–213.

O'Barr, William M. 2008. 'Children and Advertising'. *Advertising & Society Review* 9(4).

O'Loughlin Kate, Rafat Hussain, and Hal Kendig. 2020. 'Attitudes Towards Australia's Baby Boomers and Intergenerational Equity'. *The Sociological Review* 69(4): 792–811.

Orchard, Stephen and HY John. (eds). 2007. *The Sunday School Movement: Studies in the Growth and Decline of Sunday Schools*. Bletchley: Paternoster.

Ortner, Sherry B. 1995. 'Resistance and the Problem of Ethnographic Refusal'. *Comparative Studies in Society and History* 37(1): 173–93.

Oswell, David. 2012. *The Agency of Children: From Family to Global Human Rights*. Cambridge: Cambridge University Press.

Pardun, Carol J and Kathy B McKee. 1995. 'Strange Bedfellows: Symbols of Religion and Sexuality on MTV'. *Youth and Society* 26(4): 438–49.

Pavalko, Eliza K and Glen H Elder. 1990. 'World War II and Divorce: A Life-Course Perspective'. *American Journal of Sociology* 95(5): 1213–34.

Percy, Martyn. 2013. Anglicanism: Confidence, Commitment Communion. Farnham: Ashgate

Perkin, Harold. 1972. 'University Planning in Britain in the 1960s'. *Higher Education* 1(1): 111–20.

Peters, John F. 1976. 'Divorce in Canada: A Demographic Profile'. *Journal of Comparative Family Studies* 7(2): 335–49.

Pickering, W.S.F. 1972. 'The Secularised Sabbath: Formerly Sunday; Now the Weekend' In M Hill (ed), *A Sociological Yearbook of Religion in Britain* 533–47. London: SCM Press Ltd.

Portelli, Alessandro. 2009. 'What Makes Oral History Different?' In Luisa Del Giudice (ed), *Oral History, Oral Culture, and Italian Americans*, 21–30. New York: Palgrave Macmillan.

Putnam, Robert D. 2000. *Bowling Alone: The Collapse and Revival of American Community*. New York: Simon & Schuster.

Reid, Ivan. 1977. 'Sunday School Attendance and Adolescents' Religious and Moral Attitudes, Knowledge and Practice'. *Learning for Living* 17(1): 3–8.

Regnerus, Mark D, Christian Smith, and Brad Smith. 2004. 'Social Context in the Development of Adolescent Religiosity'. *Applied Development Science* 8(1): 27–38.

Ridgely, Susan B. 2011. 'Introduction'. In Susan B Ridgely (ed), *The Study of Children in Religions: A Methods Handbook*, 1–16. New York: NYU Press.

Riggs, Anne and Bryan S Turner. 2000. 'Pie-Eyed Optimists: Baby Boomers the Optimistic Generation?' *Social Indicators Research* 52(1): 73–93.

Roberts, Carol and Leslie Francis. 2006. 'Church Closure and Membership Statistics: Trends in Four Rural Dioceses'. *Rural Theology* 4(1): 37–56.

Roberts, Ken. 2012. 'The End of the Long Baby-Boomer Generation'. *Journal of Youth Studies* 15(4): 479–97.

Robinson, John. 1963. *Honest to God*. London: S.C.M.

Roof, Wade Clark. 1993. *A Generation of Seekers*. New York: Harper Collins.

Roof, Wade Clark. 1999. *Spiritual Marketplace*. Princeton: Princeton University Press.

Roof, Wade Clark. 2003. 'Religion and Spirituality: Toward an Integrated Analysis'. In Dillon, Michele (ed), *Handbook of the Sociology of Religion*, 137–48. Cambridge: Cambridge University Press.

Roof, Wade Clarke and William McKinney. 1987. *American Mainline Religion*. New Brunswick: Rutgers University Press.

Rosman, Doreen. 2007. 'Sunday Schools and Social Change in the Twentieth Century'. In Stephen Orchard and John HY Briggs (eds), *The Sunday School Movement: Studies in the Growth and Decline of Sunday Schools*, 149–60. Bletchley: Paternoster.

Rushkoff, Douglas. 1994. *The GenX Reader*. New York: Ballantine.

Riis, Ole and Linda Woodhead. 2010. *A Sociology of Religious Emotion*. Oxford: Oxford University Press.

Rice, Tom W. 2003. 'Believe it or Not: Religious and Other Paranormal Beliefs in the United States'. *Journal for the Scientific Study of Religion* 42: 95–106.

Robbins, Joel. 2004. *Becoming Sinners: Christianity and Moral Torment in a Papua New Guinea Society*. Berkeley: University of California Press.

Robbins, Joel. 2006. 'Afterword: On Limits, Ruptures, Meaning and Meaninglessness'. In Matthew Engelke and Matt Tomlinson (eds), *The Limits of Meaning: Case Studies in the Anthropology of Christianity*, 211–24. Oxford: Berghahn Books.

Robbins, Joel. 2007. 'Continuity Thinking and the Problem of Christian Culture'. *Current Anthropology* 48(1): 5–17.

Robbins, Joel. 2012. 'Transcendence and the Anthropology of Christianity: Language, Change, and Individualism (Edward Westermarck Memorial Lecture, October 2011)'. *Journal of the Finnish Anthropological Society* 37(2): 5–23.

Robbins, Joel. 2014. 'The Anthropology of Christianity: Unity, Diversity, New Directions'. *Current Anthropology* 55(S10): S292–S301.

Robbins, Joel. 2015. 'Dumont's Hierarchical Dynamism: Christianity and Individualism Revisited'. *HAU: Journal of Ethnographic Theory* 5(1): 173–95.

Roof, Wade Clark. 2000. 'Spiritual Seeking in the United States: Report on a Panel Study'. *Archives de sciences sociales des religions*, janvier–mars, pp. 49–66.

Ruel, Malcolm. 1982. 'Christians as Believers'. In J Davis (ed), *Religious Organization and Religious Experience*, 9–32. London and New York: Academic Press.

Savage, Sara, S. Collins-Mayo, B. Mayo, and B. Cray. 2006. *Making Sense of Generation Y: The Worldview of 15-25-Year-Olds*. London: Church House Publishing.

Savage, Mike, Fiona Devine, Niall Cunningham, Yaojun Li, Johs Hjellbrekke, Brigitte Le Roux, Sam Friedman and Andrew Miles. 2013. 'A New Model of Social Class: Findings from the BBC's Great British Class Survey Experiment'. *Sociology* 47(2): 21–5. https://doi.org/10.1177/0038038513481128.

Said, Edward W. 1979. *Orientalism: Western Conceptions of the Orient*. New York: Pantheon.

Satterlund, Travis and Christine Mallinson. 2006. 'Practical Realities and Emotions in Field Research: The Experience of Novice Fieldworkers'. *Social Thought & Research* 27: 123–52.

Saussure, Ferdinand de. and Charles Bally, Albert Sechehaye and Wade Baskin. 1961. *Course in General Linguistics*. London: Peter Owen.

Schofer, Evan and John W Meyer. 2005. 'The Worldwide Expansion of Higher Education in the Twentieth Century'. *American Sociological Review* 70(6): 898–920.

Sherkat, Darren E. 1998. 'Counterculture or Continuity? Competing Influences on Baby Boomers' Religious Orientations and Participation'. *Social Forces* 76(3): 1087–114.

Sherkat, Darren E and Christopher G Ellison. 1999: 'Recent Developments and Current Controversies in the Sociology of Religion'. *Annual Review of Sociology* 25(1): 363–94.

Shute, Neville. 1957. *On the Beach*. New York: Morrow.

Silverstein, erriland Roseann Giarrusso. 2010. 'Aging and Family Life: A Decade Review'. *Journal of Marriage Family* 72(5): 1039–58.

Singleton, Andrew. 2017. *Making Sense of the Generational Decline of Anglican Identity*. Geelong: Deakin University. dro.deakin.edu.au.

Slee, Colin. 2004. *Honest to God: Forty Years On*. London: SCM Press.

Small, Christopher. 1998. *Musicking: The Meanings of Performing and Listening*. Middletown: Wesleyan University Press.

Smith, Christian and Melinda Denton. 2005. *Soul Searching: The Religious and Spiritual Lives of American Teenagers*. Oxford: Oxford University Press.

Snape, Michael. 2005. *God and the British Soldier: Religion and the British Army in the First and Second World Wars*. London: Routledge.

Snape, Michael and Callum G Brown. (eds). 2016. *Secularisation in the Christian World*. London: Routledge.

Solms, Mark. 2021. *The Hidden Spring: A Journey to the Source of Consciousness*. London: Profile Books.

Spencer, A and Siobhan McAndrew. 2016. *Youth Research Council Survey of Young People's Religion and Lifestyles, 1957*. [data collection]. UK Data Service. SN: 7933, http://doi.org/10.5255/UKDA-SN-7933-1.

Spickard, James V. 1993. 'For a Sociology of Religious Experience'. *Our House Book Chapters and Sections*. 37. https://inspire.redlands.edu/oh_chapters/37

Stacey, Marilyn. 1969. 'The Myth of Community Studies'. *British Journal of Sociology* 20: 134–47.

Stanton, Naomi. 2011. 'From Raikes' Revolution to Rigid Institution: Sunday Schools in Twentieth-Century England'. In Ruth Gilchrist et al. (eds). *Reflecting on the Past: Essays in the History of Youth and Community Work*, 71–91. Lyme Regis: Russell House Publishing.

Stocking GW. 1971. 'Animism in Theory and Practice: E.B. Tylor's Unpublished "Notes on Spiritualism"'. *Man* 6(1): 88–104.

Storm, Ingrid. 2009. 'Halfway to Heaven: Four Types of Fuzzy Fidelity in Europe'. *Journal for the Scientific Study of Religion* 48(4): 702–19.

Stringer, Adrian. 2015. 'Addressing the Problem of Socio-Economic-Classification'. *In* Abby Day (ed), *Contemporary Issues in the Worldwide Anglican Communion: Powers and Pieties*, 149–68. Farnham: Ashgate.

Supicic, Ivo. 1987. *Music in Society: A Guide to the Sociology of Music*. New York: Pendragon Press.

Sutcliffe-Braithwaite, Florence. 2016. 'The Decline of Deference and the Left: an Egalitarian Moment for Localism'. *Juncture* 23: 132–7.

Sutcliffe-Braithwaite, Florence. 2018. *Class, Politics, and the Decline of Deference in England, 1968–2000*. Oxford: Oxford University Press.

Taris, Toon W and Gun R Semin. 1997. 'Passing on the Faith: How Mother-Child Communication Influences Transmission of Moral Values'. *Journal of Moral Education* 26(2): 211–21.

Tarlo, Emma. 2017. *Entanglement: The Secret Lives of Hair*. London: Oneworld Publications.

Taylor, Charles. 2007. *A Secular Age*. Cambridge: Belknap Press of Harvard University.

Thompson, Naomi. 2017. *Young People and Church Since 1900: Engagement and Exclusion*. AHRC/ESRC Religion and Society Series. New York: Routledge.

Thompson, Paul. 2017. *The Voice of the Past: Oral History*. Oxford and New York: Oxford University Press.

Tilley, J and A Heath. 2007. 'The Decline of British National Pride'. *The British Journal of Sociology* 58(4): 661–78.

Tonkin, Elizabeth. 1992. *Narrating our Pasts: The Social Construction of Oral History*. Cambridge: Cambridge University Press.

Tremlett, Paul-François, Graham Harvey, and Liam T Sutherland. (eds). 2017. *Edward Burnett Tylor, Religion and Culture*. London: Bloomsbury.

Tuchman, Barbara. 1978. *A Distant Mirror: The Calamitous 14th Century*. New York: Alfred A. Knopf.

Turner, Victor. 1977. 'Symbols in African Ritual'. In JL Dolgin, DS Kemnitzer, and DM Schneider, David. (eds), *American Kinship: A Cultural Account*. Chicago: Chicago University Press.

Schneider, David. 1980. *Symbolic Anthropology: A Reader in the Study of Symbols and Meanings*, 183–94. New York: Columbia University Press.

Twenge, Jean. 2014. *Generation Me*. New York: Atria.

Twenge JM, Sherman RA, Exline JJ, Grubbs JB. 2016. 'Declines in American Adults' Religious Participation and Beliefs, 1972–2014'. *SAGE Open*. 6(1), January 2016. doi:10.1177/2158244016638133.

Tylor, Edward Burnett. 1958 [1871]. *Primitive Culture*. New York: Harper.

Utriainen, Terhi and Päivi Salmesvuori. (eds). 2014. *Finnish Women Making Religion: Between Ancestors and Angels*. New York: Palgrave McMillan.

Utrianen, Terhi. 2014. 'Angels, Agency and Emotions: Global Religion for Women in Finland?' In Terhi Utrianen and Pävi Salmesvuori (eds), *Finnish Women Making Religion: Between Ancestors and Angels*, 237–54. New York: Palgrave MacMillan.

Van Gennep, Arnold. 1960. *The Rites of Passage*. Chicago: Chicago University Press.

Varon, Jeremy, Michael S Foley, and John McMillian. 2008. 'Time is an Ocean: The Past and Future of The Sixties'. *The Sixties* 1(1): 1–7.

Voas, David and Alasdair Crockett. 2005. 'Religion in Britain: Neither Believing nor Belonging'. *Sociology* 39(1): 11–28.

Walter, Tony. 2019. 'The Pervasive Dead'. *Mortality* 24(4): 389–404.

Ward, Keith. 1992. *In Defence of The Soul*. Oxford: Oneworld Publications.

Ward, Pete. 1996. *Growing Up Evangelical: Youthwork and the Making of a Subculture*. London: SPCK.

Warner, Rob. 2008. 'Autonomous Conformism: the Paradox of Entrepreneurial Protestantism (Spring Harvest: A Case Study)'. In Abby Day (ed), *Religion and the Individual*, 151–78. Aldershot: Ashgate.

Weber, Max. 1922. *The Sociology of Religion*. Boston: Beacon Press.

Williams, Sarah C. 1996. 'The Problem of Belief: The Place of Oral History in the Study Of Popular Religion'. *Oral History* 24(2): 27–34.

Williams, Rowan C (2019) *'What sweeter music': issues in choral church music c.1960-2017, with special reference to the Christmas Eve carol service at King's College Chapel, Cambridge, and its new commissions*. MA by research thesis, University of York.

Wilson, Bryan. 1966. *Religion in Secular Society*. London: C.A. Watts & Co. Ltd.

Wilson, Bryan. 2001. 'Salvation, Secularization, and De-moralization'. In Richard K Fenn (ed), *The Blackwell Companion to Sociology of Religion*, 39–51. Oxford: Blackwell.

Wingate, Andrew, Kevin Ward, Carrie Pemberton, and Wilson Sitshebo. (eds). 1998. *Anglicanism: A Global Communion*. London: Mowbray.

Wink, Paul and Michele Dillon. 2003. 'Religiousness, Spirituality, and Psychosocial Functioning in Late Adulthood: Findings From a Longitudinal Study'. *Psychology and Aging* 18(4): 916–24.

Woodhead, Linda. 2016. 'The Rise of "No Religion" in Britain: The Emergence of a New Cultural Majority'. *Journal of the British Academy* 4: 245–61. doi 10.5871/jba/004.245.

Woodhead, Linda and Rebecca Catto. (eds). 2012. *Religion and Change in Modern Britain*. Routledge: London.

Woodhead, Linda. 2001. 'Feminism and the Sociology of Religion: From Gender-Blindness to Gendered Difference'. In Richard K. Fenn (ed), *The Blackwell Companion to Sociology of Religion*, 67–84. Oxford: Blackwell.

Woodspring, Naomi. 2018. *Baby Boomers: Time and Ageing Bodies*. Bristol: Policy Press.

Wuthnow, Robert 1994. *Sharing The Journey: Support Groups and America's New Quest For Community*. New York: Free Press.

Wuthnow, Robert. 1998. *The Restructuring of American Religion: Society and Faith Since World War II*. Princeton: Princeton University Press.

Wuthnow, Robert. 2020. *What Happens When We Practice Religion? Textures of Devotion in Everyday Life*. Princeton and Oxford: Princeton University Press.

Yeo, Stephen. 1976. *Religion and Voluntary Organisations in Crisis*. London: Croom Helm Ltd.

Yin, Robert K. 2003. *Case Study Research Design and Methods*. Thousand Oaks and London: Sage.

Zuckerman, Phil. 2010. *Society Without God; What the Least Religious Nations Can Tell Us About Contentment*. New York: New York University Press.

Index